Money and Plan

This volume is sponsored by

THE PROJECT ON COMPARATIVE STUDY
OF COMMUNIST SOCIETIES *of*
THE CENTER FOR CHINESE STUDIES *and*
THE CENTER FOR SLAVIC AND EAST EUROPEAN STUDIES,
UNIVERSITY OF CALIFORNIA, BERKELEY.

RUSSIAN AND EAST EUROPEAN STUDIES

•

•

•

Money and Plan

FINANCIAL ASPECTS OF EAST EUROPEAN ECONOMIC REFORMS

•

•

Edited, with an introduction, by

Gregory Grossman

UNIVERSITY OF CALIFORNIA PRESS ·
· 1968
BERKELEY AND LOS ANGELES ·

UNIVERSITY OF CALIFORNIA PRESS
BERKELEY AND LOS ANGELES, CALIFORNIA

CAMBRIDGE UNIVERSITY PRESS
LONDON, ENGLAND

RUSSIAN AND EAST EUROPEAN STUDIES

CHARLES JELAVICH, *Tsarist Russia and Balkan Nationalism. Russian Influence in the Internal Affairs of Bulgaria and Serbia, 1879–1886*

NICHOLAS V. RIASANOVSKY, *Nicholas I and Official Nationality in Russia, 1825–1855*

RICHARD A. PIERCE, *Russian Central Asia, 1867–1917. A Study in Colonial Rule*

GREGORY GROSSMAN, ed., *Value and Plan: Economic Calculation and Organization in Eastern Europe*

CHARLES AND BARBARA JELAVICH, eds., *The Education of a Russian Statesman. The Memoirs of Nicholas Karlovich Giers*

JERZY F. KARCZ, ed., *Soviet and East European Agriculture*

ALAN A. BROWN AND EGON NEUBERGER, *International Trade and Central Planning*

Contents

Introduction
Gregory Grossman, *University of California, Berkeley*   1

Forced-Draft Industrialization With Unlimited
Supply of Money: Poland, 1945–1964
Andrzej Brzeski, *University of California, Davis*   17

Bank Lending and Fiscal Policy in Eastern Europe
John M. Montias, *Yale University*   38

The Role of Monetary and Credit Policy in the
Reform of Hungary's Economic Mechanism
János Fekete, *National Bank of Hungary*   57

Financial Aspects of the Czechoslovak
Economic Reform
Václav Holešovský, *University of Massachusetts*   80

The New Economic Model in Czechoslovakia
Boris P. Pesek, *University of Wisconsin, Milwaukee*   106

The International Bank for Economic Cooperation
Eugene Babitchev, *Federal Reserve Bank of New York*   129

East European Credit and Finance in Transition
George Garvy, *Federal Reserve Bank of New York*   153

Index   185

GREGORY GROSSMAN

- •
- •
- •
- •
- •

Introduction

As the economic reforms in the USSR and Eastern Europe[1] progressed from the stage of discussion and limited institutional experiments, through a series of formal, programmatic declarations by the ruling parties and governments, to initial realization of the reforms,[2] it became evident that these developments bore significant and perhaps profound implications for the role of money and finance in the "socialist" countries. It is generally held by Western (and many Eastern) students that hitherto in the Soviet-type economy money has played a "passive" role in the production sector, that little resembling monetary policy in the Western sense of the phrase could be discerned, that credit policy has been largely subordinate to the dictates of physical planning, and that both micro-economic and macro-economic instruments have occupied only a secondary, if not negligible, place in the planning, steering, and control of the economy.[3]

The various measures of decentralization of decision-making that are

[1] Hereafter in this chapter, "Eastern Europe" will be meant to include the USSR, but not Yugoslavia or Albania.

[2] For a general overview and analysis of East European reforms, see Gregory Grossman, "Economic Reforms: a Balance Sheet," *Problems of Communism* (November–December 1966), pp. 43–53, and "Economic Reforms: The Interplay of Economics and Politics" in R. V. Burks, ed., *The Future of Communism in Europe* (Detroit: Wayne State University Press, 1968).

Formal announcement of the reforms took place in 1963 in East Germany and in 1965 in Czechoslovakia, Poland, the Soviet Union, Hungary, and Bulgaria. No comprehensive reform has been announced in Rumania as of early 1968, although an "experiment" in planning and management — reminiscent of "experiments" that preceded reforms in other East European countries — was introduced in 71 industrial enterprises in July 1967, and limited changes in planning and management were voted by a Central Committee plenum in October 1967.

[3] An excellent concise yet comprehensive survey of this topic as of the eve of reforms is Dr. George Garvy's *Money, Banking, and Credit in Eastern Europe* (New York: Federal Reserve Bank of New York, 1966).

1

at the center of each reform, occasionally extending so far the reintroduction of at least a limited market mechanism (especially in Czechoslovakia and Hungary); the enhancement of the role of profit as both a
guide to resource allocation and a source of material incentives for the
firm and its personnel; some new departures in price and wage policy;
the new emphasis on efficient resource use; the heightened awareness of
inflationary danger; the attempt to rationalize foreign trade — all these
measures have posed new questions in regard to the role of monetary
and financial instruments and institutions in the reformed East European
economies. The economists, planners, and leaders of the countries in
question have not been oblivious of this. Indeed, the blueprints of the reforms — and especially of the two most far-reaching reforms in the mentioned countries — contain explicit provisions on the financial side, and
the specialized literature has carried many articles on these and related
questions. Still, serious investigation of the financial aspects of the reforms
apparently is only beginning, and the evolution of actual monetary and
financial institutions and policies is still a task for the future in Eastern
Europe — a task that will no doubt continue to be redefined as the broader
economic reforms continue to evolve.[4]

To discuss this range of problems two parallel meetings were held in
the San Francisco area in late December 1966. One was a session under
the auspices of the American Finance Association at the annual meeting
of the American Economic Association and allied societies, chaired by Dr.
George Garvy of the Federal Reserve Bank of New York. The other was
a two-day "Workshop on Communist Money and Finance" at Berkeley,
organized by the Project on Comparative Study of Communist Societies
and chaired by the editor of the present volume. The main papers read
at the A.F.A.-A.E.A. session formed part of the material discussed at
the Workshop.

Some of the papers gathered in this collection are revised versions of
the main papers presented at the Workshop. Those by Professors Montias and Pesek grew out of comments by discussants. Mr. Babitchev's contribution was not submitted or discussed at the time but is included here
because of its intrinsic interest and relevance to the general topic. Dr.

---

[4] A pioneering essay on the financial aspects and implication of the reforms is
George Garvy's "Banking and Credit in the Framework of New Economic Policies
in Eastern Europe," *Banca Nazionale del Lavoro Quarterly Review*, No. 78 (September 1966), pp. 3–29.

Garvy's "Concluding Observations" are summing up and evaluating the proceedings of the Workshop. Some of the papers presented and discussed at the Workshop are not included in this volume in order to preserve a sharper focus for its contents.[5]

It is a pleasure to acknowledge the material and moral assistance of many institutions and individuals to this undertaking. The mentioned project (a joint venture of the Center for Chinese Studies and the Center for Slavic and East European Studies of the University of California, Berkeley) provided the main part of the funds and of the administrative assistance. Some clerical help was also furnished by the Department of Economics at Berkeley. The travel expenses of several participants were generously furnished, in whole or in part, by the universities or other institutions employing them, as was some of the clerical assistance, not to mention the participants' time for research, writing, and attending the Workshop. Special mention should be made of the contribution by the Bundesminister für gesamtdeutsche Fragen (Bonn, Germany) toward Dr. Gert Leptin's travel expenses from Berlin to California. To all these institutions and persons we express our appreciation.

To Mr. Andris Trapans, a doctoral candidate in Economics at Berkeley who was the Workshop's rapporteur, and to Miss Joanne Ward, secretary of the project, go our sincere thanks for valuable assistance. To Professor Benjamin Ward, Professor of Economics at Berkeley, goes our full appreciation for help and advice over many months. Lastly, we owe a special debt of gratitude to Dr. Garvy for his continuous encouragement from the moment of conception of the undertaking to the completion of this volume, for close interest and much good advice, for careful reading of the papers and many comments communicated directly to their authors, and for his concluding observations both at the Workshop itself and (in much elaborated form) in the present volume.

Money is a "bearer of options"[6] — for its bearer. As much as any other point of view, this one helps explain the restricted place and role of money and finance in the traditional Soviet-type economy. And conversely, it

[5] All participants were Western economists with the exception of Mr. János Fekete of the National Bank of Hungary. The State Bank of the USSR was invited to send a representative to the Workshop. Its reply did not arrive until after the session and, unfortunately, was negative.

[6] Thanks are due Professor Wayne A. Leeman for introducing this phrase into the discussion at the Workshop.

is its option-bearing quality that promises money its new and enhanced role under the reforms of the second half of the sixties.

In areas where the freedom of economic choice is wide, Soviet-style money retains a high degree of "moneyness." Thus, in the household sector, under normal conditions, the degree of freedom of choice with regard to the goods placed on sale to consumers is relatively high. With comparatively few exceptions — of which housing is the most important — there has been no formal rationing in Eastern Europe for some time, although informal rationing ("one to a customer") and what the Russians euphemistically call "interruptions in consumer supply" are common. Similarly, the individual has considerable freedom of choice of job, especially if he is not a *kolkhoznik*. (Indeed, a major problem in the USSR at the moment is excessive voluntary movement of labor.) The individual is also free to save, although the forms in which he can (legally) invest his savings are limited by Western standards: savings accounts, government bonds (of limited variety), life insurance, and a relatively narrow range of capital goods (housing, agricultural implements, some livestock). Therefore, in the household sector, money is allowed to have a high degree of moneyness. That it can be spent only on a few kinds of physical capital goods and a few kinds of financial valuables does not seriously impair our conclusion so long as it can be spent relatively freely in exercising lawful options.[7]

That all Communist regimes should subscribe to the principle of freedom of household — especially, consumer — choice is not surprising: it is politically the wisest course because this goods-distribution method is the most acceptable to the public, and it is administratively more effective than either the physical doling-out of War Communism or the rationing that obtained during extraordinary periods. Fundamentally, the moneyness of money in the household sector is derivative from freedom of household choice. Money is allowed to be a bearer of options in the consumer's purse because options are allowed to the consumer. It hardly requires adding that by spending his money the consumer in a Soviet-type economy does not dictate, or even necessarily decisively influence, what

---

[7] Even in the most highly monetized and commercialized societies *some* things can be purchased for money only in contravention of law or the prevailing mores. Although the following observation is not quite germane to the point being made in the text, it is still worth noting that "no society is fully monetized, and a moment's reflection will bring to mind many things that derive their value from the fact that money *cannot* command them . . ." (Manning Nash, *Primitive and Peasant Economic Systems* [San Francisco: Chandler, 1966], p. 27.)

consumer goods will be produced, in what amounts, and when. Freedom of consumer choice should not be confounded with "consumer sovereignty."[8]

Not so in the case of the production sector in the traditional Soviet-type system. Here, the range of options permitted to lower-level economic agents, that is, enterprise management, has been severely and deliberately restricted. It is here that the "segmentation of money balances and compartmentalization of financial flows" has been carried to great lengths, and moneyness has been considerably impaired.[9] The reasons are rooted in the system of the "command economy" with its centralization of all important economic decisions, physical planning and physical disposition of producer goods, and the imposition of the leaders' values and will on the economy. In this setting, money and finance have often done little but passively reflect economic decisions taken with reference to physical quantities or to crypto-physical magnitudes, that is, aggregates in an ostensibly monetary dimension where the monetary unit serves little purpose except to permit aggregation of physical quantities.

Yet this is not to say that money and finance have been unimportant in the production sector. They have been certainly more than a decorative gloss on the real substance of the economy, even if their role has been short of an "active" one in providing the indispensable wherewithal and the positive inducement for the allocation of resources over the short or long term as in market economy. What the Communists call "control" is second to none among the functions performed by money and finance in the production sector of a Soviet-type economy. In East European usage, "control" does not mean guidance; rather, it refers to the full range of activities aiming to ensure, *ex ante*, that the positive directives are followed and that laws and regulations are observed, and *ex post*, that the deeds of omission and commission are discovered and the culprits identified. It is thus a combination of supervision, surveillance, inspection, audit, and administrative prophylaxis. "Control by the ruble

[8] We do not mean to imply that consumer sovereignty is a simple phenomenon that either does or does not obtain. For some of the attendant complexities in the Soviet case see Alec Nove, "Planners' Preferences, Priorities and Reforms," *The Economic Journal*, LXXVI (June 1966), 267–277.

[9] In "The Structure and Organization of the Soviet Economy," *Slavic Review*, XXI:2 (June 1962), 212ff., we spoke of the partial demonetization of the Soviet economy, referring to the just-mentioned impaired moneyness of Soviet money as well as to the significant areas of transactions in kind in the Stalinist system. We also drew attention to the contrast with the often rising monetization during rapid industrialization in the West.

(or another Communist currency)" is the well-known generic term for control with the aid of monetary magnitudes or financial institutions.[10]

Perhaps the most effective form of financial control over the socialist enterprise is the requirement of solvency, which imposes a budget constraint, an upper limit on the value of society's resources that the given enterprise can consume.[11] Moreover, it is typical for the enterprise's moneys to be segregated according to purpose, so that there is a separate budget constraint for each type of activity: acquisition of materials, wage payment,[12] investment, repair, incentive payments, and so forth. This kind of budget control — to use a more familiar phrase — is well known and widely practiced in formal hierarchical organizations in the West as well, from giant governments and their subdivisions, through business corporations, and to other formal organizations, such as universities.[13] The remarkable thing is not that budget control of this kind exists in Soviet-type economies; rather, that it should be so severe and constraining in regard to major units of formal organization that are virtually coterminous with whole — and in the Soviet case, gigantic — national economies.

These budget constraints have been traditionally supplemented, often redundantly, by profit targets, "planned" average unit costs, "planned" average wages, "planned" physical input-utilization norms, and so forth. The purpose of all these targets and norms has not been to guide economic activity in desired directions — this much is performed by the production, supply, and investment plans — but rather to enforce prudent management of preassigned activities and to help identify the points of deviation from standardized resource use. Again, parallels — and contrasts — with Western practice suggest themselves.

Another form of control by the ruble is the provision for regular

---

[10] Cf. Garvy, *Money, Banking, and Credit in Eastern Europe.*

[11] Since socialist enterprises are frequently deliberately subsidized, solvency here refers to the condition after the predetermined subsidy. The solvency requirement, however, is weakened because enterprises not infrequently consume capital to cover current losses, only to recoup the depletion later by a capital grant from the state treasury.

[12] The enterprise has a separate budget for wages, the so-called wages fund. It can be effectively supervised by the State Bank because the enterprise must convert its bank money into currency before each pay day.

[13] For example, the American academic community is familiar with the practice of "segmentation of money balances and compartmentalization of financial flows" in at least the larger universities. For practice in a large corporation, see the vivid account in Alfred P. Sloan, Jr., *My Years with General Motors* (Garden City, N.Y.: Doubleday, 1964), chap. 8.

supervision and audit by a financial authority. The State Bank (the "mono-bank" in Garvy's apt coinage) holds a veto right over any inter-enter-prise payment that does not conform to law, regulation, or plan. Obviously, the State Bank cannot delve into the circumstances and legal-ity of every transaction; this form of control does not seem to be effective. Probably more significant is the monobank's inquiry into the enter-prise's affairs in conjunction with extending credit (which happens fre-quently, and deliberately so as to invite the bank's attention) and the release of currency for wage payment. The various investment banks are expected to supervise construction projects that they finance. And the Ministry of Finance audits for compliance with fiscal requirements. In all these cases, the sanctions for wrongdoing may be financial, or they may be administrative or legal applied by another authority to whom the matter may be referred.

In both senses just indicated, control by the ruble is really a variant of administrative control; its distinguishing characteristics from other forms of administrative supervision are that in the first case it uses the device of budget constraint, and in the other case the supervising agency is an outside financial authority.

A major reason for the importance of control in Soviet-type econo-mies is the poor articulation of particular values and interests (at the enterprise level and even at higher levels) with the values and interests of the state, that is, of the regime, coupled with the intense determination of the regime to safeguard its values and to promote its interests. The regime is a most demanding one, requiring the fullest commitment of all to its own aims, jealous of competing values, and insisting on the maximal fulfillment of its exigent assignments. True, the individual eco-nomic agent — manager, worker — typically earns a reward for carrying out his appointed tasks. But, as is now well known, this does not ensure harmonization of particular interests with those of the state; on the con-trary it often exacerbates their conflict. Among the circumstances aggra-vating this conflict of interests is a price structure in the producer-goods sector that — it is now realized in both East and West — reflects poorly the relative importance of individual goods and resources as contribu-tors to the attainment of the state's goals. This fact intensifies the need for control (in the Soviet sense) over the actions of individual economic agents, while contributing to the difficulty of using financial instruments to guide economic activity effectively toward the state's objectives.

There are essentially three ways in which a complex economy can be guided toward centrally posited goals. The first is to "internalize" the goals and the attendant values; that is, to educate every citizen and each economic agent to accept the regime's values as his own, to be aware of and sensitive to the priorities of the moment, and to subscribe fully to the regime's objectives. Even if this had been accomplished in the Communist countries — which patently it has not been — in itself it would not suffice to run a complex economy for it cannot bring about the coordination of the innumerable economic acts, or to choose the most efficient combination of resources. Mastery of the classics of Marxism, awareness of the latest *Pravda* editorial, and a high spirit of *partiinost* and Soviet patriotism, may minimize the need for Communist-style control and for wage differentials, but they will not indicate the best octane rating of gasoline, the optimal capital intensity of a production process, or the desirable mix of ladies' dress sizes. The requisite coordination must be provided either by planning at the center and corresponding directives to lower echelons (the "command principle"), or by financial instruments in conjunction with a more or less automatically functioning price system (market mechanism), or some viable combination of the two, for both short-run and long-run resource allocation.

If coordination is accomplished primarily by the command principle, then — as we have argued elsewhere [14] — planning is necessarily biased in the direction of physical magnitudes. The, economic calculation at all levels proceeds largely in physical or crypto-physical (in the above-indicated sense) units of measure. Calculation in the monetary unit recedes in importance. Moreover, under such conditions it becomes difficult to use financial instruments for the guidance of economic decisions even within limited areas, especially if a degree of decentralization of these decisions is to take place at the same time. (The two go together inasmuch as decentralization almost by definition means reduction of guidance by directive, and replacement of the latter by guidance by means of financial instruments.) The flexibility that is a chief virtue of guidance by financial instruments tends to be negated by the rigidity of the rest of the economy operating on the command principle, just as the dispersed initiative and incentive which financial guidance presupposes are damp-

---

[14] "Notes for a Theory of the Command Economy," *Soviet Studies*, XV:2 (October 1963), 109ff.

ened by the weight of surrounding administrative controls.[15] Risk taking, especially, has been a virtually alien concept both for the socialist borrower and the socialist lender.

To recapitulate, in the traditional Soviet-type economy, in the production sector, the main role of finance has been that of "control," while its function as an active tool of resource allocation has been severely restricted, both by design and by the "logic of things" in the command economy. The monobank has been an "inventory checker," not a "risk taker," in Garvy's characterization, and Soviet-style money — in the production sector at least — has been less a bearer of options than a carrier of administrative responsibility.

So much for micro-economics. On the macro-economic level, as has been noted by Western observers, no Communist monetary policy is identifiable. This is hardly surprising in the absence of both the appropriate institutions (e.g., a capital market) and a mechanism to translate changes in the supply or cost of money into changes in real variables. On the other hand, over the decades East European planners have developed a technique of *monetary planning*, especially in regard to currency (as against bank money), which is the money of the household sector. The chief purpose of this planning has been anti-inflationary (and presumably, though operationally less significant, also anti-deflationary). The main planning technique has been the drawing up of so-called

[15] Elsewhere we have examined the Soviet experience of financing *decentralized* investment for technical modernization by bank loans and found that the program has been seriously constrained by conflict with the system of centralized physical allocation of materials and equipment, by want of incentive on the borrower's part, and by the legal requirement of a quick "pay-out" of investment (G. Grossman, "Gold and the Sword: Money in the Soviet Command Economy," *in* Henry Rosovsky, ed., *Industrialization in Two Systems* [New York: Wiley, 1966], pp. 219–226). These points have since been also stressed by a Soviet authority: cf. V. S. Gerashchenko, *Kredit i ekonomicheskoe stimulirovanie promyshlennogo proizvodstva* (Moscow, 1966), pp. 12ff. The 1965 Soviet economic reform provides for an increase in bank financing of decentralized investment for technical modernization — and a subsequent measure extends the maximum pay-out period to six years (*Ekonomicheskia gazeta*, No. 17 [1967], p. 3, par. 6) — and may offer greater incentive to management to avail themselves of such loans thanks to the greater emphasis on profit. But the conflict with the command structure as represented by materials allocation remains, as may be also understood from Gerashchenko's conspicuous silence on this point when discussing the 1965 reform (pp. 20ff.).

The partial substitution of bank-financed, repayable loans for nonrepayable budget grants for financing *new* investment projects, as introduced by the 1965 Soviet reform, does not entail any decentralization of investment decisions. Hence, this measure does not raise the mentioned problems.

"balances of money receipts and expenditures of the population," which
are *ex ante* accounts of currency flows to and from the household sectors
and of the resultant increase or decrease of currency in the public's hands
during the plan period. This is not the place for more detailed discussion of this technique of monetary planning; the interested reader is
referred to any elementary description of Soviet planning or finance.[16]
But it is important to note that a chief method of keeping the flow of
currency to households during the plan period within the limits of the
planned amount has been a tight control by the bank over currency withdrawals by enterprises for wage payments, these withdrawals being in
turn geared to the individual's enterprise's rate of production (in relation
to the planned rate).[17] This procedure — whose inflexibility has been
frequently criticized in the Eastern literature — is notable for our purpose in that it amounts to a *macro*-economic (anti-inflation) control
by means of a *micro*-financial control closely linked to the traditional
management of the economy by micro-economic directives. That is to
say, measures that would eliminate or significantly dilute management
of the economy by the traditional administrative ("command") methods,
would also require a fundamentally new technique of anti-inflationary
control.

In the production sector, within which currency is hardly used, and
bank money is the medium of payment, standard policy has been to
allow the enterprises only minimal general-purpose cash balances in order
to enhance the bank's opportunities for close "control" (as already discussed) and to minimize their potential for misdirection of resources.
But this approach is in large measure vitiated by the ease with which
credit has been generally made available to enterprises.[18]

In the present volume, Andrzej Brzeski analyzes empirically Poland's
record under the Communist regime in regard to inflation, and John M.
Montias presents a model of the inflationary process in a Soviet-type
economy. Several other contributions in this collection (especially George

[16] In addition, see Joseph S. Berliner's "Monetary Planning in the USSR," *The
American Slavic and East European Review*, IX:4 (December 1950), which is
still a valid account.

[17] Garvy ("Banking and Credit in the Framework . . . ," p. 10) points out
that the success of bank control over wage payments has been uneven in the different countries, having "proved largely ineffective" in Poland, and given up alto-
gether in Hungary.

[18] See Andrzej Brzeski's observations below. In the discussion at the Workshop
János Fekete stressed that in Hungary hitherto "credit has not been granted, it has
been taken."

Garvy's concluding remarks) touch on this problem — a problem that is important not only historically or theoretically, but also as one of the chief determinants of the prospects and limits of East European economic reforms.

Three essays refer to the two most liberal reforms, those of Hungary and Czechoslovakia. Here, the blueprints explicitly call for the reintroduction of the market mechanism on a large scale. János Fekete, Managing Director of the National Bank of Hungary, sketches a sanguine picture of the fundamentally new and much enhanced role of financial instruments for the macro- and micro-guidance of the Hungarian economy under its "new economic mechanism." His contribution is of special interest because of his key position in the financial system of his country, and because it was formulated at the height of the preparatory work on Hungary's "new economic mechanism" (since then put into effect on January 1, 1968).

The Czechoslovak blueprint, though still far-reaching in the East European context, is somewhat less so than the Hungarian; and the realization of the Czechoslovak reform in its first two years has been even more cautious. Václav Holešovský and Boris P. Pesek delve into the complexities of this reform and inquire into its limitations as well as its potential.

Eugene Babitchev offers a description and analysis of the so-called COMECON Bank, where many of the national financial problems and reform measures are elevated to and interrelated on the international level. Finally, George Garvy pulls the many strands developed by several authors together into a concluding essay.

We shall not duplicate in the Introduction what is being said in this volume about the interrelationship between East European economic reforms and monetary or financial policies and institutions. Instead, we shall limit ourselves here to a few broad observations that may add some perspective to what is to follow.

The impairment of moneyness and the partial demonetization of the Stalinist economic system [19] stand in stark contrast to the typical Western experience at early stages of industrialization. The latter we generally visualize to be associated with a *monetization* of the economy and a broadening of the options open to the holders of money. The paradox is indeed striking, but it is not inexplicable. In the Western case, monetization expanded the range of options of the entrepreneurs and investors, in-

[19] See note 9, above.

creased the attractiveness of earning money for all, and thereby helped enhance the mobilization and mobility of resources for industrialization. In Stalin's model, resources were mobilized and deployed on a vast scale, but primarily by directive. Even human resources were mobilized and distributed (or, as in the case of *kolkhozniki*, kept put) on a large scale not by inducements and incentives but by coercion and compulsion. Mobility of resources was desired by the planners and necessary for the plan, but it had to be centrally managed. Spontaneous response to monetary incentives would have brought about — so the planners feared, often perhaps correctly — insufficient mobilization of resources, tardy responses, over-reaction, and misdirection of effort. In addition, reliance on monetary incentives may have aggravated inflationary pressures. In sum, although the system's directors retained all options for themselves, they deemed their industrialization policy to require that the options of the immediate resource holders be severely restricted. This is not to say that they thereby succeeded in achieving the desired degree of resource mobilization, or the desired distribution of resources and intensity of their use, or successfully avoided inflation. As we well know, often they did not, and their coercive methods often proved to be counterproductive. This was especially bad for over-all economic efficiency. Nor was the coercion dictated by economic considerations alone. The fact remains that the partial demonetization of the Stalinist economy did have some rationale in terms of its ambitious goals and its extreme centralization.

Between 1955 and 1965 the degree of demonetization in the production sector in the USSR was somewhat reduced — the economy began to be gradually remonetized.[20] This was especially noticeable in agriculture,[21] not to mention the drastic and rapid reduction in the extent of forced labor. But until the mid-sixties, progress in this direction in the USSR and most of Eastern Europe was still slow.

The reforms of the mid-sixties represent a new departure. Even at their most conservative, as in the USSR, they still introduce the payment of interest ("payment for funds," or "production-assets levy" in East

[20] One of the first doctrinal reverses after Stalin's death was to deny that progress toward full communism entails the gradual replacement (in Marxist terminology) of "commodity exchange" by "product exchange" in the production sector, and to affirm instead that there would be a development of "commodity-money" relations. Cf. "Gold and the Sword," pp. 209ff.

[21] See, for example, Frank A. Durgin, Jr., "Monetization and Policy in Soviet Agriculture since 1952," *Soviet Studies*, XV:4 (April 1964), 375–407.

Germany) for the assets at the enterprise's disposal, the repayment of at least some capital grants from the state, economic rent for the use of natural resources other than land, and considerable discussion of payment of land rent as well. All these steps aim at greater efficiency of resource use *within* the firm. On the other hand, those practices which contribute to central "control" over enterprises are little affected by the more conservative reforms.

Reforms that would introduce a degree of the market mechanism into the socialist economy — that is, the Czechoslovak and Hungarian reforms — must afford to the enterprise considerably broader options than heretofore. They must, therefore considerably enlarge the useability of, and restrict administrative controls over, the money balances of enterprises. This much the reform blueprints of the two countries do seem to indicate, or at least to imply. To what extent these blueprints will be realized remains to be seen.[22]

Such a change, however, bears major implications not only for the enterprise but also for the bank, as Garvy notes in his contribution. The bank would have to become concerned not only with the legality of its customers' intentions, but also with their economic effectiveness, commercial promise, and financial risk. The bank-customer relation would be radically changed. Perhaps even competition on the banking side as well might be considered.[23]

Moreover, the — even partial — substitution of financial guidance for administrative direction on the micro-economic level implies a more active macro-economic stabilization policy. Whether the decentralization of any of the socialist economies will go so far as to throw the main weight of central guidance on macro-economic policy — a kind of "fi-

---

[22] We have argued that — for both political and economic reasons — the realization of every reform is likely to be more conservative than its blueprint; see "Economic Reforms: A Balance Sheet," p. 54. Experience so far seems to bear this out.

[23] Competition among the monobank's branches might impair the bank's "control" function, and for this reason it would not seem imminent. The East German solution, the creation of special branches of the monobank to serve individual industries, maximizes the banker's competence in his clients' affairs while it avoids competition on the banking side. It thus seems to concord with the spirit of the more conservative reforms, namely, enhancing micro-economic efficiency while preserving the structure of traditional "control." The manager of the Moscow Province branch of the State Bank has called for separate banks (under the State Bank's supervision) to serve individual "leading branches of the economy, resting his case on considerations of both efficiency and 'control.'" (I. Chernov, "Bank v novykh usloviiakh," *Kommunist*, No. 8 [June 1966], 94ff.)

nance socialism" — seems to be an academic question at this time. Nevertheless, insofar as decentralization of economic decisions is taken seriously, an entirely new role must be given to macro-economic financial instruments, and indeed to the concept of monetary policy. The conduct of stabilization policies by financial instruments will probably occasionally clash with the pursuit of the leaders' real objectives for the economy.[24] Would these clashes be resolved more successfully in the Communist system than they now are in the West?

It is not unreasonable to expect that in the foreseeable future all countries of Eastern Europe will continue to experience heavy pressure on their resources. To mention only one reason: their regimes are likely to continue to see economic advance (the exact pace and nature varying from country to country) as its chief domestic mission and the prime legitimation of the regime's power. If we are correct, then the main stabilization problem will be the avoidance of inflation. Significant and widespread increase in producer-good prices is, per se, a nuisance to effective planning and a cause of resource misallocation, especially if substantial decentralization occurs. What is more, it is an important source of upward pressure on *retail* prices.

Furthermore, costs of consumer goods may be pushed up by a number of structural readjustments, some directly under the reforms and some not. Some wages may be raised in order to achieve more effective wage differentials for incentive reasons (as now officially recognized in Hungary and Czechoslovakia). Farm prices may continue to be raised throughout Eastern Europe in further attempts to strengthen agriculture and to respond to increasing internal and export demands. But the margin between costs and retail prices is now often quite narrow, in contrast to the heavy though uneven incidence of turnover taxes about a decade earlier. Many important consumer goods are subsidized, for example, meat and dairy products in the USSR. Housing has been subsidized throughout Eastern Europe all along. So have been many consumer services, such as passenger transport. In sum, rising costs may quickly pose the dilemma for the government of either subsidizing ever-widening ranges of consumer goods, and subsidizing more heavily, or raising retail prices.

Both courses of action are likely to be resisted: subsidies on fiscal and efficiency grounds, retail price increases on internal political grounds. The

[24] Holešovský, pp. 100–101, below.

latter consideration, by all appearances, now exerts much force in Eastern Europe; it may do so even more if the regimes should be internally divided or feel mounting political uncertainty in connection with the reforms themselves. Under such circumstances the politically easier course may well be to cling to the traditional controls over wages, prices, production, and producer-goods supply. In other words, the fear of inflation may well be — indeed, has already been (as evidenced by, say, the retention of "wages fund" targets for enterprises in the Soviet Union) — a significant *economic* limitation to the realization of the reforms. If so, the ability to learn and willingness to implement effective macro-economic stabilization policies may yet prove to be a significant factor in the success or failure of at least the more liberal reforms. (As we have noted, the more conservative reforms do not call for much innovation on the macro-economic level.) Keynesian economics may yet come to the rescue of *socialist* "free enterprise" as it once did for its capitalist cousin!

Lastly, it is worth stating the near-obvious. The fuller monetization of East European economies and the other closely related aspects of at least the more far-reaching reforms — such as enhanced role of profit-making and heightened material incentives geared to it, new financial instruments and institutions, transition from planning and economizing in physical terms to doing so in monetary terms, the new *active* power of the Bank and the Fisc,[25] and so forth — are fraught with serious implications for all sides of social existence. We should not wish to suggest any simple causal nexus between remonetization and (shall we say) socialist commercialization on one hand and psychological, social, political, and ideological developments on the other. But whatever the effects, the existence of a complex connection of this sort can hardly be denied. It is surely taken for granted by both the bolder proponents and the more tenacious opponents of economic reform in all East European countries. Yugoslavia serves at once as a model and an object lesson in this regard; a careful, objective study of the impact and effects of remonetization and marketization in that country might be most suggestive for discerning the likely sociopolitical developments in Eastern Europe as a result of

[25] Nothing illustrates the unimportance of the Ministry of Finance in the Soviet regime as vividly as the fact that the post of Minister of Finance was held continuously (with the exception of one year) for a quarter of a century, under Stalin and under Khrushchev, by one person, A. G. Zverev.

major economic reforms.[26] Likewise, historical or even socioanthropo-
logical studies of the effects of monetization and commercialization in
nonsocialist societies that have undergone or are undergoing rapid development might be suggestive.[27]

This is not the place to do more than mention the intriguing extra-
economic implications. The contributions that follow do not range much
outside the economic realm either; they have enough to say on this score
alone. But the interested reader will surely have no reason to restrain
his curiosity or imagination.

[26] Nor should too much be made of the Yugoslav paradigm, either. Its internal
dynamic, thanks especially to its multinational character that also reflects differences in economic development and cultural heritage, is not duplicated even approximately in other East European countries.

[27] Cf. an anthropologist's observation that "money promotes the divergence of
the socially most esteemed from the socially most influential" (Nash, p. 27). In
regard to Eastern Europe, for "socially most esteemed" read "ideologically most
esteemed and politically most entrenched." It may be added that some anthropologi-
cal studies of "primitive money" are quite suggestive for understanding Soviet-
style money; for example, the distinction between "general-purpose money" and
"limited-purpose money" (where the function of the limitation on money's role
is to protect tradition, rather than hierarchical authority as in Communist countries). Cf. Manning Nash, *ibid.*, and George Dalton, "Primitive Money," *American
Anthropologist*, LXVII:1 (February 1965), 44–65, reprinted in G. Dalton, ed.,
Tribal and Peasant Economies (Garden City, N.Y.: The Natural History Press,
1967), pp. 254–281.

ANDRZEJ BRZESKI

•

•

•

•

•

Forced-Draft Industrialization with Unlimited Supply of Money: Poland, 1945-1964

East European economists are exploring "bourgeois" theory and practice in quest of clues for reform. Conversely, some lessons can also be drawn by the West from the experience of socialism. Among problems rendering themselves to such a study, finance is neither most important, nor — as a concomitant of specific institutions — most fruitful in conclusions. And yet, here too, a few insights can be gained by looking across the divide. An examination of Poland's monetary performance during two postwar decades contributes, if marginally, to a better understanding of the Western dilemma of creeping inflation. Moreover, given the diverse monetary impact of seemingly uniform policies and institutions in Eastern Europe, it merits attention of comparative economists.

THE "FINANCIAL SYSTEM"

Polish financial institutions (patterned on the usual continental principles) had been practically annihilated in World War II. With the restoration of statehood in 1945, a few major banks were reactivated along with the Ministry of Treasury. There was no room for a stock exchange; more or less planned allocation of treasury funds replaced the rudimen-

I had the benefit of discussing some of the ideas in this paper with Professors Thomas Mayer, Henry Y. Wan, Jr., and Leon Wegge, my colleagues at the University of California at Davis. Expressing my gratitude to the aforementioned, I should like to exonerate them from any responsibility for the remaining errors and misrepresentations.

17

tary capital market of the prewar period. But otherwise, through 1948, banking and treasury followed tradition as closely as possible under the novel conditions of wholesale nationalization and central planning.[1] All that was soon to change. In a series of sweeping reforms, paralleling more general political and economic developments, Poland adopted a Soviet-type financial organization. Its salient characteristics can be summarized as follows:[2]

1. The banking system is subordinate to the Ministry of Finance, which itself is an adjunct of the Planning Commission. The core of the system is the National Bank of Poland (NBP) — a multibranch institution combining functions of central and commercial banking. A small number of auxiliary banks perform specialized tasks, especially the General Savings Bank (PKO) — serving private depositors — and the Investment Bank (BI) — administering capital funds.

2. Credit operations are concentrated in the NBP. Most lending is to socialist firms, on short-term, for specific inventories and accounts receivable. The total and its allocation are planned quarterly, presumably in conformity with production and other targets. Interest, though higher on overdue loans, is a fixed service charge, not a rationing device.

3. Credit creates "money": currency and deposits.[3] Strict regulations separate their circular flow into two spheres. Currency is used in intersectoral payments (socialist to private units and *vice versa*) and in private transactions. All other payments (among socialist units) must be made by deposit transfer or, rarely, offset. The till reserves of socialist units are constrained by a small maximum. Excess must be siphoned off daily to the bank. Currency for approved outpayments, with minor exceptions, must be obtained from the bank. The outgo and ingo of currency — and hence, also the amount in circulation — are planned quarterly, according to appropriate targets (wages, procurement of farm produce, sales, and the like).

[1] For an account, cf. W. Jaworski, *Zarys rozwoju systemu kredytowego w Polsce Ludowej* (Warszawa, 1958), and Z. Pirożyński, *System budżetowy Polski Ludowej* (Warszawa, 1952).

[2] A short and lucid presentation can be found in G. Garvy, *Money, Banking, and Credit in Eastern Europe* (New York: Federal Reserve Bank of New York, 1966). More information on special Polish arrangements is contained in A. Brzeski, "Inflation in Poland, 1945–1960" (unpublished Ph.D. dissertation), Berkeley: University of California, 1964.

[3] Saving deposits are summarily classified as "money" here, but see the discussion in "Demand for Money" below.

4. Surveillance over firms ("control by the zloty") is at the heart of banking. Not only are the loans compartmentalized and tied to the plans of borrowers, but equal scrutiny applies to *all* financial transactions and assets. The local branch of the bank, with which firms in a designated territory must do business, is primarily an auditing office.

5. A score of interlocking financial balances, linked to national economic targets, provide a unified framework for monetary and fiscal planning. In addition to the mentioned quarterly credit and currency plans of the NBP, there are annual plans prepared by the Ministry of Finance. The state budget, with a scope of half or more of the national income, is at the center, redistributing funds — mainly through turnover and profit taxes — as required by government and investment outlays (financed predominantly from grants). Still more comprehensive, however, is the financial program of the state — a net statement of sources and uses of funds of the entire socialist sector. The latter, supplemented by an equally broad balance of private monetary income and expenditure, is equivalent to complete national accounts in *ex ante* terms.[4]

With small modifications, this system — designed as a setting for the industrialization drive of the Six-Year Plan for 1950–1955 — has survived until recently. In 1955, bank loans became available for modernization and other projects with quick payoff.[5] A 1958 reform simplified borrowing (twenty-odd credit categories dwindled to seven) and gave firms more leeway in finance. It also stressed profit as a source of working capital.[6] But this left the essential features of the "financial system" largely intact. Further, considerably more radical changes were announced in 1966 as a part of the over-all planning and management reform. Henceforth, all but priority capital projects are to be internally financed by firms and their associations, assisted in this task by extensive investment loans. Generally, the access to bank credit is to be facilitated and the latitude of firms in financial matters substantially increased. On the other side, to prevent misuse of these privileges, the bank is to

[4] Cf. J. M. Montias, "Inflation and Growth: the Experience of Eastern Europe" *in* W. Baer and I. Kerstenetzky, ed., *Inflation and Growth in Latin America* (Homewood, Ill.: Irwin, 1964), esp. p. 223.

[5] Cf. W. Jaworski, "Rola kredytu krótkoterminowego w finansowaniu drobnych inwestycji," *Finanse*, V:6 (June 1955).

[6] Cf. W. Jaworski, *Obieg pieniężny i kredyt w gospodarce socjalistycznej* (Warszawa, 1961), pp. 181ff., and W. Pruss, "Zmiany w systemie . . . ," *Finanse*, VIII:2 (1958)

exercise a good deal of discretion in dealing with clients, whose credit-worthiness will be judged by commercial standards. Sanctions — from differential interest charges to refusal of credit — are to discourage delinquency.[7] Some of the incipient changes seem to border on a revolution, but it is yet early for an assessment of their real significance. Institutions, financial or other, must be judged by efficacy. A wait-and-see attitude is warranted by the uncertainties surrounding the conditions on which the success of the financial reform so heavily depends. In this respect, neither Poland's past record nor more general considerations are reassuring.

GOALS AND ACHIEVEMENTS

On the surface, a "financial system" like that of Poland, appears ironclad. Its objectives are twofold: to reinforce the micro-economic regime of the plan within the firm and to prevent disequilibrium in a high-invest-ment economy. For this, Polish "hundred-percent-reserve" banking and credit rationing, imbedded in comprehensive financial planning, coordi-nated with physical targets and supported by fixing of wages and prices, could be held ideally suited.

The function of finance in a Soviet-type economy is clearly secondary if not to say "passive." [8] Direct implementation of the plan, through ad-ministrative order and physical allocation, takes precedence over finan-cial measures. This sometimes leads to the belief that East European "financiers" have an easy task.[9] But such a notion is mistaken. The banker's life in Poland does not lack in professional frustrations, even though some responsibilities as well as excitements of *haute finance* may be amiss, where decisions are made by engineers and material bal-ances experts of the Planning Commission.

Despite exhortations to "financial discipline," the formidable appara-tus of the "financial system" — with a staff of nearly sixty thousand in banks only — has failed to secure the avowed micro- and macro-objec-

---

[7] Cf. J. Albrecht, "Budżet Państwa na 1966 rok," *Finanse*, XVI:1 (1966), esp. pp. 3–4 and G. Garvy, chaps. 8 and 10.

[8] Cf. G. Grossman, "Gold and the Sword: Money in the Soviet Command Economy," in H. Rosovsky ed., *Industrialization in Two Systems: Essays in Honor of Alexander Gerschenkron* (New York: Wiley, 1966), p. 216, for the discussion of "passive" vs. "active" money.

[9] Cf. B. U. Ratchford, "The Government and the Central Bank in a Free So-ciety," in R. S. Smith and F. T. de Vyer, eds., *Economic Systems and Public Policy: Essays in honor of Calvin Bryce Hoover* (Durham: Duke University Press, 1966), p. 60.

tives of financial planning. Polish journals [10] reveal numerous loopholes in the seemingly foolproof controls over firms. Production cost, prime and overhead alike, are running above the norm. Spending on capital projects exceeds estimates. Unplanned inventories of finished goods and raw materials accumulate. As a corollary of that, on the macro-level, are the known indications of disturbed equilibrium: shortages and inflationary pressures.

A few data illustrate the extent of these phenomena. Between 1953 and 1960 unplanned business inventories of the socialist sector increased by 55 million zlotys.[11] Again in 1963 and 1964, notwithstanding remedial action, inventory accumulation in the socialist sector overshot the plan by 6 billion zlotys.[12]

Wage payments (and hence production costs) have been running ahead of targets since the inception of Polish planning. Not even the Draconian labor laws of the early 1950's brought this situation to an end. Due to decreed rate changes, wage drift, and above-the-plan employment, the wage bill limits set in the Six-Year Plan soon lost all operational significance. Under the Five-Year Plan for 1956–1960, wage controls just about collapsed. Total payments in 1957–1960 topped the originally planned wage bill by 42 billion zlotys. The more realistic corrected annual wage targets were consistently "overfulfilled" as well.[13] For one reason or other, this seems to have continued in recent years too. The 1961 wage payments were 8.3 billion zl (5.3 percent) in excesss of the year's plan. Corresponding figures for 1962 and 1963 were 5.7 and 7.8 billion zl (3.3 and 4.2 percent) respectively.[14] *Partly*, the extra payments can be accounted for by additional production: when output targets are exceeded, firms are entitled to a higher wage bill. But this is only a part of the explanation. In 1962, for instance, industrial output targets were overfulfilled by a trifling 0.6 percent, whereas the extra wage payments in industry reached 2.4 percent. And in 1963, when industrial wages

[10] See particularly the official organs of the Ministry of Finance (*Finanse*) and of the National Bank of Poland (*Wiadomości Narodowego Banku Polskiego*, hereinafter cited as *W.N.B.P.*).

[11] Computed from *W.N.B.P.*, IX:12 (1959), 568; X:7 (1960), 320 and *Finanse*, XV:10 (1965), 7.

[12] Cf. *Finanse*, XV:10 (1965).

[13] Cf. "Inflation in Poland, 1945–1960," pp. 301–305.

[14] Cf. S. Wilczyński, "Problemy kształtowania funduszu płac," *Finanse*, XV:4 (1965), 32.

topped the plan by 4.1 percent, output targets were barely met.[15] Notably, these aggregates do not properly reflect micro-economic transgressions against wage planning. Many firms must have drastically overspent their wage quotas to produce such over-all results.

In an already overcommitted economy, investing one-fifth to one-fourth of its gross national product on top of heavy military and administrative expenditures, all this could not fail to engender inflationary pressures. Ever-increasing price levels as well as various symptoms of repressed inflation (formal and informal rationing, empty shelves, industrial subsidies) have become a permanent feature of Poland's postwar economic history. Neither the confiscatory monetary reform of 1950, relieving the population of two-thirds of their currency holdings,[16] nor a host of other counterinflationary measures — a forced internal loan of 1951, obligatory delivery quotas for farm produce, and conservative fiscal policies — managed to put a stop to inflation. Whether through general price-wage reforms (in 1949 and 1953), or through piecemeal revisions of official price lists, the price index of goods sold by socialist retail quadrupled since 1946. Consumer-price rises were partly repressed, for political reasons, at the expense of endemic shortages, but producer prices — mainly of goods sold to peasants — had to be raised by 70 percent or more between 1955 and 1964, increasing the respective index seven-fold since 1945. At the same time, free market prices for privately sold food (still an important item in Poland) kept creeping up during most of the period. And to wipe out mounting industrial losses, the government introduced several price revisions (1956, 1957, and 1960) for raw materials and equipment.[17] Only in 1960, prices of industrial inputs — the so-called Group A commodities — were upped by 26 percent,[18] but reportedly many firms and whole industries have continued in the red, prompting new upward revisions of prices.

Poland's record of inflationary pressures sharply contrasts with the avowed policy goals. Price stability has been as much emphasized in Warsaw, albeit perhaps for less convincing reasons, as it is in Washington. Its preservation is manifestly a principal function of the financial system.

[16] Cf. H. Wronski, *Le rôle économique et social de la monnaie dans les democraties populaires. La reforme monétaire Polonnaise 1950–1953* (Paris: Rivière, 1954).

[17] For a detailed report of price changes, see "Inflation in Poland, 1945–1960," chaps. 4, 5 and Appendix A.

[18] Cf. A. Płocica, "Jeden czy dwa poziomy cen," *Finanse*, XV:1 (1965), 29.

[15] *Ibid.*, note 4.

SUPPLY OF MONEY

Money is a mere *fiat* of Poland's "financial system." But it also is an organizational input in the process of social production As a means of exchange, it is required in all transactions involving goods and services. As a standard of value, it is indispensable in enforcing some kind of "efficiency," through *khozraschet* or through market regime.[19] A less frequently mentioned peculiarity of the money input is the fact that its supply depends exclusively on institutional arrangements.

For a variety of reasons, the analytical usefulness of the concept of money supply in Soviet-type economies is sometimes negated.[20] With due allowances for the unique features of Soviet-style planning, one may plausibly argue the opposite case.

In the short run (here defined as a period insufficient for price-wage adjustments and financial reorganization), any curtailment of the money supply can lead — because of a paucity of means of payment — to reduced levels of activity. Such is the logic of "tight money" in a monetary exchange economy, be it of Soviet-type.[21] Symmetrically, and again in the "short run," an increasing scale of output will ordinarily necessitate more money. This is a straight-forward Fisherian argument, singularly appropriate under the circumstances (rigid payment techniques and frequencies, virtual elimination of commodity loans, and insulation of the "financial system" from abroad) prevailing in Poland.

"Long-term" effects of monetary contraction are questionable inasmuch Polish workers too have ways of resisting a cut in nominal wages. Likewise, peasants are able to resist lower nominal prices for their produce. However, "long-term" results of monetary expansion can be predicted with more assurance. If money supply outpaces total demand for money balances, inflationary pressures ensure. This is a consequence of a Quantity-Theory-type mechanism of price-level determination.[22] Polish experience provides one more test of the propositions of this theory.

For two decades, the NBP has been rapidly expanding loans. Com-

[19] Cf. G. Grossman, "Notes for a Theory of the Command Economy," *Soviet Studies*, XV:2 (October 1963), 117.

[20] Cf. G. Garvy, p. 44.

[21] Certain components of total money supply (notably treasury deposits accumulating as a result of the perennial budget surplus) could be written off, say against "normative loans," without repercussions.

[22] See Friedman's generalized version of the theory in his "The Quantity Theory of Money — A Restatement," in M. Friedman, ed., *Studies in the Quantity Theory of Money* (Chicago: University of Chicago Press, 1956).

parability of data is impaired by several bookkeeping operations trans-
forming firms' indebtedness into their (budget-financed) capital. Still,
the available data suffice as a rough measure of this growth. From 1946
to 1949, total loans outstanding (approximately equal to "money supply") increased almost 15 times, when national product less than trebled.
These were extraordinary conditions, of course: the supply of money was
built "from scratch." At a slower pace, from 1950 to 1960, the corresponding growth rates were 6.7 times for loans and 2.6 times for product.
Subsequently, from 1960 to 1964, loans appear to have expanded by 65
percent against a 26 percent increase in product.[23]

Since the Soviet-type "financial system" and particularly banking, is
presumably designed to minimize liquidity,[24] Polish monetary expansion
has been rather striking. The elasticity of money supply with respect
to income, $\Delta M/\Delta Y \cdot Y/M$, for 1950–1964 was about 6.3. A similar
estimate for another Soviety-type economy, East Germany, yields for
the same period an elasticity of only 3.8.[25] This rough comparison probably does not fully bear out the relatively higher rate of Polish monetary
expansion.[26]

Lax credit was at the root of the phenomenon. Behind the stern
façade of rules and regulations, the supply of loans has been elastic. Statutory sanctions against financial transgressions (overspending of wage
funds, excessive inventories, delinquency in payments for deliveries)
have remained ineffectual. Somehow, when the "chips were down," that
is, after a real transaction occurred, loans were always forthcoming. And

[23] Estimates of loans outstanding for 1946–1960 from "Inflation in Poland;
1945–1960," Appendix B; for 1964 from S. Majewski, "Rozwój działalności Narodowego Banku Polskiego w latach 1945–1965," *Finanse*, XV:4 (1965), 6, combined with data in *Rocznik statystyczny 1965*, pp. 88, 501, and in T. Zaczek,
"Zmiany w strukturze źródeł finansowania inwestycji w 1966 r.," *Finanse*, XVI:1
(1966), 23. National product data are from *Rocznik statystyczny 1965*, p. 69.
[24] Cf. D. R. Hodgman, "Soviet Monetary Controls Through the Banking System" in G. Grossman, ed., *Value and Plan* (Berkeley and Los Angeles: University
of California Press, 1960), pp. 109–113.
[25] Effects of the 1957 currency reform were eliminated from the estimate of
money supply growth. The latter was computed from currency and private saving
deposit statistics, rather than from loans outstanding. All data came from *Statistisches Jahrbuch für die Deutsche Demokratische Republik 1966*, pp. 21, 423,
and 424.
[26] Product (Marxian "gross national income") growth has been notoriously
overestimated in Poland. That the degree of exaggeration was greater in Poland
than in East Germany, can be inferred from a comparison of official and recom-
puted indices of industrial output. (The latter weighs heavily as a component of
the Marxian "product.") Cf. A. Zauberman, *Industrial Progress in Poland, Czechoslovakia, and East Germany, 1937–1962* (London: Oxford University Press, 1964),
chap. iii, esp. pp. 120–121.

once granted, they were hard to recall. New loans could not be refused for wage payments and raw material purchases, even if borrowers were already in arrears. In those rare cases where sanctions had been invoked, the bank was eventually overruled by ministerial planners. The preponderance of real targets defeated all efforts of the bank to check monetary expansion. Production had to go on at any cost.[27]

The incomplete banking statistics corroborate this diagnosis, now widely accepted by financial planners. "Overdue loans," the last escape of delinquent borrowers, have always constituted a sizeable proportion (from 3.3 to 13.6 percent during 1949–1959) of the outstanding total. This was in contrast with the significantly lower share of such loans in Czechoslovakia, practicing monetary restraint with more vigor.[28]

Interfirm settlements have been extended beyond the prescribed period in many cases (from 11 to 70 percent during 1951–1960), leading to additional credit extension on accounts receivable.[29]

Not sparing effort, the bank has managed, on occasions, to reduce both the proportion of "overdue loans" and that of lagging settlements (though the latter has again risen after 1957). But this was a Pyrrhic victory. The apparent improvement was achieved mainly by granting delinquent firms additional credit from regular loan accounts. At times this credit was forced on firms in financial trouble. To sum up: credit and currency plans notwithstanding, Polish banking lacked effective controls over the supply of loans. The latter adjusted itself rather passively to the "requirements of trade," as defined by borrowers. Unplanned real transactions (including pure waste) and financial irregularities were ratified *ex post* by new loans. To quote a vice chairman of the NBP, "credit automatism was an inherent built-in feature of the Polish system.[30]

DEMAND FOR MONEY

Deflationary operations of the treasury served primarily the purpose of neutralizing the abundance of credit. The postwar deficits were eliminated in 1947. Since then, through 1964, the state budget produced a huge cu-

[27] Cf. *W.N.B.P.*, VII:1 (1957), 4–9; VII:2 (1957), 60; VII:3 (1957), 111–112 and *Finanse*, VII:4 (1957), 21–31.
[28] Cf. W. Jaworski, *Obieg pieniężny* . . . . , p. 182 and *Zarys rozwoju* . . . , pp. 170–201; *W.N.B.P.*, VII:8 (1957), 396 and *Statistickà rŏcenka Č.S.R. 1964*, p. 492.
[29] Cf. W. Jaworski, *Obieg pieniężny* . . . , pp. 106, 108, 110 and *W.N.B.P.*, X:12 (1960), 579.
[30] Cf. L. Gluck, "Nowe kierunki systemu kredytowego," *W.N.B.P.*, VII:7 (1960), 324.

mulative accounting surplus of 90 billion zlotys.[31] Much of this surplus
(exceeding the original budget forecast) was written off against "normative loans" to industry. A large part is a result of counting private
savings deposits as "budgetary" revenue. Some of it arises from bookkeeping conventions in treatment of the zloty equivalent of foreign loans.
The remainder may be said to represent treasury "demand for money."
But naturally only the transitory accumulation of treasury *working* funds
affects the monetary situation. The rest — consisting of "frozen surpluses"
of previous years — might as well be canceled out with notional assets
of the banking system.

The demand of socialist firms for money is chiefly for transaction purposes. Yet, in view of the standby availability of bank loans, one would
not expect here any stable relationship. In state-owned industry, with
steady output growth, the changes in money balances are indeed erratic.
In retail trade, sales and money holdings grow frequently together, but
again no regular pattern seems to emerge.[32] In both cases, the size of
money holdings by firms depends on fluctuating rules of the "financial system" and bank procedures, rather than on the volume of transactions.
Fortunately, it is not necessary to be further concerned with the determinants of monetary balances of firms. Relevant is that they need not hold
more money than desired; the excess can always be used to pay off loans.
In aggregate, *and* in virtually every individual case, the indebtedness of
firms to the bank exceeds by far their monetary assets. And the bank welcomes every opportunity to extinguish outstanding loans.

Private demand for money is of more interest. Unlike socialist firms,
the private sector as a whole has only one way of ridding itself of unwanted money that cannot be spent on goods: to cut back on the supply
of effort (labor and farm produce). No observer of Poland, and especially
of Polish farming, can escape the impression that this has happened at
times. But normally, as in all similar cases — short of hyperinflation —
the supply of effort has continued, and increased, while the public was
trying to unload its excess balances on the market. Resultant shortages,
directly or by official edict, drove up prices and wages throughout the
economy. This was mentioned before.[33] Central price and wage setting can

[31] Cf. J. Drewnowski, ed., *Mały słownik ekonomiczny* (Warszawa, 1958), p. 111
and *Rocznik statystyczny 1965*, p. 490.

[32] Cf., *Rocznik statystyczny 1965*, p. 406.

[33] See "Goals and Achievements," above.

temporarily repress, or slow down, the inflationary momentum. But it cannot eliminate the classical spirals and spillovers, if the "financial system" keeps producing too much money.

Ever since a limited amount of war time currencies ("Cracow zloty" and Reichsmark) was exchanged for the notes ("Lublin zloty") of the National Bank of Poland in 1945, money holdings of the private sector — a residual difference between total money supply and the socialist sector's demand for money — have been rapidly augmented. The October 1950 monetary reform, introducing the present "Warsaw zloty" (at the currency exchange rate 100:1 with prices and wages rescaled at the 100:3 ratio), interrupted the trend only for a short time. Estimated from official quarter-end statistics, *annual average* money balances of private units have grown from 1945 through 1964 almost *eighty times!* [34]

This was more than private units were willing to hold as can be inferred from the discussed inflationary processes. Luckily, the inflationary potential of the monetary excess was in part absorbed by the public's growing "liquidity preference." A Cambridge-type coefficient (average annual money holdings as a fraction of expenditures, both at 1961 prices) computed for the private sector, rises from 0.05 in 1946 to 0.24 in 1964 — an almost steady climb, interrupted by the 1950 monetary change-over (confiscation of nominal balances) and the 1953 price-wage reform (government decreed reduction of real money balances). Had the proportion of private income (expenditures) held in money been fixed at, say, the 1946 level, Poland might have experienced once again, as in the 1920's, a runaway inflation despite central planning.

A number of formulae were fitted to the data. Statistically satisfying results were obtained from $M = AY^{\alpha}N^{\beta}\epsilon$, with M and Y standing for (real) average annual balances and (real) expenditures, and N for private non-farm employment (a proxy for volume of trade). The random term ϵ reflects unspecified influences including speculative demand for money. Regression, for t = 1946, . . . , 1964, yields $\alpha = 2.30$ and $\beta = 0.57$, both significant at the 0.005 level. R^2 is 0.967 and the assumptions of homoscedasticity and no autocorrelation pass the appropriate tests (F and Durbin-Watson) at the 0.05 level of significance. Possibly, a still better fit could be obtained with other formulae. However, even these results suggest that a Quantity-Theory-of-Money type of analysis throws

[34] See Appendix at the end of this essay.

some light on the determinants of private demand for money. In Poland this approach is nowadays unpopular. Most economists favor instead an Aftalion-like "income theory" of money.[35] But this is because they wrongly associate the Quantity Theory with a constant velocity of circulation.

The elasticity of private demand for money with respect to expenditures (2.30) merits special attention. Obviously, when no other financial assets, such as securities, are available to the public, some such result should be expected when there is private saving. Moreover, with little consumer credit, an elastic demand for money must be a by-product of increasing *per capita* incomes and shifting expenditure patterns.[36] The same factors that account for this are behind the rising proportion (from 16 to 56 percent between 1955 and 1964) of private balances held in savings accounts: money for future purchases is safer in the bank. Similarly, they explain the increasing average denomination of bank notes (by 133 percent in the same period): hoarders prefer larger notes.[37]

The inclusion of saving deposits in private demand for money may appear objectionable. That, however, is a definitional question to be decided on grounds of operational convenience. Here, a broad concept of money serves an analytical purpose. First, the bulk of Polish saving deposits constitutes short-term liquidity reserves easily convertible to cash. Besides, savings deposits with the PKO can be directly used — in lieu of rarely held checking accounts — to make certain payments.[38] Secondly, the more recent spread of genuine time deposits,[39] leading to long-term immobilization of private money balances, is fully consistent with, nay, a logical offshoot of, the advanced hypothesis. When cars begin to come on the market at prices equivalent to four or five years of average wages, one may as well accumulate money toward their future purchase in a blocked account, especially if this can earn privileged access to a limited supply as well as bonuses.

[35] Cf. M. Kucharski, "Teoria pieniądza a wzrost gospodarczy," *Finanse*, XVI:5 (1966).

[36] Cf. F. A. Lutz, "The Demand for Money," *International Economic Papers*, No. 11, pp. 155–156, and for similar interpretation of the Polish case: Rada Ekonomiczna przy R. M., *Główne problemy sytuacji gospodarczej kraju* (Warszawa, 1958), p. 135.

[37] Cf., *Rocznik statystyczny 1961*, p. 404 and *Rocznik statystyczny 1965*, p. 501.

[38] Cf., *Rocznik polityczny i gospodarczy 1959* (Warszawa, 1960), p. 685.

[39] Cf., G. Garvy, pp. 88–91.

THE BASIC MECHANICS OF INFLATION

The mechanics of inflationary processes is never simple: "a complete account of . . . inflation . . . would deal with the whole of the dynamic analysis."[40] Where the interaction of "demand pull" and "cost push" is additionally complicated, as in Poland, by administrative manipulation of relative prices and income shares, the developments defy orderly analysis. So do — under most conditions — the effects of inflation. A disaggregated model of the economy, with specification of many technological, behavioral, and institutional relationships, would be necessary to deal with the subject realistically. This is not possible here.

Grossly oversimplifying the picture,[41] one can construct a "naïve model" of the strategic interdependencies among the flow and stock variables of an inflationary economy.

This might be:

(i)	$Y(t) \equiv C(t) + I(t)$	product identity
(ii)	$Y(t) = f[N(t); K(t)]$	production function
(iii)	$N(t) = g[C(t); \lambda(t)]$	labor supply function
(iv)	$M^d(t) = h[C(t)]$	demand for money function
(v)	$M(t) = M(0) + \int_0^t j[I(\tau); p(\tau)]d\tau$	supply of money function
(vi)	$M^d(t)p(t) = M(t)$	equilibrium condition

Here — t (and τ) for time as usual — Y, C, and I have standard meaning. K is capital stock equal to an initial value plus cumulated investment, $K(0) + \int_0^t I(\tau) \, d\tau$. N is employment. The shift parameter λ reflects exogenous demographic factors, say $\lambda(t) = \lambda^{rt}$, where r is a given rate of population growth. M^d is demand for money, and M its supply, with M(0), the initial stock. Finally, p is a price index. Except for M and p all variables are in "real" terms.

---

[40] Cf., B. Hansen, *A Study in the Theory of Inflation* (London: Allen & Unwin, 1961), p. 199.

[41] Apart from complete aggregation, the crudest simplifications are as follows: (a) all production and investment are carried out by the socialist sector; private units supply labor only; (b) capital does not wear out; there is neither depreciation no technological change; (c) there is no government spending (and, hence, no budget); (d) all money is held by households; socialist firms' receipts are immediately used to pay off debt; finally (e) price adjustments are instantaneous. Given the focus of this paper, assumptions (c) and (d), eliminating the complexities of the "financial system," may seem inadmissible. Yet they may be analytically harmless: the "model" deals with the *net* supply of money to the private sector — certainly a crucial variable in a Soviet-type economy.

With investment, $I(t) \equiv dK/dt$, predetermined by central planners, as it presumably would be in a Soviet-type economy, the six equations in six unknowns (Y, C, N, M_d, M, and p) trace out a unique growth path. Under the strong assumptions of the Quantity-Theory of Money,[42] the eqilibrium condition in (vi) is *always* satisfied due to instantaneous price adjustments. But *noninflationary* growth, with $dp/dt = 0$ throughout, occurs only for a particular investment sequence determined by the exact shape of the functions (ii) through (v).[43] Not surprisingly, under normal conditions — and given the characteristics of monetary behavior — the higher the marginal productivities and the labor supply, the steeper the rate of increase in investment compatible with price stability. Furthermore — with marginal productivities, labor supply, and money stock fixed — this rate varies with the public's liquidity preference.

The role of monetary institutions, and more generally of the "financial system," in steering the economy along a noninflationary path is clear, too. Other things (technology and private behavior) held constant, the inflationary impact of an investment stream can be reduced or neutralized through modifications of (v).[44] In a realistic setting — budget, taxes, and some flexibility in credit — this is feasible, at least within some range. In any case, however, monetary laxity — as in the Polish case studied here — undoubtedly magnifies the inflationary potential of the "big push" in investment.

Given enough data, a simultaneous equation model built along similar lines — appropriately disaggregated and specified, including a complete description of monetary and fiscal institutions — might lay bare the structural underpinnings of Poland's inflationary performance. One important relationship, corresponding to (iv) of the naïve model," was directly estimated in the preceding section. A more complete formulation might possibly reveal that in addition to price-level determination, the supply

---

[42] See (e) in preceding note.

[43] Substituting (v) into (vi) and differentiating with respect to time (dotted variables), one obtains:

$$\dot{M}^d(t)p(t) + M^d(t)\dot{p}(t) = j[\dot{I}(t);p(t)].$$

On the assumption of the simplest linear $j = \alpha I(t)p(t)$, further substitutions from (i) to (iv) yield for $\dot{p} = 0$ after rearrangement of terms:

$$\frac{\dot{I}(t)}{I(t)} = \frac{\partial Y/\partial N \cdot \partial N/\partial \lambda \cdot \dot{\lambda}(t)}{I(t)} - \frac{\alpha(1 - \partial Y/\partial N \cdot \partial N/\partial C)}{dM^d/dC} + \frac{\partial Y}{\partial K}$$

This is the condition for noninflationary growth.

[44] In the simple case developed in note 43, by reduction of the supply coefficient α.

of money, and more generally the "financial system," have a bearing on the real variables of a Soviet-type economy.

MONEY AND THE REAL ECONOMY: PLAUSIBLE TOPOLOGY

What, then, is the nexus between monetary institutions and the real economy? How does money supply affect economic growth and efficiency? These are difficult questions. At best one can hope for tentative answers relating to specific situations. A few loosely argued suggestions — arrived at in the course of a preliminary study of the Polish experience — are offered.

Inflation and Growth

The direct influence of an inflationary expansion of money supply on the growth process in Soviet-type economies may be relatively small. Investment and foreign trade — ordinarily singled out as main impact areas of rising prices and wages, are, if not wholly immune to, largely insulated from their adverse effects.[45] One can even plausibly argue — as Pigou and Mikoyan did! — that a modicum of inflation is beneficial to industrialization efforts. Thus, a negative real balance effect of rising prices, might induce increased labor supply at a given level of real wages. This was disregarded in (iii) of the "naïve model." Or, one can consider inflationary pressures of an overcommitted economy, a useful element in the trial-and-error search for "optimum tautness" in central planning. This would have to be included in (ii) of the model.[46]

Generally, the alleged developmental advantages of a mildly inflationary milieu,[47] may have some degree of validity also for socialist Poland. But it would seem that rather than inflationary pressures *per se*, more important for Polish growth were those characteristics of monetary institutions that made inflation possible — namely the highly elastic supply of loans.

[45] Cf., P. Wiles, "Soviet-type Inflation," (Milano: CESES, 1966), mimeographed.

[46] Both problems are discussed in "Inflation in Poland, 1945–1960," pp. 317–329.

[47] Cf., especially A. O. Hirschman, *The Strategy of Economic Development* (New Haven: Yale University Press, 1958) and the contributions of Latin American "structuralists." See also, T. Wilson, "Inflation and Growth," in *Planning and Growth* (London: Macmillan, 1965) for a different interpretation.

*Supply of Loans and
the Feasible Growth Rate*

The link between bank loans, as a sole source of means of exchange, and economic activity[48] assumes new dimensions in an economy embarking on forced-draft industrialization. Here, as during the Six-Year-Plan period in Poland, large amounts of workers must be extracted from farming and low-priority urban pursuits that offer an alternative way of making a living. When nominal wages (and agricultural procurement prices) are downward rigid, such a massive manpower transfer and a smooth distribution of labor force within industry may be helped by monetary expansion. This, of course, on the premise that behavioral schedules are different from the classical version in (iii) of the model. Real balances, as an additional argument in the functions, might suffice if rural-urban and occupational liquidity-preference differentials exist,[49] to take one example. Or, within bounds, money illusion may be present. Much theoretical, let alone econometric, spadework ought to be done to clarify this. Nonetheless, it is conceivable that without the extra elbow room provided by permissive credit, the relative income readjustment needed for creation and allocation of Poland's industrial labor force might have been more difficult than it actually was. Thus, by obviating the special strain of "tight money" in an economy abounding in rigidities and bottlenecks, and beset by political tensions, the generous supply of loans might have been a useful instrument of industrialization. If so, the successful implementation of the Polish growth program was, in part at least, contingent on apparent shortcomings and loopholes of the "financial system." Briefly, and contrary to the classical dichotomy of the simple model, it might have just so happened that within the relevant range of variation, $\dot{Y}/\dot{M}$ was positive!

It has been observed long ago that "easy money" may be grease for the wheels of the Soviet-type industrialization engine.[50] Pertinent Polish developments support this view. Nominal average net wage was allowed nearly to quadruple between 1946 and 1964 — through reforms, regulations, and drift. Behind the climbing average were differential advances for various industries and categories of labor.[51] Ever-expanding loans

[48] See "Supply of Money," above.
[49] Cf. *W.N.B.P.*, V:4 (1965), 159; V:12 (1955), 632; and VI:9 (1956), 449.
[50] Cf., W. B. Reddaway, *The Russian Financial System* (London: Macmillan, 1935), pp. 83–84.
[51] Cf., *Rocznik statystyczny 1965*, pp. 467–468.

supplied the indispensible instrumentation for "ratchet" and "spillover" mechanism of rising wages to assure industry of adequate supplies of new workers, and to keep the already employed ones on the job. The vast net increment in employment in the socialist sector (4½ million, that is, more than doubling between 1949 and 1964) has been managed by such methods. Symptomatically, East Germany took another course. From 1949 to 1964 nominal average wage hardly changed and monetary expansion was kept in check. However, this was accomplished with an established industrial labor force and with a mere 26 percent increase in total employment.[52]

Agricultural policies, boosting private farm proceeds 4½ times between 1951 and 1964[53] can be interpreted in a similar fashion. This time, strictly on order of the planners, Poland's monetary system was functional in alleviating a drastic food shortage and the resultant balance-of-payment crisis. Insofar as these were serious hurdles to industrialization, elastic supply of money made a contribution to growth here, too. Partly, as in industrial labor, it was through inducing more productive effort. Aside from this, another mechanism was at work — diversion of the peasants' own demand for their product (increasing the proportion of farm output destined for the market).

Supply of Loans and Efficiency

The elastic supply of loans may have been functional in performing the socialist miracle of forced-draft industrialization of Poland. It was no help, however, in imposing a regime of efficiency.[54] In the wake of efficiency-oriented reforms of industry and finance, this is a timely topic that cannot be pursued here beyond a few preliminary, summarizing remarks.[55]

a) Easy access to money was prerequisite to such vestigial freedoms that were left to Polish managers under physical command planning. Consequently, it might be considered a factor injecting a measure of

[52] Cf., *Statistisches Jahrbuch für die Deutsche Demokratische Republik 1966*, p. 23.

[53] Roughly estimated from *Nowe Rolnictwo*, No. 18 (1958), 734; L. Zienkowski, *Dochód narodowy Polski 1937–1960* (Warszawa, 1963), p. 255; and *Rocznik statystyczny 1965*.

[54] This coincides with Reddaway's appraisal of the Soviet financial system in the early Five-Year Plan.

[55] See, however, A. Brzeski, "Finance, Central Planning and Economic Reform in Eastern Europe" (Milano: CESES, 1966), mimeographed.

flexibility into an otherwise rigid structure of bureaucratic centralism. At times, no doubt this was to the best. But more often, managerial choices dictated by a host of "success indicators" and bonus schemes, and based on misleading prices, were in conflict with priorities of market *and* plan alike. The Law of Value controversy of 1956–1957 and the present reform movement have been prompted by recognition of this fact.

b) Secure in their knowledge that loans would be forthcoming when needed, and indifferent to real cost, Polish managers engaged in all the hedging practices familiar to students of the Soviet firm.[56] Raw materials were hoarded everywhere (which was a major cause of unplanned inventories). Overstaffing of plant and office was widespread.

c) Inflationary pressures accompanying elastic credit, and particularly repressed inflation, by creation of a seller's market, blunted incentives for quality and proper output mix. This, again, is an endemic phenomenon of East European socialism, much discussed in literature. Worse yet, the ability of the firms to finance above the plan inventories, made it possible to produce defective goods for which there were no users. Such outright waste, temporarily disguised as "inventory accumulation," was widespread in the early 1950's.

Neatly summed up in terms of the model (but this time frankly without any prospect for more precise formulation, let alone estimation), all this means that neither the marginal product of capital, nor that of labor, were free from monetary impact: $d(\partial Y/\partial K)/d(dM/dt)$ and its labor analogue, might have been negative. Paradoxically, through such a chain of causation, lax credit would have prevented industrialization — that it otherwise fostered — from full fruition.

A SOMEWHAT MORE
DOWN-TO-EARTH CONCLUSION

Monetary explanations alone are insufficient for an understanding of the vicissitudes of production and distribution of the wealth of nations. But neither must they be neglected. This is true of Soviet-style socialism, as it is of capitalism. There, as here, money is more than a mere veil.

Poland, like other East European countries, is believed to have dis-

---

[56] Cf., J. Berliner, *Factory and Manager in the USSR* (Cambridge: Harvard University Press, 1957), and D. Granick, *Management of the Industrial Firm in the USSR* (New York: Columbia University Press, 1957).

pensed with "monetary policy." This is not so, unless very narrow definitions are accepted. Policy — according to Webster — is "a settled course adopted and followed by a government, institution, body or individual." Hence, it must be judged by actions rather than pronouncements. From this point of view Poland's monetary policy appears clear: nearly perfect flexibility — an unlimited supply of money in the service of industrialization.

Consistently pursuing this policy, albeit not so much by preference as under external pressure, Polish bankers were not free of equivocations and confusion. Nor are their Western colleagues. Inherent complexity of monetary economics makes any course of action a Hobson's choice. Like their counterpart in Western countries, Poland's bankers have had to live always eyeing the two alternatives: price stability (and perhaps improved efficiency) or growth. Never ceasing to talk about the first, they obviously had to opt for the second. Perhaps, through ineptitude ("real bills" doctrine?) or misjudgment, they sacrificed more stability (and efficiency) than was necessary to achieve the planned rate of growth. Possibly, they might even have adversely affected the economy's growth potential. No one will ever know.

Unquestionably, the policy of unlimited supply of money, by feeding inflationary price-wage spirals, led to a much desired opening for socio-economic bargaining, foreign to Marxist principles and authoritarian ideals of statecraft. Inflation, of the creeping kind, it has been said, "acts as a great social mollifier."[57]

POSTSCRIPT

Professor Franklyn D. Holzman commented extensively and critically on this essay during the Workshop. His criticism can be summarized in three points: (1) the changing relationship of the rate of monetary expansion, the consumer index and the coefficient k suggests that the student of the Polish economy deals with three heterogenous subperiods — 1946 to 1953, 1953 to 1957, and 1957 to 1964 — which must not be lumped together in the analysis; (2) the relatively small increase in consumer prices after 1953 was due to the repression of inflationary forces rather than to the public's willingness to hold larger real balances; and (3) given

---

[57] Cf., M. Bronfenbrenner, F. D. Holzman, "Survey of Inflation Theory," *American Economic Review*, No. 4 (1963), 626.

an elastic supply of money, its quantity is determined by demand, hence
it is improper to argue that an increase in liquidity preference kept prices
from rising. I think that the third point stems from a common misunder-
standing. When I speak of the elastic supply of money, I have in mind
its *nominal* quantity which, under the Polish conditions, adjusts itself
more or less passively to output or, operationally, to the borrowers' re-
quests. The demand for money, however, is always that for *real* balances
and depends on some such variables as the level and the distribution of
private income, the availability of goods, and so on. The public's liquidity preference (demand) affects, through market pressures which cause
price adjustments, the real rather than the nominal quantity of money.
Holzman's second thesis contradicts the facts. All evidence indicates
that the symptoms of repressed inflation were most acute before 1953 —
the year of the price-wage regulation, which raised consumer prices by
40 percent. Even in a Soviet-type economy the public cannot be forced
to hold much more *real* money than it desires, if there is a significant
free market sector (food) and the possibility of withdrawing the supply of
labor (e.g. housewives quitting their jobs). Still, I am in sympathy with
Professor Holzman's doubts, since the assumptions of a Quantity-Theory
of Money-type of price adjustment mechanism are hard to reconcile with
the existence of repressed inflation. But perhaps this is a matter of reaction lags and degrees of disequilibrium. If this is taken into account, a
subdivision of the postwar two decades into the subperiods suggested by
my critic in (1) might have greatly enriched the analysis and clarified its
results. In my less ambitious attempt to interpret the facts, I restricted
myself to *an* analytical "least common denominator" which, I believe, I
found in current monetary theory. Even so, I must admit that without
assuming the existence of some repressed inflation, it would be difficult
to explain the fact, pointed out by Holzman, that my data imply a private
marginal propensity to spend over the period 1958–1964 of less than
one-third, with negative propensities in four of the seven years. Holzman's understandable dissatisfaction with purely monetary interpretations
of inflation led him to suggest that in Poland too, as in the Soviet Union,
its deeper causes were in the excess demand for labor. Despite the plausi-
bility of this view (well known from the Holzman-Powell controversy), it
raises a "chicken-or-egg" problem inasmuch as the excessive claims on
labor were made effective through the medium of the elastic credit. With
tighter credit, growth would perhaps have been stymied or achieved

through more severe regimentation, but the overambitious plans could hardly have resulted in rising wages and prices. I was interested mainly in the consequences of the actual policies, that is, of a permissive monetary regime.

APPENDIX

REAL PRIVATE MONEY BALANCES AS FRACTION OF REAL PRIVATE INCOME

1946–1964

Year	Nominal average private money balances[a] (M)	Price deflator[b] (P)	Average private money balances at 1961 prices (M̂)	Private income at 1961 prices[c] (Y)	Fraction (k) Magnitude	Index	Year-to-year percent average
1946	987	.27	3,655	68,725	0.0531	100	
1947	1,939	.40	4,847	87,179	0.0555	104	4
1948	2,997	.41	7,310	104,502	0.0699	132	26
1949	4,113	.50	8,226	123,626	0.0665	125	−5
1950	5,178	.54	9,589	132,953	0.0721	136	8
1951	5,316	.59	9,010	140,885	0.0639	120	−13
1952	5,971	.68	8,781	145,347	0.0604	114	−6
1953	7,674	.97	7,911	150,285	0.0526	99	−15
1954	10,205	.91	11,214	177,102	0.0633	119	20
1955	12,377	.88	14,065	194,671	0.0722	136	14
1956	16,660	.88	18,932	217,150	0.0871	164	21
1957	24,657	.94	26,231	245,384	0.1068	201	23
1958	29,605	.96	30,838	251,897	0.1224	230	15
1959	36,349	.98	37,091	267,156	0.1388	261	13
1960	41,534	.99	41,953	270,938	0.1548	291	11
1961	49,496	1.00	49,496	285,719	0.1732	326	12
1962	58,769	1.02	57,617	291,979	0.1973	371	14
1963	59,158	1.03	57,435	305,384	0.1880	354	−5
1964	79,103	1.05	75,336	318,555	0.2364	445	26

[a] From quarter-end figures.
[b] Price index for all goods and services purchased by the private sector.
[c] Consumption and investment, including subsistence components.
SOURCES: Official data and author's estimates. Details (to be soon published elsewhere) available on request.

JOHN M. MONTIAS

- •
- •
- •
- •
- •

Bank Lending and Fiscal Policy in Eastern Europe

It is characteristic of the stage reached in the study of Soviet-type economies that quite a few efforts are now being made to construct models simulating the behavior of the decision makers in these centrally planned systems. Many students of central planning think that more insights will be gained from systematization, quantification, and prediction than from the further accumulation of specific details and instances about institutions whose general patterns of behavior have already been studied. Professor Brzeski's dynamic model (in this book) describes what he calls the "strategic interdependencies" among the flow and the stock variables of an inflationary economy based on Poland's postwar experience. My contribution lies in the same general area as Brzeski's, but differs from his in its degree of quantification. I have attempted to find numerical answers to specific questions, for plausible levels of the exogenous variables and of the parameters, in a simplified representation of a Soviet-type economy. In particular I wish to calculate the budget surplus that would maintain or restore aggregate market equilibrium for a volume of banklending to enterprises corresponding to given rates of inventory accumulation. I also contrast the quantitative impact of various fiscal and monetary policies in a situation of repressed inflation and in one in which full consumers' choice prevails (i.e., where no aggregate surplus demand exists). I shall peg my discussion, to begin with, on Brzeski's model, which provides a convenient standard for differentiating my product.

I am indebted to Raymond P. Powell for valuable criticism at several stages in the preparation of this essay. I am, however, solely responsible for any remaining conceptual or numerical errors. I also wish to thank Mrs. M. Weaver for programing the simulations in the second part of this essay.

In Brzeski's model, the real variables include consumption and investment, without distinction between additions to fixed assets and to inventories, and labor supplied for employment. The supply of labor depends on real consumption and on exogenous demographic factors. National income is a function of the capital stock, the cumulative sum of past investments, and of employment. The demand for money is a function of the level of consumption in real terms. The supply of money is determined by the past stream of investments and by the price level in each period. The level of investments is set autonomously by the planners in each period. Prices of investment goods adjust in such a way as to preserve equality between the demand for and the supply of money. The system is determinate — there are as many equations as endogenous variables — and, for given levels of the exogenous variables, it "traces out" a growth path of the endogenous variables.

In my opinion, the structure of this model is so simplified that it fails to capture some of the essential aspects of the inflationary mechanism in a Soviet-type economy. The money supply in reality is not determined by investments — at least not by investments in fixed assets, which are financed in large part from the budget.[1] It is determined simultaneously by the volume of credits and by the behavior of enterprise and budget deposits, which, together with currency in circulation and savings deposits, form the principal liabilities in the consolidated balance sheet of the national bank in each country and of the specialized banks. A theory of inflation must be capable of showing, on the one hand, how the total volume of bank assets is determined and, on the other, how the corresponding volume of liabilities is distributed among its principal components. It should also be capable of explaining how enterprise deposits get to be converted into currency in the hands of the public and under what circumstances the budget may increase its deposits at the expense of currency holdings or enterprise deposits.

Even a crude model must recognize the fact that "real variables" are or may be influenced by the decisions of households and of the government, which in turn are conditioned by their monetary receipts. The level of consumer-goods inventories is in part determined by consumer saving and consumption decisions. The government may scale down investments to counteract inflationary pressures generated by the monetary system.

---

[1] In the first postwar years, when both fixed investments and additions to working capital were financed in part from budget deficits, investments and monetary circulation were more directly linked.

Besides this interdependence between monetary and real variables, there is also a feedback of prices on the other variables in the system. This feedback, as Professor Raymond Powell pointed out in his study of the Soviet monetary system, is due to the impact of changes in prices and wages on the current value of inventories, which in turn affect the volume of credits issued to enterprises and, withal, monetary circulation.

One aspect of the behavior of the managers of the monetary system in a Soviet-type economy that is especially difficult to postulate is the determination of the size of the budget surplus. Is the surplus used as a flexible instrument to offset unplanned excesses in household incomes? Is the surplus "autonomous," in the sense that shortfalls on the receipts side are matched by a corresponding curtailment of expenditures, so that the planned and realized surplus tend toward equality? Or does the Ministry of Finance allow the budget surplus to be determined "passively" by realizing expenditures at planned levels, no matter what the state of receipts may be or the need for deflationary fiscal measures to offset the consequences of credit policy or of extraordinary wage disbursals? It is evident that our models will behave differently under these divergent assumptions. The budgetary statistics in the table that follows cast some light on the problem.

Although no firm conclusions can be drawn from the evidence in Table 1, it does suggest that the treasury tended to offset above-average yearly increments in credits with larger-than-usual budgetary surpluses and conversely for below-average credit expansions. From 1951 to 1953 the deflationary policy was carried out by raising receipts above plan and maintaining expenditures at anticipated levels. In 1954 and 1963, however, receipts were kept close to target, but expenditures were raised substantially in the first year and lowered in the second in inverse relation to the credit expansions of these two years.[2]

If it is correct to assume that the budget acts as a flexible instrument for blotting up excess liquidity, then a mechanical theory of the inflationary process, such as Brzeski's, cannot explain year-to-year changes in monetary circulation and prices.

---

[2] The only year, it seems to me, when the monetary situation got clearly out of hand was 1956. Here, incidentally, excessive wage disbursals associated with an extraordinary political situation, rather than the unplanned extension of credits, were chiefly to blame. (For details, see J. M. Montias, "Inflation and Growth: The Experience of Eastern Europe," *in* W. Baer and I. Kerstenetsky, eds., *Inflation and Growth in Latin America* [Homewood, Ill.: Irwin, 1964], pp. 241–246.)

The interaction between "real" and financial variables is illustrated in a simplified manner in the models that follow.

Three basic types of fiscal policy may be envisaged, depending on the degree of repressed or open inflation the government is willing to tolerate:

1) If the government wishes to maintain equilibrium in retail markets without queues or other symptoms of repressed inflation and is unwilling to raise the level of consumer-goods prices, then it must manipulate disposable household incomes and the aggregate supply of consumer goods and services in state and cooperative stores so as to keep all markets cleared while maintaining a "normal" level of inventories. (Inventories

TABLE 1

DIFFERENCES BETWEEN ACTUAL AND PLANNED BUDGET RECEIPTS AND
EXPENDITURES IN SELECTED YEARS

(billions of zlotys at current prices)

Year	Actual budget receipts minus planned	Actual budget outlays minus planned	Planned surplus	Actual surplus	Increase in currency in circulation	Increase in savings bank deposits	Increase in credits outstanding	Deposits of socialized enterprises at end of year
1951	+7.6	+ .3	4.1	12.0	n.a.	0.2	+ 6	n.a.
1952	+6.7	− 1.7	0.9	9.3	1.0	0.2	+10	7.5
1953	+4.2	− 0.7	1.7	6.6	2.3	0.4	+15	n.a
1954	+1.4	+13.0	11.9	0.3	1.6	0.6	+ 2.7	11.3
1962	+8.6	+ 4.8	3.6	7.4	2.0	7.1	+20[a]	11.2[b]
1963	+1.8	− 9.2	3.2	14.2	0.7	9.7	+34[a]	28.8[b]
1964	+7.5	+ 7.5	4.9	9.2	3.4	9.0	n.a.	14.9[b]

[a] Estimate.
[b] State enterprises in industrial and trade sectors only.

NOTE: All increments in credits and monetary circulation are measured as differences between the level of the stock on December 31 of the preceding year and on December 31 of the given year. Budgetary receipts and surpluses, both planned and actual, include increases in household deposits in savings banks.

SOURCES: 1951 to 1954: W. Jaworski, *Zarys rozwoju systemu kredytowego w Polsce Ludowej* (Warsaw, 1958), pp. 118, 122–123, 178–199, 199; *Ekonomista*, No. 3, 1961, pp. 184–185; *Finanse*, No. 9, 1961, p. 12. Planned budgets are from the yearly statement on the budget by the Minister of Finance. 1962–1964: planned budgets: *Finanse*, No. 1, 1962, pp. 3–6, No. 1, 1963, pp. 3–5; No. 1, 1964, p. 4. Budget fulfillment, currency in circulation, savings deposits and deposits of enterprises are from *Rocznik statystyczny 1966*, pp. 523, 531, 533. The year-to-year increases in credits were estimated from the index of short-term credits extended by the National Bank in *Wiadomości Narodowego Banku Polskiego*, No. 1, 1965 (back of front cover) and from the total liabilities of all banks on December 31, 1962 in the same periodical No. 2, 1965, p. 47. Data in *Finance a úvěr*, No. 10 (Prague, 1965), p. 629, *Finanse*, No. 7, 1964, p. 29 and No. 12, 1964, p. 5 helped to estimate changes in total credits outstanding from the increments in short-term credits of the National Bank.

are at a "normal" level if they stand in desired proportion to consumer-goods output.)

2) The government may raise (or lower) the level of consumer-goods prices to achieve the same aims as in type (1).

3) If some degree of repressed inflation is permissible, then the authorities may set a given ratio of consumer-goods inventories to output, ration formally or informally the limited supplies of these goods coming on the market, and use the budget to keep forced saving — undesired increases in currency and savings deposits — within certain limits.

I shall only consider models consonant with types (1) and (3), on the justification that across-the-board increases in the level of consumer-goods prices tend to be a measure of last resort, which most East European governments have successfully avoided since 1956. I recognize that among the budgetary policies open to the government, some might lead to such a degree of repressed inflation that price increases would be unavoidable; but I believe that the authorities would not adopt them or, if they did, that they would quickly abandon them when they became aware of their consequences (for example, the curtailment of investments in Poland in the summer of 1959 and 1963). This ruling out of price increases implies that my models do not apply to the Polish situation in the late 1940's and in 1952–1953 when inflation was allowed to emerge in the open. I believe, however, that an equation representing the government's price response to certain conditions of repressed inflation could be grafted onto my second type of model and that it would be capable of yielding more realistic results than Brzeski's scheme.

In all model types, I consider the effects on consumer-goods inventories and household saving of varying a parameter, denoted k, which represents the proportion of increments in bank loans covered by the budget surplus. To raise k for a given level of bank loans and for given rates of taxation, the government must curtail investments in fixed capital.[3] This will cause employment in the producer-goods sector to contract. I shall assume that any labor released from this sector will be employed by the consumer-goods sector and will make a net addition to the initially postulated output of these goods. (This initial level, denoted $\bar{C}_0$, is ap-

---

[3] The curtailment of investments will have a feedback on bank loans *via* producer-goods inventories, but this secondary effect will normally offset only a small part of the original change. Note also that for k to be inversely related to investments, the surplus *net of the increment in bank savings* must rise with k (see below, pp. 53–54).

proximately that which would obtain if the budget were just balanced, that is, if k were zero.) The wage bill in the model consists of two components: one centrally determined, W_0, linked to the outputs of the two sectors by known labor-input coefficients, and the second arising from enterprises' unplanned outlays, financed by idle bank deposits, denoted ΔW.

I make the following simplifying assumptions:

1) The ratio of producer-goods inventories to investments in fixed capital is given. (It is independent of the forces interacting in the system.) Thus increments in inventory accumulation are tied to increases in investment.

2) Budgetary receipts are made up exclusively of taxes on enterprises and of increments in household saving deposits transferred to treasury account. Budget outlays comprise only investments in fixed capital and additions to working capital of enterprises (a fraction of enterprise increases in inventories).

3) Investments in fixed capital can only be made from budget grants.

4) Enterprise deposits not required for transaction purposes are spent on wages without effect on the supply of labor or on its allocation between consumer and investment goods. Their only effect is to bid up wages.[4]

5) The economy is closed to foreign trade.

6) The model's structural relations are all taken to be linear.

Additional assumptions about household and enterprise saving propensities are built into the following system of equations, which corresponds to the first situation envisaged (in which consumers' choice prevails).

In the equations below, the variables are either dated by the subscript $t-1$, in which case they correspond to the period preceding the current period, or they are undated, in which case it is understood that they belong to the current period, or "year." All exogenously determined variables are marked by a bar placed over them.

---

[4] For any one enterprise, of course, excess wage outlays are likely to help overfulfill the output plan. But for the system as a whole, as long as the labor supply is fixed and the marginal value productivity of labor is not too different in the various sectors, there is little chance that a higher-than-planned wage bill would have a substantial effect on output measured at constant prices. Indeed, except for the impact of higher wages on some agricultural goods, *via* the free market, and on some inventories held at cost, the value of national income at current prices should not be significantly affected either by these excess disbursements.

We first consider the changes in the assets and in the liabilities of the banking system.

The increment ΔM in currency in the hands of the public and in savings deposits is given by equation (1).

1) $\Delta M = a(W - \overline{W}_{t-1})$

where a is a coefficient smaller than 1, W is the actual wage bill in the current period and $\overline{W}_{t-1}$ the wage bill in the preceding period.[5]

The budgetary surplus, which adds to the treasury balances deposited in the banking system, equals a fraction k of the increase in loans to enterprises.

2) $ki(I_i^t + I_i^c) = t(Y - W_p) + b(W - \overline{W}_{t-1}) - I_t - g(I_i^c + I_i^t)$.

The left side of equation (2) shows the budget surplus in its relation to the increase in bank loans; the right side shows the surplus as the difference between budget receipts and expenditures. The symbol letter i stands for the fraction of increases in inventories of producer goods, I_i^t, and of consumer goods, I_i^c, credited by the banks; Y is the gross value of output of enterprises; W_p is the centrally determined wage bill; W is the total wage bill; I_t are investments in fixed capital financed by the budget; t is the fraction of $(Y - W_p)$ taxed by the state;[6] b is the ratio of increments in savings deposits to increases in the wage bill over the preceding period;[7] and g is the fraction of inventories financed directly by the budget.

The increase in enterprise deposits ΔE is set automatically by enterprises on the basis of their transactions requirements.

3) $\Delta E = d(Y - \overline{Y}_{t-1})$

where d is the constant ratio of increments in deposits to increments in output and $\overline{Y}_{t-1}$ is the preceding year's output.

Now ΔM, ΔE, and the increase in budget deposits (equal to the budget surplus) all represent increments in the liabilities of the banking system. Their sum must match the increment in assets, that is, the net addition

[5] The assumption here is that the public desires to maintain a constant ratio of currency holdings to current income.

[6] Taxes here depend on the value of output minus the centrally determined wage bill. A model variant where the tax base was equal to $(Y - W)$ rather than $(Y - W_p)$ was also examined. (See p. 48–49.)

[7] This assumption implies that s, the marginal propensity to save, is constant, while the average propensity rises from 0 when income is constant all the way to s when $\frac{\overline{Y}_{t-1}}{Y} \to 0$. A variant with a constant average propensity to save was also tried out. This change in assumptions had no discernible effect on the operation of the model.

to bank loans.[8] After substituting the expressions in equation (1) to (3) for the three sources of increments in deposits, we obtain equation (4):

4) $i(I_i^t + I_i^c) = d(Y - \overline{Y}_{t-1}) + a(W - \overline{W}_{t-1}) + ki(I_i^t + I_i^c)$.

The following structural relations are also given.

5) $I_i^t = e(I_t - \overline{I}_t^{t-1})$

where e is the constant ratio of increments in inventories of producer goods to the increase in investments in fixed capital over the preceding period ($\overline{I}_t^{t-1}$ stands for investments in the last period).

The demand for labor due to the tentatively planned output of consumer goods $\overline{C}_0$ and from the producer-goods sector is determined in equation (6):

6) $L_p = c\,\overline{C}_0 + f(I_t + I_i^t)$

where c and f are the labor inputs per unit of output in the two sectors.

When this labor demand is subtracted from labor supply $\overline{L}_s$, the residual ΔL represents the otherwise unemployed labor force that is to be allotted to the consumer-goods sector.

7) $\Delta L = \overline{L}_s - L_p$

The manpower released by the producer-goods sector and assigned to the consumer-goods sector, in order to maintain a market equilibrium through a budget surplus, may be thought to have a lower productivity than the previously employed labor force in the receiving sector. Instead of adding $\Delta L/c$ to the output of that sector, we shall therefore assume that it adds only $\Delta L/(c + v)$, where v is a non-negative number. If these extra laborers are paid according to their marginal productivity, they will receive wages equal to $\overline{w}_c\,c\dfrac{\Delta L}{c+v}$, where $\overline{w}_c$ is the average wage in the industry.[9] The total centrally determined wage bill is given by equation (8):

---

[8] Total liabilities of the consolidated balance sheet of the banks include, in addition to the three items mentioned, the savings deposits of households. The asset corresponding to the deposits is a government obligation to the banks. Both the deposits and the obligation should be subtracted from the total assets and liabilities of the system to arrive at the equality described in the text.

[9] In simulating the behavior of the model, I did not try to distinguish the average wage in the two sectors. Note that $\frac{c}{c+v}$ expresses the ratio of the average wage of the incremental workers to the average wage of workers already employed. An alternative assumption, which was not explored in the simulations, would be to make the wages of all workers equal to $\overline{w}_c$. This alternative assumption, if v were strictly positive, would presumably make it necessary to run a larger budget surplus (in proportion to the increase in loans) in order to achieve equilibrium in the consumer-goods market than in the solutions to the programs that were actually run. This would not, however, change the mechanism of interaction in any substantive way.

8) $W_p = \overline{w}_c L_p + \overline{w}_c c \dfrac{\Delta L}{c+v} + \overline{w}_c f(I_t + I_i^t)$

The total wage bill W equals W_p plus the increment in the wage bill due to unscheduled outlays of enterprises:

9) $W = W_p + \Delta W$.

National income is defined in equation 10):

10) $Y = \overline{C}_0 + \dfrac{\Delta L}{c+v} + I_t + I_i^t$.

Finally, we introduce a behavioral equation for households:

11) $(a+b)(W - \overline{W}_{t-1}) = W - (\overline{C}_0 + \dfrac{\Delta L}{c+v} - I_i^c)$

In the equation above, total household saving appears on both sides. On the right it is derived as the difference between household incomes and sales of goods and services, equal in turn to the total output of consumer goods minus increments in the inventories of these goods. Saving on the left is split between additions to currency holdings and additions to savings deposits, both of which depend on increments in incomes.

ΔW, the unscheduled outlays on wage and salaries of enterprises, is determined by the solution of the equations above. But it may also be computed independently as a residual in the enterprises' balance of receipts and expenditures:

12) $\Delta W = Y - W_p - t(Y - W_p) - (1 - i - g)(I_i^c + I_i^t) - d(Y - \overline{Y}_{t-1})$

This equation requires a few words of explanation. The receipts of enterprises from the household sector equal the sales of consumer goods and services. Enterprise receipts from the government sector equal I_t, on the assumption that all investments are financed by budget grants, plus working-capital subsidies $g(I_i^c + I_i^t)$. Total output Y (equal to $\overline{C}_0 + \dfrac{\Delta L}{c+v} + I_t + I_i^t$), minus additions to inventories $(I_i^c + I_i^t)$, equals total enterprise receipts from the household and government sectors, exclusive of working-capital subsidies. Hence, the gross receipts of enterprises amount to $[Y - (I_i^c + I_i^t)]$ plus credit increments $[i(I_i^c + I_i^t)]$, plus working-capital subsidies from the government $[g(I_i^c + I_i^t)]$. This boils down to $[Y - (1 - i - g)(I_i^c + I_i^t)]$. Disposals of these receipts include centrally determined wages W_p, taxes $t(Y - W_p)$, and desired additions to bank deposits $d(Y - \overline{Y}_{t-1})$. The entire residual is spent on unplanned wages or ΔW. This equation was used in all variants as a check on the solution of the simultaneous equations.

Solutions for various values of k are tabulated below for the following values of the coefficients and exogenous variables: $i = 0.8$, $e = 0.5$,

$f = 0.8$, $c = 0.6$, $g = 0$, $v = 0.4$, $t = 0.8$, $a = 0.1$, $b = 0.2$, $\overline{C}_0 = 105$, $\overline{W}_{t-1} = 90$, $\overline{L}_s = 115$, $\overline{I}_{t-1} = 35$, $\overline{w}_p = 1$. These parameters and those selected for the variants examined later were chosen to illustrate the situation prevailing in Poland in the early 1960's and are at least plausible in their magnitudes. (All variables except employment and wages are measured in billions of zlotys at prevailing prices; wages and employment are in arbitrary units, but the total wage bill in each sector stands in approximately the right proportion to the value of output.)

TABLE 2

k	Y	Increase in credits	ΔM	Increase in savings deposits	I^c_i	I_f	ΔL ($= \Delta C$)	ΔW	Budget surplus
0	169.9	5.3	3.3	6.5	− 7.4	50.6	0.4	7.7	0
0.2	169.4	6.4	3.2	6.3	− 4.9	49.3	2.2	7.5	1.3
0.5	168.2	9.4	2.9	5.8	+ 1.9	46.0	7.3	7.0	4.7
0.6	167.4	11.3	2.8	5.5	+ 6.0	44.0	10.3	6.8	6.8
0.7	166.3	14.0	2.5	5.1	+11.9	41.1	14.7	6.3	9.8
0.8	164.5	18.2	2.2	4.4	+21.5	36.4	21.8	5.6	14.6
1.0	152.3	47.7	−0.2	−0.5	+87.3	4.3	70.7	1.0	47.7

This simulation suggests that inventory accumulation in the consumer-goods sector is sensitive to changes in the parameter k. A balanced budget would cause inventories to drop by 7.4 units; at the other extreme, if the budget simply covered the entire increase in bank loans, inventories of consumer goods would rise by 87.3 units, at the expense of fixed investments and producer-goods inventories. If the inventory-to-output ratio in the consumer-goods sector necessary to maintain market equilibrium happened to be equal to 0.5 and if consumer-goods output in the preceding period had been equal to 90 units, then the desirable increase in inventories would come to approximately 5 units. A little less than 60 percent of the increase in bank credit would have to be covered by the budget surplus to arrive at this equilibrium.[10] A characteristic feature of this variant of the model was that the leverage exerted by a given small change in k on inventories of consumer goods was much greater at high than at low values of the budget surplus. The reason for this is that a deflationary policy causes total inventories to *rise* (the drop in producer-

[10] For k equal to 0.6, the increase in consumer-goods output over the preceding period would be 10.3 units (11.4 percent). To this increase there would correspond an inventory accumulation of 6 units, or slightly more than was needed to maintain equilibrium.

goods inventories being outweighed by the increase in consumer-goods inventories). Thus loans increase, and a small change in k generates a larger increase in the budget surplus than when k is low and investments high. However, if the inventory-to-output ratio in the producer-goods sector were appreciably larger than in the consumer-goods sector, the opposite effect might be observed: total loans would drop as k increased, and the impact of k would be inversely related to its size.[11]

In general, the main effect of increasing k is to reduce the "accumulation ratio" (the ratio of total investment to national income) and to increase the ratio of inventory accumulation in consumer goods to total investment. When full employment is maintained at all times, k — at least within the plausible range of its variation — exerts relatively little influence on the size of national income and on the total wage bill.

Four other variants of the basic model were investigated. In the first, the coefficient g, the proportion of inventory accumulation financed by budget subsidies, was raised from zero to 0.2, with a simultaneous decrease in the coefficient i (the ratio of inventory accumulation financed by the banks) from 0.8 to 0.6. Thus $(1 - g - i)$, the fraction of inventory accumulation financed by the enterprises themselves, was held constant.

The effect was deflationary, compared with the standard variant where 80 percent of inventory accumulation was financed by bank loans. For $k = 0.5$, I_i^c rose from 1.9 in the standard model to 7.2 in this variant. For $k = 0.6$, the corresponding values were 6.0 and 11.2. (Investments in fixed capital had to be curtailed to make room for subsidies. Approximately the same budget surplus was generated in the two cases.)

Next, the proportion of inventory accumulation financed from enterprises' own funds was raised from 0.2 to 0.5 (with $i = 0.4$ and $g = 0.1$). With the budget surplus equal to 50 percent of the value of loans to enterprises, this alternative financing of inventories virtually eliminated ΔW and raised I_i^c from 7.2 (with $i = 0.6$, $g = 0.2$) to 11.2. In all variants considered, a reduction in the sum of i plus g turned out to be the most powerful way of forcing down ΔW and curbing wage drift.

The next variant traced out the effect on the simultaneous determina-

[11] The fragmentary data for Poland would seem to indicate that high values of k were associated with large increases in loans. But this is not provable. A large budget surplus may have been necessary to offset an extraordinary increase in loans that was due to an unanticipated increase in producer-goods inventories (due, for example, to poorly coordinated plans). A detailed inventory and credit analysis would be required to identify cause and effect.

tion of the endogenous variables of taxing enterprises according to their actual gross profits $(Y - W)$, instead of their gross profits net of unscheduled wage outlays $(Y - W_p)$ as in the standard model. This apparently slight change had an unexpectedly powerful deflationary impact. With k equal to 0.5, it caused an increase in I_i^c from 7.23 in the standard model to 33.6 (investments in fixed capital fell from 43.4 to 17.4, ΔW rose from 6.7 to 41.2). The reason for this becomes apparent when we consider the following equations:

13) $\Delta W = Y - W_p - t(Y - W) - (1 - i - g)(I_i^c + I_i^f) - d(Y - \overline{Y}_{t-1})$

The only difference between equations (12) and (13) is that $+ tW_p$ occurs in the first and $+ tW$ in the second. When enterprises transmute their unrequired deposits into ΔW, this causes a contraction in tax receipts, which in turn induces a drop in investments. Labor is transferred from the producer-goods to the consumer-goods sector. But the net effect of this transfer is to diminish W_p (due to the lower-than-average productivity and wages of transferred workers). The reduction in W_p being smaller than in Y, enterprises are left with increased funds at their disposal which they again spend on wages. With the parameters selected, equilibrium can only be attained by reducing investments to a very low level. The interaction here is so complex, however, that generalizations are hazardous.[12]

In all discussed simulations, a subvariant was introduced, wherein the value of inventories of producer goods was raised by a coefficient equal to the ratio of ΔW to W. In other words:

$I_i^f + e(1 + \frac{\Delta W}{W})(I_f - \bar{I}_f^{t-1})$

This adjustment was meant to allow for the "Powell effect" or at least for a part of it, since the adjustment implicitly assumes that wage drift influences only the *increment* in producer-goods inventories rather than the costs of holding the entire stock, an alternative, and perhaps more plausible hypothesis.[13]

[12] Note, for instance, that when v was reduced from 0.4 to 0 (so that the productivity of the transferred workers was equal to the average in the consumer goods sector), the cutback in investments necessary to restore equilibrium was substantially smaller than before.

[13] The impact of cost increases on existing inventories will depend on accounting methods. "First-in-first-out" accounting practice would cause a larger portion of existing inventories to be revalued at present, higher costs than "last-in-first-out" practice. As a partial compensation for this omission of the effect of higher wage costs on the existing stock, it should be noted that inventories of finished goods ("finished" from the viewpoint of the enterprise selling them) are normally valued at existing prices rather than at cost and should therefore be invariant to the rise in wage costs.

Turning again to Table 2, we recall that when k was set at zero, ΔW was equal to 7.7 and I_i^c to -7.4. Allowing for the feedback of ΔW on the increment in inventories in producer goods causes inventories of consumer goods to fall by 8.8 units — a further slight deterioration in the market situation. The fact that ΔW was virtually the same in the two variants suggests that it is sufficient to calculate the first-round impact of the feedback. When k was raised to 0.5 and ΔW was equal to 7.0, I_i^c turned out to be $+2.0$. Allowing for the feedback caused the increment in I_i^c to decline to $+1.25$, a rather considerable effect in relative terms. Further experimentation showed that the relative effect on I_i^c was inversely proportional to the absolute level of the latter. In any event one can easily imagine that in a situation where wage controls were loose (that is, where the coefficients c and f were liable to rise above plan), and where fiscal policy failed to offset, or *a fortiori*, reinforced the inflationary effect of automatic credit extension, ΔW might be large enough to have a significant effect on increments in inventories of producer goods and hence might seriously disrupt market equilibrium. If the authorities were moved to raise prices in the producer- or the consumer-goods sector to restore equilibrium, this would raise the value of inventories in one or both sectors and cause a further expansion of credit. A cumulative inflationary mechanism might then be set in motion (through the interaction of wage drift, inventory reevaluation, and corrective price-level adjustments).

So far, the discussion has adhered to the somewhat utopic assumption of untrammeled consumer choice. While consumer rationing does not prevail in "normal times" in Soviet-type economies — it was formally abolished in the Soviet Union in 1947 and in Eastern Europe in 1953–54 — it has been widely observed that shortages, queues, and other forms of non-price allocation have persisted in all these economies. Whether these disequilibria reflect imbalances in the markets for individual consumer goods or an over-all excess in aggregate demand has not always been clear. It is, in any event, instructive to study the interaction of monetary and fiscal variables in a situation where repressed inflation prevails and compare the results with the previous model where consumer-goods inventories bore the brunt of changes in aggregate demand.

I shall dwell on two variants; the difference between them turns on the mode of household saving. In the first, households behave as if they wished to deposit in savings banks a given fraction of their increase in incomes and to hold the residual forced saving in the form of currency. In the second, residual savings, after currency requirements have been satisfied, are all deposited in the banks. We have for the first variant:

$\Delta S = b(W - \overline{W}_{t-1})$ and ΔM residual,

and for the second:

$\Delta M = a(W - \overline{W}_{t-1})$ and ΔS residual.

For both variants the increment in consumer-goods inventories is set at a fraction q of the increase in the output of consumer goods over the preceding period. Thus we have a new equation:

$$14) \quad I_i^c = q(\overline{C}_0 + \frac{\Delta L}{c + v} - \overline{C}_{t-1}).$$

For the first variant, the number of equations is the same as in the basic model, since equation (14) replaced equation (1), in which ΔM was determined as a function of the increment in disposable household income in the basic model. In the second variant, there are twelve equations, including number 1, which is pertinent, since ΔS rather than ΔM is residual.

The first variant yields results that parallel those of the basic model, in the sense that a rise in k, the fraction of credits covered by the budget surplus, mops up excess currency in circulation, reduces investment in fixed capital, and raises the output and inventories of consumer goods. These changes are brought out for five values of k and for alternative methods of financing inventories in Table 3.

The comparative statistics of repressed inflation and of free consumer choice are similar. Raising k, besides cutting down on currency in circulation, reduces fixed investment and compels a transfer of manpower from the producer- to the consumer-goods sector. The magnitude of GNP is hardly influenced by the change in assumption regarding the accumulation of consumer-goods inventories (given k and all the other parameters and coefficients). The main difference is the volume of currency outstanding, which is, of course, much larger for a low value of k when inflationary pressure is repressed than when the inventory-to-output is allowed to vary. As in the basic model, enterprises' unscheduled wage outlays are relatively insensitive to changes in k.[14]

As before also, an increase in the fraction of inventory increments

---

[14] For the parameters chosen, it happens that ΔW *rises* with k, but this is due to the particular constellation of parameters selected, and is not an inherent feature of the model.

TABLE 3

EFFECTS OF VARYING k, i, AND g ON ΔM, ΔW, I_i^c, I_t, Y AND THE
BUDGET SURPLUS WHEN ΔM IS RESIDUAL

	I_i^c	ΔM	I_t	ΔL	ΔW	Y	Budget Surplus
1) $i = 0.8$, $g = 0$							
$k = 0$	3.0	11.3	50.2	0.9	5.7	169.8	0
$k = 0.2$	4.8	8.5	47.8	4.6	6.0	168.9	2.6
$k = 0.5$	7.4	4.6	44.3	9.8	6.4	167.6	6.3
$k = 0.65$	8.7	2.7	42.7	12.3	6.6	166.9	8.1
$k = 0.8$	9.9	0.8	41.1	14.7	6.7	166.3	9.9
$k = 1.0$	11.4	−1.6	39.1	17.8	7.0	165.5	12.0
2) $i = 0.6$, $g = 0.2$							
$k = 0$	5.2	7.9	47.2	5.5	6.1	168.6	0
$k = 0.2$	6.6	5.9	45.5	8.1	6.3	168.0	1.9
$k = 0.5$	8.4	3.0	43.0	11.9	6.5	167.0	4.7
$k = 0.65$	9.4	1.6	41.8	13.7	6.7	166.6	6.0
$k = 0.8$	10.3	0.2	40.6	15.5	6.8	166.1	7.3
$k = 1.0$	11.4	−1.6	39.1	17.8	7.0	165.5	9.9
3) $i = 0.6$, $g = 0$							
$k = 0.2$	4.8	5.9	47.8	4.6	2.7	168.9	2.0
$k = 0.65$	7.7	1.6	43.9	10.4	3.3	167.4	6.1
$k = 1.0$	9.9	−1.6	41.1	14.7	3.7	166.3	9.2
4) $i = 0.5$, $g = 0.1$							
$k = 0.2$	5.7	4.6	46.6	6.4	2.9	168.4	1.6
$k = 0.65$	8.1	1.0	43.4	11.2	3.3	167.2	5.1
$k = 1.0$	9.9	−1.6	41.1	14.7	3.7	166.3	7.7

NOTE: The values of the exogenous variables for all solutions were: $\overline{C}_0 = 105$, $\overline{C}_{t-1} = 100$, $\overline{Y}_{t-1} = 150$, $\overline{W}_{t-1} = 90$, $\overline{I}_{t-1} = 35$, $\overline{L}_s = 115$, $\overline{w}_p = 1$. The coefficients used were: $q = 0.5$, $f = 0.8$, $c = 0.6$, $e = 0.5$, $b = 0.1$, $v = 0.4$, $t = 0.8$, $d = 0.1$.

financed by the government, when it is matched by an equal decline in the fraction of inventories financed by the banks, reduces ΔM and raises I_i^c for a given value of k. For a given i (the fraction of inventory financed by the banks), an increase in g (the fraction of inventories financed by the government) leaves ΔM unchanged; but it does drive up ΔW. Our earlier conclusion on wage drift still stands: *the only effective way of preventing wage increases caused by enterprises' spending of otherwise idle deposits is to force them to finance a larger share of their total inventory accumulation.* For this purpose, budget surpluses are sometimes totally ineffective and, in all cases examined, manifestly inefficient (in the sense that they require an extraordinary curtailment of fixed investments to absorb a small ΔW).

Now we broach the last variant of this paper where I assume that households' bank saving is a residual item. Households behave as if their aggregate income in excess of the volume of consumer goods available for sale to households — equal to the output of these goods minus a fixed share earmarked for inventory accumulation — was saved in the banks, with the exception of a predetermined fraction of the increase in incomes going into currency hoards. This system, for low values of k and for an inventory-to-output ratio in the consumer-goods sector equal to 0.5 (as where ΔM was residual), turns out to be unstable, in the sense that the solution of the relevant simultaneous equations yields negative values for almost all variables including investments and bank saving.[15] When k is raised to 0.5, possible but implausible values arise, which denote an intolerable degree of repressed inflation, with fixed investments amounting to more than half of GNP, additions to bank savings equal to half of total household incomes, and I_i^c strongly negative. Raising k to 0.65 is sufficient to reduce investments in fixed capital to about a quarter of GNP, to drive the increment in bank savings down to 5.5 units (a reasonable magnitude), and to bring consumption and inventories in the consumer-goods sector into harmony with the wage bill. When the fixed inventory ratio q is lowered from 0.5 to 0.2, the system reacts to changes in k, in the range 0 to 0.8, in a manner opposite to that observed in all other variants of the model: as the budget surplus rises, investments increase, consumption falls, and forced savings accrue in bank accounts. As in all other variants ΔW remains insensitive to small changes in k.

The key to these anomalies is found in the budget equation — equation (2) — and, in particular, in the inclusion of ΔS, the (residual) increment in bank saving, in government receipts. We first remark that the higher the inventory-to-output ratio in the consumer-goods sector, the smaller will be the marketable supply of consumer goods. For a given wage bill, a high q and a small "market fund" will generate a large ΔS, which will be incorporated in budget receipts. A large ΔS allows the government to spend more on fixed investment, thus deflecting resources from the consumer-goods sector and further depressing its output. This self-feeding mechanism is explosive for low values of k. Moreover, as we have just seen, for certain values of q the budget will accumulate a sur-

---

[15] The coefficient i was set at 0.8 and g at 0 for this simulation.

plus more readily by curtailing consumption and inflating household bank deposits than by trimming investments for a given level of tax receipts. Thus a higher k will be associated with a larger ΔS. This is what makes the system operate "in reverse gear" for certain constellations of parameters. The paradox vanishes when we consider that the budget surpluses assimilated by "taking over" household saving are fictitious. When these accruals are eliminated from budget receipts a deficit is revealed, whose size is indeed proportional to the volume of forced saving.[16] Consumption and investment only react perversely to a rise in k when the surplus is defined to include government borrowing from the public.

In reality, of course, repressed inflation will seldom cause households to put all their surplus income either in currency hoards or in bank savings. The mixture of the two propensities that will be observed in a concrete situation will depend partly on the distribution of the increments in incomes in urban and rural areas. The evidence that can be collected from the Eastern European economies suggests, in any case, that bank savings have tended to rise faster in recent years than currency holdings.[17] If the residual-saving variant of the model is at present the more realistic one, then we should expect these economies to be more inflation-prone than in the past when currency was the favorite hoarding medium, *provided the basic assumptions of the model are fulfilled*: (a) that the choice of consumers is significantly limited, and (b) that the government treats increments in the public's savings deposits as spendable receipts.

The first assumption surely holds at least part of the time. So far I have seen no arguments in the writings of East European specialists in monetary theory that would indicate any awareness of the potential inflationary impact of a policy consonant with the second assumption. Neither have I any reason to believe that treasury receipts from savings banks are treated differently from taxes or any other receipts.

A closer look at the extraordinary credit expansion of 1963 and at its consequences brings to light a complication that was not envisaged in any

[16] With $q = 0.2$, the surplus net of increments in savings equals 11.3 when k is set at 0.2; 5.8 with k at 0.4; −18.0 with k at 0.65; and −193 with k at 0.8. Curiously enough, when k is brought up to unity, the net surplus becomes positive again (+99.5) and produces a situation of extreme deflation.

[17] For Poland, see Table 1. In Russia savings deposits rose 5.4-fold from 1959 to 1963, compared with a 59 percent increase in currency outstanding (*Revista de statistica*, No. 8 [1965], 67, 70).

of the variants of the model, namely that the inflation may on occasion be repressed not by limiting market supplies available to consumers but by preventing enterprises from spending their idle funds. In 1963, loans rose by approximately 34 billion zlotys. At the end of the year, 17 billion zlotys in enterprise deposits were held in blocked accounts.[18] This extraordinary measure was introduced in addition to, rather than in lieu of, the normal increase in k necessary to absorb at least a part of the excess liquidity injected into the monetary system. The actual increase in k, incidentally, was achieved mainly by trimming budget expenditures, especially on investment projects.[19]

In 1964, the volume of deposits of state enterprises in the industrial and trade sectors contracted by nearly 14 billion. I have no information about credit extension in that year, but I infer from the changes in liabilities of the banking system that it was unusually small. The planning authorities, by blocking deposits in the first year and by forcing enterprises to use some of their own free funds to finance inventories in the second, managed to forestall any serious disturbance in the Polish "money market." (In the light of the model, the authorities' course of action was more judicious than if an attempt had been made to force down the level of enterprise deposits by running an enormous budgetary surplus at the expense of fixed investments or of other budget outlays.)

The combined increase in currency and in savings deposits averaged about 20 percent per year from December 1962 to December 1964. This was certainly high but by no means catastrophic. There was no run on stores. Retail inventories continued to increase although at a slower pace than before. (They rose from 39.7 billion zlotys at the end of 1962 to 48.1 billion zlotys at the end of 1964.) The index of free prices on the peasant market, which had hit a record high of 129.1 in 1962 (on a 1955 basis), receded to 114.5 in 1963 and to 111.6 in 1964.[20] There is no evidence that the inflation was more tightly repressed than before the extraordinary credit expansion.

On the whole my conclusions are less pessimistic about the Polish authorities' ability to check inflationary tendencies than Brzeski's. Although

[18] *Wiadomości Narodowego Banku Polskiego,* No. 11 (1965), 47. According to the Minister of Finance, 15 billion zlotys were blocked in 1963 (*Finanse*, XIV:1 [1964], 6).

[19] Even "key investment projects" were hit by this deflationary move (*Finanse,* XIV:1 [1964], 3).

[20] *Rocznik statystyczny 1966*, pp. 338 and 512.

I do not think that either the managers of the National Bank or the Ministry of Finance officials have a comprehensive view of the complex interactions between monetary and fiscal policy, I submit that, between the two, they are capable of making correct decisions *post factum* to offset the inflationary consequences of their collective mistakes. Whether or not free consumer choice prevails, the state can use budget surpluses to drain the excess liquidity released by bank lending; on the other hand, the banks, by applying relatively slight pressure on enterprises to finance a greater share of their inventory accumulation, or, in the last instance, by temporarily blocking deposits, can prevent surplus liquidity from seeping into the household sector through unscheduled wage increases. What is essential in the first case is that the state should be willing to counter inflation by manipulating the "real" variables in the system — either *ex ante* by placing an appropriate ceiling on planned investments and social outlays or *ex post* by trimming budget expenditures below their originally targeted levels in order to redress an existing disequilibrium. Likewise, the banks, if they are to collaborate successfully with the fiscal authorities to curb inflation, must be willing to moderate their adherence to the "real bills" doctrine by easing or tightening their loan policy in the light of the monetary situation (and, especially, of the volume of enterprise deposits.) One reason why a mechanical dynamic model such as Brzeski's cannot cope with Poland's postwar monetary history is that the fiscal and monetary authorities are now willing to resort to counterinflationary remedies that would have seemed excessively prudent, if not downright revisionist, in the first period of frantic industrialization.

JÁNOS FEKETE

-
-
-
-
-

The Role of Monetary and Credit Policy in the Reform of Hungary's Economic Mechanism

Is there anything like an independent monetary and credit policy? I would think that this could not be contended. Monetary and credit policy is only one instrument of general economic policy — though a very important one. Its tasks are determined by the over-all targets of economic policy. What do we understand by monetary and credit policy? Its connotation is wider in Hungary than generally in Western countries. In addition to influencing economic activity by credit instruments we include in it also budgetary and income policies as well as price and foreign-exchange policies. The subject matter of this contribution — the role of monetary and credit policy in the new system — I would nevertheless think it difficult to deal properly with this question without at least a brief historical survey. Indeed, during the past twenty years we also pursued a "monetary and credit policy." Therefore, I will begin by examining, in broad outline, monetary and credit policy in Hungary's economic evolution.

I.

What did Hungary's balance sheet look like at the conclusion of World War II? The country had come to an almost complete standstill after the big war effort and the continuous spoliation by the German and Hungarian fascists. Forty percent of the national wealth was destroyed, corresponding to the aggregate national income of five years. Half of the capital invested in transport, two-thirds of the animal population, about half of the establishments of the manufacturing industry, and a yet higher part of the stocks of materials and produce was annihilated. The national income fell to 45 percent of that before the war. Out of it Hungary had to cover the needs of reconstruction and enormous international liabilities under the head of reparations and occupation costs. The receipts of the state budget and the accumulation of monetary capital by the private economy were not able to provide cover for such a volume of expenditure, thus inflation became unavoidable. Within eighteen months Hungary set up a world record of money depreciation: on July 31, 1946, 1.4 quintillion of pengoes was equal to one gold pengoe of 1938.

In this plight the men responsible for the direction of monetary and credit policy were faced with the extraordinary task to create a new, stable currency. The stabilization of August 1, 1946, represented a "feat of arms" which was to exercise a fundamental influence upon our entire future development. Even now, looking at it from a distance of twenty years, it is worth while to review its main features.

The stabilization was carried out with the aid of new methods on the basis of a comprehensive economic conception under particularly difficult conditions, when Hungary had to rely almost entirely upon her own resources. The stabilization plan provided for the creation of the economic preconditions: in the course of land reform estates of more than 57 hectares (34 percent of the country's territory) became the property of 640,000 working peasants; by the time of the stabilization the production of industry rose to 52 percent, coal output to 60 percent, the production of the iron and metal industries to 75 percent of the prewar level; 90 percent of the railway network was again put into operation; by way of taxation in kind, stocks in industrial consumer goods were accumulated by the authorities; the government assisted the accumulation of goods stocks by the granting of credit; and Hungary succeeded in recovering part of her National Bank's gold reserves, which had been removed to the West. As part of the stabilization plan, the distribution of the national income by end use was determined, as well as the conditions of the expected dynamic equilibrium for the first year. In addition to the setting of prices and wages and the establishment of a par value for the new currency, another important decision involved the determination of the maximum level for the issue of banknotes, in such a way as to provide for a considerable tightness of money at the outset. The bulk of forint amounts by which the stocks previously accumulated in the economy could be bought was put into circulation against the surrender of gold and foreign exchange hoarded by the population during the inflation. These could be used for essential imports without delay.

After some months, state expenditure was almost entirely covered by the receipts. Stimulated by a high rate of interest, deposits increased rapidly, whereas the control of credit was extended to almost the entire volume of credit.

This credit policy was essentially deflationary but, being accompanied by the selective granting of credits, it did not represent a brake on production. Indeed, it made possible adequate control of the investment activity even in this extraordinarily tight situation.

Within one year, industrial capacity increased to more than double and exceeded the 1938 level by 15 percent. National income rose by 36 percent and real wages of industrial workers by 43 percent. The model of a directed, controlled market economy thus proved a complete success in Hungary by the experience of the stabilization.

From the point of view of economic policy and consequently also from that of monetary and credit policy, the twenty years which have elapsed since then may be divided into two major periods: from 1947 to 1956 and from 1957 to the present — up to the introduction of the reform.

At the beginning of the first period, the most important objective of economic policy was the closing of the war wounds and to get economic activity moving again. Hungary had to rebuild — and in a more up-to-date manner than before — the destroyed factories in order to provide an adequate basis for liquidating her centuries-old industrial backwardness. In addition, dwelling houses and bridges, lying in ruins, were awaiting reconstruction, and the population stood in need of food and clothing. All this required huge quantities of raw materials, machinery, food, and industrial goods.

It proved necessary to effect a maximum concentration of all resources at Hungary's disposal. The completion of the gradual taking into public ownership of industry, the establishment of the state monopoly of foreign trade, the nationalization of the banks and the setting up of the centralized banking system[1] created the possibility of planned action under centralized direction.

---

[1] Previously the National Bank of Hungary performed only the duties of a bank of issue. An important part of economic activity was under the direction and fi-

Methods of planned economy were needed that would lend themselves to overcome the shortage of goods as quickly as possible. The method which appeared to be most suitable for this purpose was the stimulation of a rapid increase in production by highly centralized measures and a comprehensive central control of the economy. The organs responsible for the direction of the national economy set the targets to be achieved by the individual economic units. The planning instruction given to each enterprise specified in detail (for one year, and also by quarter and even by month) which goods were to be produced and in what quantities, to whom and at what price their products were to be sold, which raw materials and in what quantities might be used, how many workers and technical and administrative employees might be engaged, the wages to be paid, the machines to be used, and so on.

The enterprises were then judged according to their fulfillment of these plans prescribed by the central authorities, especially regarding the quantitative production targets. According to the degree of plan fulfillment, the enterprises obtained various benefits, the managers and workers received rewards and premiums, welfare services for the benefit of staff were widened, and so on.

As the property conditions prevailing in agriculture made such a system of detailed targets only partly feasible, central control was implemented by requiring that all peasants surrender a considerable part of their produce to the state purchasing agencies at fixed prices.

In this period, the basis of the monetary and credit policy was a detailed plan broken down to individual enterprises. In judging the credit demands of the economic units, the decisive criterion was whether the purposes for the accomplishment of which the funds were required figured in the plan of the enterprise. All items figuring in the plan were financed practically automatically, both as regards current production costs and the required investments. This did not, however, give rise to

nancial control of the biggest banks (Hungarian General Credit Bank, Hungarian Commercial Bank of Pest, First National Savings Bank Corporation of Pest, Hungarian Discount and Exchange Bank) which had considerable foreign participations. In December, 1947, the public law dealing with the nationalization of the banks was promulgated. Thereby the National Bank of Hungary — while keeping its functions as the bank of issue — became the central organ for the implementation of the monopolies of money circulation, credit, and foreign exchange.

In 1948, the Hungarian Investment Bank was set up to handle the budgetary funds to finance investments and renovations. The National Savings Bank caters for the needs of the population. It collects savings and grants credit to the population.

unusual problems, and the realization of the goods produced — in view of the fact that demand was far in excess of production — proceeded without a hitch although there were qualitative shortcomings.

Simultaneously, measures were introduced aiming at ensuring the central control and allocation of monetary and credit media. Thus, enterprises paid almost all their profits to the budget; at the same time, however, they received budgetary allocations, not to be repaid, for investment purposes. The funds permanently needed for the current activity of the enterprises were made available by the National Bank of Hungary from deposits belonging to the Treasury and kept with the bank. Temporary monetary requirements were covered by the bank by short-term credits granted from the deposits of the enterprises, the savings banks, and the State Insurance Corporation as well as from its own assets.

Moreover, the centralized banking system became an important basis for the control of the economic units. The entire monetary circulation passed thus, for instance, through a so-called single account of the enterprises kept with the bank, which supervised monetary settlements item by item. In order to control the volume of the purchasing power put into circulation and to ensure the stability of the currency, the bank also controlled the disbursement of wages — this control being related to the fulfillment of the production plans. During this period characterized by a high degree of centralization, monetary and credit policy thus represented an important instrument of economic direction.

In 1949 it was possible to reach and even somewhat to surpass the level of 1938, the last year of peace, in volume of industrial production and in real income of the population. In 1950–1955, in keeping with the large-scale industrialization program, more than one quarter of the national income was used for investments, and nearly one hundred new industrial enterprises came into being. By increasing the capacity of the existing units, by putting into operation of new plants, and by large-scale construction activity Hungary succeeded in eliminating the oppressingly high rate of unemployment of prewar days and practically reached full employment. The number of employed persons in the national economy rose by 600,000 (almost equivalent to the entire population growth) of which more than 500,000 represented the increase of the labor force in industry and building which together exceeded the 1938 level by roughly two-thirds.

Increases in capacity and labor force, however, were not yet sufficient by themselves. The satisfaction of the need of raw materials and energy consumption which greatly increased represented a decisive problem since Hungary in this respect is a poor country. In the solution of Hungary's big problems the ever-increasing shipments of the CMEA countries — above all the Soviet Union — proved very helpful. More than two-thirds of Hungary's raw material imports came from the USSR; our import requirements in basic materials — such as coal, mineral oil, iron ore, wood and cotton — were primarily filled by the Soviet Union. The Soviet market for the products of our industry is stable and favorable because Hungary is able to pay for her imports with Hungarian industrial articles (machinery, consumption goods, rolling stock, pharmaceutical articles) which she can produce economically. Financial conditions have from the outset been also favorable: within the framework of bilateral clearing accounts interest-free, mutual technical credit lines related to the volume of turnover became available. Trade is conducted on the basis of mutual advantage. Foreign-trade turnover rose to more than double during this period at the end of which almost one-fifth of the national income was realized through the intermediary of the foreign market.

Thanks to the gradual increase in wages and earnings, but mostly to the rise in employment, real income, in 1955, exceeded that of 1949 by more than a quarter.

We are not claiming that these achievements were the result of a completely uniform and uninterrupted development. From time to time, periods of slow-down, minor setbacks, and unexpected difficulties occurred. Thus, in spite of the large-scale investment efforts, the increase of the industrial output was due chiefly to a rise in employment, whereas productivity increased only to a lesser degree; agriculture likewise did not develop at sufficient speed. The production of consumer goods was not able to keep pace with the growing demand, and so on. The detailed instructions of the plans impeded the freedom of decision of the enterprises, sometimes even when this was unnecessary. Initial steps to eliminate the shortcomings which made themselves felt during this period were introduced but could not be fully developed.

The next major period also started under difficult conditions. In 1956 Hungary's national economy sustained substantial damage. Apart from the material damage, production amounted during several months to a mere fraction of its former volume, and consumption at the same time considerably exceeded its previous level. At the end of 1956 and the beginning of 1957 inflation represented a real threat. It was overcome within a short time because of grants-in-aid and loans received from the Soviet Union and the other socialist countries. Assistance was granted partly in the form of raw materials for industry and consumer goods for the population, and partly in the form of long-term loans in freely convertible currencies to be repaid by commodity shipments.

Backed by this international aid, the new government consolidated the political and economic situation within a short time. Without relinquishing the fundamental objective of economic policy — the building of socialism — the specific economic targets of the new era were characterized by many new features. Taking account of the country's economic possibilities, the government pursued the aim of gradually bringing about a structural change in Hungary's industry which would ensure the supply of the population on an adequate level and the increased participation in the international division of labor. A more moderate growth of the volume of production was to go hand in hand with quality requirements and giving more weight to postulates of productivity and economical production. To satisfy the increased demand for farm products, a transition to large-scale production methods had to be brought about in agriculture without a setback in the level of output. The successful realization of all these objectives was to provide the basis for a considerable and lasting increase in the standard of living of the population.

Having learned from the mistakes of the preceding period, Hungary wanted to ensure the fulfillment of the objectives by a new approach to the problems. The time had come to loosen the administrative ties and gradually to replace them by measures based on the acceptance of more responsibility by the managers and on the material interest of the workers. To mention some of these measures without endeavoring to place them in a precise sequence of time or importance: the excessive ties on production were reduced, the ministries in charge of production got practically a free hand regarding the setting of mandatory target figures for the individual enterprises, the former labor-force and wages control was replaced by a simpler supervision of average wages, prices were regulated in such a way as to reduce the previous disproportions and to allow them to follow cost relations more closely, a system of profit-sharing was introduced which made it possible for enterprises to distribute a part of their profits among their workers. The enterprises have to pay a so-called fee for the use of assets (a kind of interest on capital) in proportion to the amount of fixed and working capital used by them; the mandatory surrender of crops, livestock, and animal products was abolished and replaced by state purchases on the basis of market relations; in order to promote a more economical import policy a dual customs-tariff system was put into force.

The monetary and credit policy in this period, too, followed the changing methods of economic management, and measures in keeping with them were introduced also in the field of banking. The former financing of production — which had an essentially automatic character and was closely tied to the plan — was thus improved by the introduction of various "target credits." Moreover, a wide range of differential rates of interest (from 0.5 to 18 percent) was established, depending upon the economic aim to be achieved. Preferential rates were granted for the production of important raw materials, export goods, and prime necessities, whereas high rates of interest were applied to stocks of goods in respect of which no movement had occurred for some time and to needlessly tied-up and redundant stocks.

The measures taken in monetary and credit policy played an important role in ensuring that the large-scale transformation of agriculture which had started in 1958 could be concluded successfully without a setback in production. At the end of 1961, roughly 96 percent of the arable land was accounted for by state and cooperative farms and a beginning was made to ensure step by step also the other prerequisites of mass production, namely a high degree of mechanization, large-scale equipment, the development of agricultural technique, an improved supply of specialists, and so on. The state budget made available large amounts of nonrepayable investment funds; the cooperatives were granted large amounts of medium and long-term investment credits under favorable conditions. The budget undertook to refund incidental losses incurred by cooperatives until they got economically stronger. In connection with sale contracts concluded with purchasing agencies, the bank has been granting short-term credits to bridge over liquidity problems stemming from the seasonal character of agriculture.

Hungary tried to support a more intensive participation in a favorable international division of labor also on the financial side. In the past twenty years, even under the most difficult conditions, Hungary has al-

ways met its international obligations without delay. This gave her the
opportunity to strengthen her ties with the credit and money markets of
Western Europe. Trade relations which after the war started on a bilateral basis are now being carried on for many years — with only minor
exceptions — with the aid of freely convertible currencies. In the past ten
years, our foreign trade turnover increased by an annual average of 12
to 14 percent, and today nearly 40 percent of Hungary's national income
is realized through the intermediary of foreign markets.

The increase in the foreign-trade turnover was assisted by the credit
policy of the bank. The bank financed production for export purposes
by cheap credits and granted short-term credits for the financing of
imports.

The new elements that made themselves felt in the methods of economic management resulted in the coming to the fore of quality postulates and drew the attention to a phenomenon which formerly had been
observed only sporadically: that of production not always being in conformity with demand. This imbalance is not a question of a lack of over-
all equilibrium between effective demand and the volume of available
goods. The problem is that Hungary's enterprises often do not produce
those goods, or not in such a quality or variety demanded at home or
abroad. As long as there was a general shortage of goods, this did not represent a problem, since consumers bought also goods which did not
in all respects meet with their requirements. But as the needs of the population were being satisfied to an increasing degree, demand switched in
the direction of goods of better quality. Industry did not respond always
adequately to the new requirements since nothing forced it to do so. Production continued on the basis of the original plans, and the bank financed
this production. This resulted in an increase of stocks not readily marketable. In 1961–1964, about 8 percent of the national income went to
the increase of inventories and reserves. Part of this was rendered necessary by the higher production, but a considerable part was in excess of
the increase needed for normal business. The accumulation of stocks in
excess of requirements immobilizes part of the national income, prevents
a rise in the standard of living of the population, and limits the desirable
growth of production.

In the interest of a reduction of existing stocks and in order to prevent
a further formation of redundant stocks, a great number of measures
were introduced, largely of a financial character. The aim was to induce

enterprises to liquidate their existing redundant stocks even at reduced prices and to prevent the production of similar new stock of unsatisfactory goods. Clearance sales of consumer goods at reduced prices have thus become a regular feature. As for products used for further processing, prices that had remained unchanged for a longer period have been freed, the actual prices being determined by free agreement between buyers and sellers, and any loss to the producer is being paid out of the budget. The bank, on the other hand, in the course of the financing of the current activities emphasizes the sale prospects of the goods to be produced and systematically makes sure to what degree the production is covered by orders and delivery contracts. Production whose realization does not seem to be assured will not be eligible for bank credit, whereas stocks turning slowly over are being financed at high rates.

The new system of delivery contracts which came into being in September, 1966, conforms with the former practice of the bank. The new system of delivery contracts strengthens the position of the buyer and contributes to the liquidation of the wrong practice which tied the production to plan figures established from above, often without due regard to actual requirements.

The mentioned measures have achieved partial results. In 1965 and 1966, a better harmony between production and demand was attained, and stocks were reduced. In 1965, only 2 percent of the national income were accounted for by the increase in stocks and reserves, and at the same time the number of articles in short supply decreased. Hungary had a considerable increase in exports without overburdening the balance of payments on the imports side. The bulk of the growth in production (about 90 percent) was derived from a rise in productivity.

Despite these encouraging results it became clearer in recent years that the methods of economic management applied up to now — the detailed plan instructions decreed from above, the allocation system, and the high degree of centralization of managment — which rendered good services in the liquidation of an economy characterized by shortages, do no longer ensure an adequate rate of development. More is needed than a simple modification and improvement of some details of an otherwise essentially unchanged method of management by centralized plan instructions. A major change became urgent also by the fact that the manpower reserves necessary for large-scale development became exhausted.

It is for this reason that Hungary tried to find ways for the transition from extensive to intensive methods of development.

On the basis of intensive research, investigation and analysis carried out with the cooperation of distinguished economists, leaders of enterprises, and the controlling state bodies, a decision was adopted by the Party and government ordering a comprehensive reform of Hungary's economic mechanism — the system of economic management. On the basis of guide lines of the reform which were discussed and adopted, and also received wide publicity in the press, the careful elaboration of the details is now well under way. The launching of the reform is planned for the beginning of 1968.[2]

The idea of a reform of the system of economic management has emerged in recent years not only in Hungary but — with a greater or lesser time lag — in practically all socialist countries. This shows that in the European socialist countries a rather long phase of development destined to liquidate a state of affairs characterized by shortages has, in general, come to an end and a new and more balanced phase has begun where the objective consists in the satisfaction of needs on a higher plane. To cope with this changed task planned economy needs more flexible methods.

In frequent talks with representatives of foreign central banks, commercial banks, and economic research institutes I heard what people abroad think about Hungary's planned reform. In most cases I met with opinions that correctly see the essential features of Hungary's ideas and follow the developments with benevolent interest. There are, however, some problems where perhaps an imperfect knowledge of the antecedents represents an obstacle to a clearer understanding. I would like to examine some of them.

There is, for instance, the question of whether the reform of the economic mechanism does represent an absolute necessity for Hungary — in other words, to what degree did the responsible leaders of the country have the freedom of decision to accept or reject the reform? Might they have chosen also another solution to raise the standard of economic performance? I may safely state that the country is in full possession of its freedom to decide these matters. Hungary is struggling with some problems, but it has a well-balanced, rapidly developing economy. Economic efficiency might be improved even by keeping or slightly modifying

[2] The reform was in fact introduced on January 1, 1968. Ed.

the existing mechanism, but by generally better organizing its operation. Hungary shall, of course, avail herself also of these possibilities. The leaders of the country, however, are not only responsible for the present, but for the future as well. If they intend radically to improve the economic performance, if they want to prepare the national economy for long-term dynamic development, the possibility for action is already largely determined.

Our investigations have demonstrated that in the long run the conditions of a more rapid and more balanced development can only be secured by the reform. The implementation of the reform is a prerequisite for an increase in Hungary's international competitiveness, for an essential change in the rational husbandry of stocks, for a speedier reduction of the costs of production, and for a broadening of the resources needed to raise the standard of living. From the point of view of the country's long-term development, the reform must thus be considered a condition *sine qua non.*

It has been said that Hungary is proceeding too cautiously and over-carefully, that she takes too much time for the preparation instead of introducing new methods already this year or at the beginning of the next. The reform can be considered as a great economic and political task, similar to the stabilization, an exciting and inspiring assignment for every economist. This present task also has to be prepared properly. For six months only the existing deficiencies were analyzed, another six months were needed by a team of several hundred distinguished economists to elaborate the principles of the new system, and eighteen months are available to work out the practical implementation in all its details of the prepared principles which were in the meantime approved by the highest authorities. Hungary's economists cannot be charged with excessive speed, but they want to carry out the reform in such a way as to forestall a setback in output, the cropping up of unemployment, a decline in the standard of living, and a deterioration of the balance of payments. And though Hungary has friends who will assist her in times of trouble — this happened once — she does not want to depend on this help again. It is for this reason that Hungary is cautious, and may be, even slow.

Though Hungary will introduce the reform on January 1, 1968, this does not mean that we are delaying all changes to that day. Ever since 1957, but especially in recent years we have taken a series of measures which were already conceived in the spirit of the new mechanism. During the remainder of the time, we shall also introduce those economic measures which do not have to be postponed until 1968. What will then exactly happen on January 1, 1968? I may perhaps define it shortly as follows: up to that date the old system of economic management will continue to function as the general framework, though it will comprise already numerous new elements; whereas from January 1, 1968, onwards the new mechanism will begin to operate in its entirety. This will constitute a new framework in which we shall have to work, though many processes and methods inherited from the old system of economic control and management will continue to make themselves felt. Their influence will thereafter have to be gradually liquidated.

I have read some evaluations according to which the reform has been rendered necessary by the failure of the former economic policy, and that the break with the past means a new orientation of economic policy. Others have only put the question regarding the inter-relation of the reform with the economic policy, carried on up to the present. The reform of the economic mechanism is the organic continuation of the line of conduct regarding general policy and economic policy on which Hungary set out in 1957 and followed ever since. Hungary, however, does not consider unalterable methods and institutions which were once necessary, but have been left behind by developments.

Finally, let me mention also those opinions according to which the reform actually means the abolition of planned economy and the introduction or rather the "rediscovery" of the market economy. This is not true. In the future, too, national economic plans will be drawn up — though by more sophisticated methods than previously — regarding the main tendencies and proportions of economic activity, the broad processes of development. These, however, will not be broken down to the level of individual enterprises and will not set plan targets from above. Economic direction by the state will therefore not be of a detailed and administrative character as at present. The system of direct guidance built upon plan instructions will be replaced by regulations relying mainly on economic measures which give wider scope to commodity relations[3] based on "value." This will render the central direction of the compre-

---

[3] Commodity relationship is the Marxian term for defining the situation where goods are produced with the aim of being sold for money on the market, as against direct bartering. The scope of commodity relations was in Hungary rather restricted owing to the allocation system, mentioned earlier, which had many features characteristic of bartering.

hensive processes of the national economy more powerful and more effective than at present. The reform does not aim at weakening the central direction of the economy by the state, nor at liquidating the planned economy, but rather at strengthening them. Hungary does not want to introduce a market economy without direction and control, but the market is going to be organized and regulated working within the framework of the planned economy where the interests of the enterprises will in a large measure be dovetailed with those of society. Properly speaking, the most essential feature of the reform consists in that Hungary shall be in a position to combine — on the basis of the socialist ownership of the means of production — the planned central direction of the national economy with the active role of the market.

On this basis Hungary wants to draw a rational delimitation between the spheres of centralized and decentralized decisions; to ensure that all those questions which can best be judged on the level of the individual enterprises, actually belong to their sphere of decision; and at the same time to maintain the say of the central authorities in respect to those questions which are of fundamental importance for the development of the economy, which demand a superior approach and comprehensive knowledge. Let us examine the essentials of the reform from this angle:

1. Under the new arrangements, what degree of independence will the socialist state, in its capacity as owner, grant to the individual enterprises?

After January 1, 1968, the enterprises will no longer receive plan tasks broken down from above. They will decide on their own most questions involving their current activity. They will thus decide (a) within their sphere of activity, how much, and in which assortment, they will produce of the different articles, how much they will offer to domestic buyers or for export; (b) in what quantity and quality, from which firms, out of domestic or import sources they will buy the raw materials and semi-finished products needed for their output; (c) how many and what kind of workers they want to employ and what wages they are going to pay within the framework of the public regulation of wages.

They will also enjoy more independence in dealing with minor questions of development and expansion.

When judging the activity of the enterprise and its workers, the basis of evaluation will not be the fulfillment or overfulfillment of its plan. The main compass and yardstick of the performance of each unit will be its profit after the discharge of their financial obligations toward the state in its capacity as owner. If the enterprise makes good use of its economic independence, that is, if it offers for sale such goods and in such quantities, of such quality and at such a price for which there exists an effective demand within the country or abroad, and if it does so with the most rational inputs, its profit will be rising. If this does not happen, it will be the enterprise's fault.

Profit is the over-all indicator of the activity of each unit, an indicator controlled by the market on the social scale. In a socialist society profit does not, of course, represent the ultimate aim of production. But we would nevertheless deem that the striving after higher profit by each unit may become an effective instrument for the attainment of the social goal, namely the best possible satisfaction of needs. It will be able to play this role if we tie the material interestedness of both the enterprises and their workers to the increase in profits. The widening of the independence of the enterprises means thus above all that they will enjoy the fruits of adequate performance more directly and to a greater degree than before; at the same time, however, the consequences of unsatisfactory performance will be reflected on their own resources.

2. What is the significance of public ownership of the means of production from the point of view of the reform?

In exercising its ownership rights, the socialist state may close down or merge enterprises; the right of ownership is embodied also in the fact that the manager of the unit is a representative of the state, nominated and relieved by state organs. The regulations applying to the structure and limits of wages in the national economy are prescribed by the state in its capacity as owner. It is the right of ownership which affords the possibility to issue direct instructions in those exceptional cases where some endeavors of an enterprise may not be entirely in line with the public interest — for instance in connection with international obligations undertaken by the state.

The socialist state in its capacity as owner of the enterprises supplies them — first of all by way of the budget — with the material means needed for their activity. The state requires, however, that for the use of these assets the enterprises pay public imposts — in the form of taxes and contributions — providing that these assets are being used with at least the minimum of efficacy to be expected.

Thus, for instance: (a) the state budget provides the enterprises with the buildings, machinery and equipment — in short with the fixed capital needed for production; on the value of this fixed capital, a fee is paid for the use of resources amounting to 5 percent per year; (b) up to the amount of the working capital permanently tied up in production the state budget provides the enterprises (in the course of the settlement of working capital funds to be effected in 1967) with working capital on which the same fee of 5 percent for the use of resources has to be paid — the temporary cash needs in excess of the working capital fund will be satisfied through credit; (c) the state provides for the supply of enterprises with the qualified labor needed for their operations; on all wages paid, enterprises have, however, to discharge a wages tax of 25 percent; this tax constitutes one of the sources for the expenses foreseen in the State budget for professional training, public instruction as well as for social welfare and the public health service; (d) part of the profits is to be paid into the state budget as a profits tax.

These obligatory payments represent the minimum return that may be expected of the enterprises in a normal performance. The profit attained in excess of this will remain at their disposal and may be used for the following purposes: (a) for the formation of reserve funds in order to enable them to assume — with adequate circumspection — rational risks in order to develop output and supply as well as to increase profitability; (b) to create a development fund which. together with the amortization of the fixed capital, forms the enterprises' own funds out of which they may replace obsolete equipment as well as develop and expand their capacity within their own competence; (c) to increase the material interestedness of the workers (the so-called profit-sharing fund); the latter may be used to supplement wages by the granting of premia and rewards and end-of-year bonuses; moreover, it is with the aid of this fund that the financing of the welfare, cultural and sport programs of the enterprise is effected; basic wages may also be augmented, within certain limits, from the profit-sharing fund.

In well-operating enterprises with above-normal profits, the managers, intermediate clerks, and workers participate in wages supplements in proportion to the responsibility borne by them. Those who are in a position to influence the development of profits to a greater degree also share in a larger measure in the benefits. If, however, an enterprise shows a deficit and is therefore not able to cover the wages due for individual work and achievements, it may only pay the minimum wages guaranteed by the state. This corresponds for the workers and lower employees to the basic wages as at the time of the introduction of the new economic mechanism; for those employees, however, who owing to their leading position are mainly responsible for the deficit, it will represent only a proportion of the basic wages.

3. What economic instruments will be available after the reform to ensure the central decisions and direction in respect of questions of fundamental importance for the development of the economy?

The most important will be: planning on the scale of the national economy; price policy; investment policy; trade and foreign-exchange policies; credit policy.

It is a common characteristic of these instruments that they do not aim at the operative influencing of, or intervention in, essentially short-term economic events, but rather serve the central control of the long-term trend of development as well as to ensure its direction into appropriate channels. Let us look at some of these instruments more closely:

Planning on the scale of the national economy. — Under the new mechanism the fundamental task of planning on the level of the national economy will consist in the drawing up of plans for defining the main objectives of economic development, the chief proportions of economic growth ensuring an optimal equilibrium and affording an adequate basis for the coordinated application of policy instruments promoting its achievement. It follows that under the new economic mechanism the center of gravity of planning will shift in the direction of long- and medium-term plans. For medium-term (5-year) plans the long-term plan serves as a basis. The medium-term plan assumes a particularly important role seeing that within its framework the decisions referring to development may already be made in a rather concrete form; whereas in respect to many of them a rather large degree of freedom still exists. The use of the instruments of economic direction is also partly linked with these medium-term plans. The annual plan, on the other hand, is to be the plan of the coordinated operative measures of the government and largely aims at influencing economic processes whose regulation is fundamentally to be left to the market mechanism.

This role of economic planning demands that the planning activities be raised to a higher level, and that the scientific foundation of the plan be strengthened.

Price policy. — It constitutes an essential element of the reform to guide the enterprises by a more rational and elastic price system toward a better use of their resources, toward the creation and maintenance of equilibrium between supply and demand, and toward rapid technical development.

In the interest of an adequate assertion of actual "value" relations a general reform of producer prices is being carried out on January 1, 1968. The price reform will be based on the actual cost of production and on the value judgments of the market, keeping in view also preferences of economic policy.

When shaping the price system Hungary takes into account that production costs and value judgments by the market are changing factors. Prices can therefore only then exercise their guiding and stimulating role in an adequate manner if official price-pegging applies only to a rather small segment,[4] while prices of most goods are determined by agreement between buyers and sellers. This, however, can only be achieved gradually. The new price system will thus for the time being apply three categories of prices, namely: (a) pegged [fixed] official prices for some important raw materials, energy and fuel, prime necessities, and basic services; (b) prices negotiated — within official limits — by the enterprises; prices of this kind will apply to some raw materials and to a variety of consumer goods; (c) freely moving prices for the other raw materials, half-finished goods and about 30 percent of the consumer goods; these prices will be determined by negotiations between seller and buyer.

The price reform will bring about a change also in the structure of consumer prices. This, however, will be implemented in such a way as not to affect the general level of consumer prices in an essential manner and not to reduce the real income of any major stratum of the population.

The liquidation of the mutual isolation of prices in the domestic market and foreign trade constitutes an important objective of the reform. With this purpose in view — on the basis of the average "production cost" of foreign exchange to the economy — so-called foreign exchange multipliers will be introduced to apply equally to exports and imports, independently of the official gold content of the forint. Users have to pay, for the materials, semifinished goods, and machinery imported by them, the actual foreign price converted into forints on the basis of the foreign-exchange multiplier. This price is to give a realistic measure of the cost

---

[4] Currently, 85 percent of all prices of goods are officially fixed.

of the import to the national economy. Producers of export goods, on the other hand, will get the countervalue of the foreign exchange received for their products also converted into forints at the rate of the foreign-exchange multiplier, independently of whether the export is transacted by them directly or by the intermediary of a foreign-trade corporation.

Correct guidance in this case is important from the point of view of the balance of payments. Hungary expects that the users — through the differences in price — will carefully examine their import requirements and prefer domestic sources of supply or imports (and the cheapest source for such imports) respectively according to relative costs. Exporters, on the other hand, are expected to shift to producing readily selling, competitive products to enhance their profit.

Investment policy. — The general trend of development and changes in the structure of the economy are above all determined by the establishment of new big enterprises or modernization. In addition, an important role is played by further production and other objectives (e.g., the development of the electric grid, road building on a national scale, major establishments in public health and public instruction). It is for this reason that Hungary intends to ensure the availability of material resources needed for these objectives — on the basis of decisions to be embodied in the medium-term plans of the national economy — also in the future by funds concentrated in the state budget.

The role of bank credit in the investment field is going to increase and will acquire considerable weight. It will also be on the basis of the medium-term national plans that the amount to be assigned for these purposes and the selection of the branches of the economy to be developed will be decided. It is incumbent upon the bank to make the evaluation of the demands for investments credits by the enterprises, subject to the guidelines laid down in the plan regarding the development of the economy. This involves not only meeting of credit demands, establishing of priorities, or rejection in some instances, but also the granting of preferences — on the basis of selective evaluation for the development of those branches which are designed by the plans with regard to conditions of capital repayment and interest. The enterprises will, of course, decide independently whether, on the conditions stipulated by the bank, it will be worth while to avail themselves of the investment credit for the specific aims, and whether they can shoulder its conditions keeping in mind their prospective profit.

Trade and foreign-exchange policies. — In order to assert adequately the national interest in trade policy and to ensure the optimal use of our foreign-exchange resources — to fulfill punctually foreign-payment liabilities — Hungary cannot dispense with central direction of foreign trade and foreign-exchange policy. However, a large measure of decentralization for the decisions of the enterprises relating to their foreign-trade activities is to be granted.

The chief manifestations of centralized policy in this field are as follows:

Foreign-trade activities may only be pursued by enterprises having received an authorization from the foreign-trade authority. Centralization extends, however, only to the right of granting this authorization, whereas the organization and activities of the enterprises concerned with foreign trade will be more varied than before. Producers can thus obtain authorization for the export of their own products, or for the import of their raw-material requirements. Specialized foreign-trade corporations will continue to operate partly on the basis of their own working capital, and partly as agencies.

Export and import deals may only be made after export and import licenses are obtained from the foreign-trade authority. The maintenance of the system of such licenses serves above all to promote the systematic information of the competent organs, while at the same time allowing adequately to assert the interest of the state in trade policy as well as the fulfillment of obligations stipulated in international agreements.

The determination of the uniform foreign-exchange multipliers applied in foreign trade is the responsibility of the central authorities.

An effective import-tariff system will be drawn up, which will serve the interests of trade policy, industrial protection, and price policy. The customs rates to be applied will be differentiated also according to whether the trade partners grant the most-favored nation clause to Hungary.

The enterprises are under an obligation to surrender to the National Bank of Hungary — which is vested with the implementation of central foreign-exchange control — all claims in foreign exchange they have obtained in the course of export operations.

The granting of export credits in excess of a set amount and recourse to import credits of all kinds is subject to the granting of a preliminary authorization by the National Bank of Hungary.

Credit policy. — In order to appraise more closely the tasks, functions, and methods of credit policy in connection with the reform of the economic mechanism, it is necessary to make some preliminary remarks about the relationship between the budget and the credit system.

As everywhere, the final distribution of state revenue takes place in Hungary through the budget, whereas the credit system operates only with funds put temporarily at its disposal. There exist, however, substantial differences regarding the length of time for which funds available from the two sources may be used. The budget makes long-term funds available. It follows that for all needs (investments, working capital funds of enterprises, long-term export credits) requiring long-term financing the funds are made available from the budget. The banks — the National Bank of Hungary and the Investment Bank — act only as intermediaries with regard to long-term financing.

The National Bank of Hungary generally possesses short- and medium-term means whose sources — apart from its own funds and those resulting from its function as a bank of issue — are formed by short-term deposits belonging to the enterprises, savings banks, and the state insurance corporation as well as to the Treasury. As a consequence, the bulk of the credits extended by the bank is short-term.

Under the new economic mechanism the volume and direction of the credits as well as the interest policy to be employed will be determined in close connection with the national economic plan by the guidelines for credit policy which have to be simultaneously approved.

The guidelines determine the general tendency to be followed by the banking system in the course of the actual extension of credit in keeping with changing circumstances and the objective needs of the economy.

Since the banks handle part of the long-term budgetary funds serving specific purposes, the guidelines of credit policy deal also with them. They thus comprise actual principles applying to the long- and medium-term financing of investments, to the short- and medium-term financing of production, services, and trade, as well as to the short-, medium-, and long-term financing of consumer needs. As for the granting of credit to production and trade, guidelines provide indications for a selective credit policy, that is, indications in what fields deviations from the general conditions of credit are justified. The guidelines lay down which branches may be granted preferential treatment with regard to interest and the extension of credit, and which branches are to be restrained. Selective credit policy is important from the point of view of the promotion of exports, of keeping imports on an even keel, and of influencing the supply of consumption goods.

Short-term credit needs may arise in connection with the expansion of production and sales, with a time gap in respect of receipts and expenditure, and so on. In granting credit, the bank — taking into account the guidelines of credit policy — examines the credit worthiness of the potential borrower. Credit will be granted to enterprises which are profitable, whose products are in demand, and which regularly meet their obligations on maturity. The bank is not bound to satisfy automatically the credit demands of any enterprise. If marketing of the output does not appear to be secured or if payment difficulties are a regular feature, the bank may refuse to extend the credit.

Interest on short-term credits is dependent on the circulating velocity [5] of the assets of the enterprise. Enterprises which produce economically and whose sales are proceeding without a hitch pay the basic rate of interest. When the basic rate of interest is determined it is important to keep in mind that it should be higher than the fee for the use of their own working capital assigned to the enterprise. If the slowing-down of the circulating velocity indicates economic problems — marketing difficulties, excessive stocks, and so on — interest is established on a higher level and may in rare, exceptional cases even reach 18 percent annually. The interest level for credit needed for the expansion of production and trade depends also on whether guidelines of credit policy envisage the stimulation of the enterprise in the interest of economic expansion.

Since enterprises will dispose over a more abundant supply of own funds than up to now, temporary surpluses of funds may arise (for example, when resources of the development fund are held in reserve for a protracted time). These funds may be kept on deposit with the bank and draw interest. The latter will vary with the time the deposit is being kept with the bank. (Up to now, no such interest was paid.)

The reform of the economic mechanism and its various aspects in the field of monetary and credit policy have many facets. It was, of course, impossible for me to deal with every one of them. I have thus not mentioned the rules applying to the activity of agricultural co-operatives and their financial side. These rules are in many respects based on principles

---

[5] Circulating velocity expresses the proportion between sales receipts and the volume of assets tied up to achieve this result.

similar to those for the enterprises, but in keeping with their nature they have also several particularities. I did not concern myself with the activity of non-profit (or public) institutions (hospitals, schools, research institutes, cultural establishments) as well as with the work of the local authorities which — though it is to become simpler and more informal than up to now — will nevertheless in the main continue to be limited and directed by the State budget. Finally, I did not have the opportunity to enlarge upon the increased demands that will make themselves felt upon the economic administration and within its framework with regard to financial administration as regards the drawing up of a more comprehensive, operative system of information composed of investigations and analyses referring to the evolution of the economic situation, to flows of money, etc.

I would hope, however, that my paper — even without aiming at completeness — has at least succeeded in acquainting you with the spirit and the most essential features of the reform of economic management in Hungary and above all — with the increased role and functions of our monetary and credit policy within its framework.

VÁCLAV HOLEŠOVSKÝ

•

•

•

•

•

Financial Aspects of the
Czechoslovak Economic Reform

It is slightly misleading to speak of financial aspects of the Czechoslovak economic reforms — as the title does — because we will primarily discuss the *activization* of money and finance, which is really the core of these reforms. With the increased importance of market relations and enterprise autonomy, money is bound to become *the* vehicle of messages triggering economic transactions, evaluating them, and changing their direction. Consequently, "in the new conditions" — as the ritualized reference to the 1967 economic model has it — everything having to do with money is acquiring a new role: prices and price calculation, enterprise finances, the tax system, state-budget operations, banking, and the credit system. Even in areas reserved for direct contracting and custom-made production, as in weapons' acquisition and public investment projects, money prices and cost-benefit calculations are likely to gain meaning. The global plans themselves are to be primarily projections of output volumes expressed in money-value aggregates. The detailed commodity content is to be filled in by market demand and supply, assisted and to some extent short-circuited by input-output analyses and forecasting of the structure of final, as well as derived, demand. In the new-style, "polycentric" planning,[1] the binding agent, the "language material" of the system is to be "active money."

A Western-trained economist comes to the task of describing and analyzing the role of money and monetary institutions in the "new model"

I wish to acknowledge the financial support of the Research Council of the University of Massachusetts in the preparation of this contribution.
[1] The expression is of Czechoslovak origin; see *Plánované hospodářství*, XIX:8–9 (August–September, 1966), p. 158.

comparatively well equipped. Western economies have had a sufficiently long experience with monetary and financial control tools in a market milieu, and the main relationships between banking and fiscal operations, on the one hand, and the real sector of the system, on the other hand, are well understood. It is reasonable to expect that, as centralized command planning is being dismantled, many monetary and financial phenomena and many policy issues familiar to Western economies will appear in some form in the "marketized" planning systems of East Europe — and that they will appear with the necessity of a logical conclusion. One might say, paraphrasing Marx, and with all the required *mutatis mutandis*, that Western economies show East European economies the image of their own future. If it is true that some sort of convergence of systems has been under way, and if West European planning receives its due and is acknowledged as an original product, then it is East Europe that is doing all the converging. A convenient lazy-man's method of organizing his impressions would be then to note instances of the "familiar new" and to gauge the distance separating the emerging Czechoslovak system from some full-fledged, well-articulated organization of polycentric planning, steered and modulated by an equally well-articulated assortment of monetary and fiscal instruments. This is what the West European varieties of planning have been trying to approximate and what the Czech economists presumably have in mind when they talk of the terminal "target solution" (*cílové řešení*).

Unfortunately, during the period of transition, the new which should be familiar to us is not always clearly recognizable among the ruins of the command system. The reason is that monetary instruments have been given a task without precedent: to assist in cleaning up the debris of the previous system, "phasing out" the institutions of the command-planning complex, and repairing the damages it had inflicted to the economy. This explains their neither-nor character: they are no longer quite the old monetary corsets of physical-output plans, but as yet they are not sensitive elements of economic servo-mechanisms or discretionary regulators either. Nevertheless, on the whole, we know what to expect or at least what to look for.

As for the damages done to the economy by centralized command planning, the repair job is enormous. I do not agree with the notion that the old system was condemned primarily because of the sales resistance of consumers and the accumulation of inventories at the retail level, at least not in Czechoslovakia. It was rather because a large number of malfunctions of different types appeared at various points of the system simultaneously, causing an authentic protracted economic recession which even the most indomitable official optimist could not argue away. Some of these well-documented malfunctions — not listed in any particular order of enumeration — are:

(1) Accumulation of inventories of intermediate products, especially of work-in-progress — a sign of disturbed flows between producing firms and domestic as well as foreign customers. (2) Accumulation of one particular type of work-in-progress, that of unfinished construction of new plants. (3) Appearance of idle capacities, and probably of hidden unemployment — hidden in manufacturing and disguised by wages playing the role of unemployment compensation. (4) Onset of the effects of a chronic policy of under-replacement of fixed capital in plants inherited from the preplan area. (5) Hidden inflation — not so much in the form of repressed inflation accompanied by swelled-up liquidity of firms and households, as in the termite-type of inflation which shows in the deterioration of the quality of products sold at fixed prices. (6) Effects of the anti-innovation bias of managerial incentives, reflected in the lag of product models as well as production methods behind world technological standards. (7) Lowered working morale of labor and cynicism among managers.

There exist obvious as well as less obvious interdependencies between these various malfunctions, but by and large they can be traced to inadequacies in the system of economic communication. One way of defining the nature of this inadequacy is to say that the system has been relying on excessive specificity of messages — excessive in relation to its capacity to generate and process detailed information and to perceive all the interdependencies and consequences of messages and, therefore, their operational significance. The proliferation of economic traffic jams finally made the system's directors give up further attempts to deal with the confusion by a new wave of specific messages, commands, interventions, administrative sanctions, and incentives. The anarchy of centralized planning was to be relieved by the newly discovered coordinating functions of the market system. Money and money flows are now expected to make the value dimensions of economic activity visible again. If the self-poisoning process of centralized planning was due to its reliance on excessive specificity of messages, the new system hopes to achieve detoxication by the generality and universality of monetary messages.

Money, the all-pervasive fluid of market systems, penetrating all corners and gears, is to flush out inefficiencies and open the old natural channels between producers and users. The retreat from "subjectivism" and "voluntarism" in the management of the national economy is to become an advance toward the principle of self-regulation. The need for subjective judgments, which risk forever to degenerate into arbitrary actions, is to be minimized. This is the meaning of the Czech economists' call for "objectivization" of economic relations. It is a good way of bringing out the essential purpose of their monetization.

This essay is meant to be a general guide to the major monetary and financial features of the Czechoslovak system of economic management which started in 1967 on a three-year trial-run basis. In the first and longest part, I will discuss how the new measures are likely to affect the behavior of managers of individual firms. In the second, I will survey the new tasks assigned to banking and to the supply of credit. The third part will be reserved for the new functions of the state budget and fiscality, in general. We have to content ourselves, at this point, with the description of promulgated ordinances and the interpretation of intentions, with few references to empirical material.

I shall refer occasionally to experiences made with certain pilot reforms and experiments introduced in 1965 and 1966, but I want to make clear that the 1967 model is to be considered as the proper beginning of reform. The partial changes and isolated experiments of the past two years were of very limited value. The reported favorable results may always be attributed to the working of the Hawthorne effect — in human affairs being watched changes the conditions of the experiment. The unfavorable results are equally inconclusive because it is impossible to test the efficiency of market incentives and processes in isolated plants as long as they are immersed in the command system. This was the painful experience of the management of the Mayak and Bolshevichka factories in the Soviet Union. The same is true of Czechoslovak industries. In reforming economic systems, rehearsals are apparently not possible.

The Nature of the Firm

The place assigned to the individual enterprise in the command system used to strike economists as contrary to the nature of the economic universe, seen as a quasi-organic entity of interdependent functions within the wider process of reproduction of human societies. Rightly or wrongly, one reached for military metaphors to convey the spirit of instructions-to-be-unconditionally-obeyed flowing down the command pyramid, of the upward flow of reports on their dutiful execution, decision-making by the manual, the crudest notion of costs, discontinuity of tasks, weak lateral ties with units on the same level, and so on. The new economic model calls for a different imagery, and biology stands ready to supply its share of well-tested similes. An individual enterprise appears as a living cell. Monetary flows mediate and regulate the interchange of inputs and outputs between one cell and other specialized cells; they control their growth, multiplication, and replacement; they maintain a balance of functions and give the enterprise an economic identity and continuity — an autonomy attuned to the common purpose of the economic structure. However, there is no such natural state into which the economy would automatically settle once the paramilitary instruments of command planning are relaxed. The transition involves the installation of new signaling devices sensitive to monetary flows, and a retraining of the human agents.

Enterprise Aims and Incentives

In a market system the correctness of decisions concerning the purchase of inputs and production is tested by the response of the users-customers and becomes visible in the net financial returns. Curiously, the new Czechoslovak model which tries to use the allocative devices of the market system fails to define explicitly the rate of return which individual enterprises shall be expected to maximize. The new "rules of the game" resemble a welter of instructions concerning the disposition of enterprise revenues, and it is up to the managers to find out where their advantage lies. Only long after July 15, 1966 — when the new rules had been adopted — did management officials and some economists start to inquire what general criterion of efficiency the legislator had in mind, or should have had in mind,[2] and whether the new rules of enterprise management were consistent with it. There was some confusion of views about the proper criterion of economic efficiency — some favored labor productivity;[3] others, the ratio of net product to gross social product[4] —

[2] Bohdan Hlaváček, "Ekonomicý cíl podniku," *Hospodářské noviny*, No. 29 (July 1966).
[3] Vladimír Nachtigal, "Jaká kriteria pro hodnocení hospodářského vývoje," *ibid.*, No. 30 (August 1966).
[4] Stanislav Vácha, "Ekonomický cíl a kriéria jeho dosahování," *ibid.*, No. 33 (August 1966).

until one Miroslav Toms convincingly showed that it is, in free translation, total factor productivity — the ratio of national income over the sum of capital stock and labor input — which is the rational measure of efficiency.[5] There is no doubt that the instructions on the disposition of enterprise revenue are broadly and crudely consistent with this view.

The coded message of the instructions tells the management: "Try for a maximum of realized value added while keeping your capital stock and manpower as low as possible." In terms of enterprise finances: "Try for a maximum of net sales after taxes — and, incidentally, the tax rates have been constructed so as to induce you to release (or keep you from buying) any assets which will not add to your disposable net sales!" The crudity of the instructions — the mark of administrative command — shows mainly in the arbitrarily set rates and in their attempts to influence factor proportions, as will be seen when we discuss the "wage-bill surtax."

Before we comment on any part of the instructions, it will be useful to take a look at the package as a whole.[6] Schematically, we may start with the enterprise gross sales and see what subtractions have to be made before the firm can call any revenue its own:

(1) Gross sales

less (2) cost of materials and capital consumption allowances

equals (3) enterprise "net sales" (value added by the enterprise, confusingly called "gross revenue" — *hrubý důchod* — in Czech),

less (4) labor cost (at wage rates according to prevailing regulations),

less (5) allocation to the "reserve fund" in the amount of 2 percent of the annual wage bill,

less (6) allocation to the fund of cultural and social needs, at the minimum in the amount of .8 percent of the annual wage-bill,

less (7) capital charge — *odvod z výrobních fondů* — calculated at 6 percent of the depreciated value of the stock of fixed capital and 2 percent of business inventory),

less (8) value-added tax — *odvod z hrubého důchodu* — calculated as 18 percent of enterprise net sales under (3), adjusted by subtracting (7), (12), and (13), which covers social security contributions),

[5] Miroslav Toms, "Kritérium hospodářské činnosti podniku a růrstový cíl ekonomiky," *ibid.*, No. 14 (October 1966) and Mojmír Hájek and Miroslav Toms, "Teorie reprodukce, produktivita práce a struktura produktu," *Politiká ekonomie*, XIV:6 (June 1966), 484–495.

[6] All references to the new measures are taken from the government decree No. 242 of July 15, 1966, reprinted and annotated in a special supplement to the weekly *Hospodářské noviny*, No. 30 (July 1966) under the title "Rámcové podmínky hospodaření podniku platné od 1. ledna 1967."

less (9) "payroll surtax" called "stabilization tax — *stabilizační od-vod* — calculated as 30 percent of the excess of the actual wage bill over a hypothetical wage bill based on $\frac{9}{10}$ of the average annual wage the firm had planned for the year 1966,

less (10) "decongestion tax" — *přirážka k stabilizačnímu fondu* — amounting at most to 2 percent of the total actual wage bill (optional, imposed by local government to discourage labor influx),

less (11) fines for external diseconomies of production,

less (12) interest on liquid working capital financed by credit (4 percent),

less (13) interest on investment credit (6 percent),

less (14) credit installments covered from net sales (another part of repayments is made from capital consumption allowances),

equals (15) disposable net revenue (*použitelný hrubý důchod*) available for payments of bonuses or reinvestment.

To obtain the magnitude of the disposable "cash flow," one would have to add to the disposable net revenue the retained portion of capital consumption allowances. Liquid funds available to the enterprise may be augmented by new bank loans and by government grants.

Business Taxation as Tool of Efficiency

It is clear from this survey that business taxation will from now on be regarded only secondarily as a source of finance of nonconsumption uses. It will be exploited primarily in its capacity to influence management decisions, as a powerful source of incentives and disincentives. Item (5) — the capital charges — have been frequently seen as the minimum rate of net return on productive assets. However, the rate of net return must be large enough to cover all other obligatory charges, so that it should be interpreted as the minimum marginal rate — a permissible but still avant-garde notion among Czech economists. It is doubtful whether the planners really wish to see capital stock accumulate until it earns 6 percent on the margin — the determinants of the rate of investment to be aimed at have not been properly clarified. Therefore, one should not attach any particular significance to the precise level of the rate but rather consider it merely as a device making the managers aware of the cost of immobilizing funds in physical productive assets by making the source of their extra compensations vary inversely with the volume of capital stock. The tax base shall include also that part of unfinished investments which had been expected to be in operation according to obligatory tasks of the plan but were not — one of the residues of command features. On the other hand, the recently discovered concern with external diseconomies — water and air pollution — is reflected in the exemption from the taxable capital of waste-processing installations. Further exemptions are housing; social, cultural, and hygienic installations; and means serving conservation. New self-financed investments (or financed from long-term credit insofar as it is being repaid from net revenue) will remain untaxed for five years — a twist encouraging the use of disposable net revenue for investments rather than for employees dividend (profit sharing?) and to invest in quickly amortizable assets. Capital charge will be perpetuated, in principle, even if the stock of capital inherited from the previous era and financed mainly by capital grants will have been fully depreciated and perhaps replaced by capital stock financed entirely from the enterprise's own funds. It will remain a tax; it is not planned to change it into a mere internal device for calculating opportunity cost. Suggestions of some economists that the portion of new investments financed from bank investment credit be burdened only by a credit charge of 8 percent, not by the capital tax, went unheeded.[7]

Enterprise managers will also be undergoing a training-on-the-job in economizing working capital, including liquid funds. For that purpose, all enterprises will have all their working capital "confiscated" as of the starting date of the new rules and will receive bank credit to finance, retrospectively, their already accumulated inventory, as well as any additional current working capital needs. Proceeds from sales of inventory-on-hand as of January 1, 1967, will be turned over to the bank as if it had been financed *in toto* from credit. This ingenious maneuver is supposed to equalize the situation of all enterprises with respect to their endowment with working-capital assets and to stimulate the liquidation of excessive inventory hoards. Enterprises will be free to use their own judgment in deciding whether to continue using working-capital credit or to get rid progressively of short-term indebtedness and build up their own interest-free liquidity and inventory position. In either case they will have a built-in motive to watch their working capital and the proportions of its inventory and liquid components.[8]

[7] *Finance a úvěr*, No. 5 (1966), 262.
[8] It so happened that the stratagem of starting firms off with a minimal cash endowment failed miserably. The price reform, described later, unwittingly pro-

Paradoxically, the traditional methods of mopping up all enterprise liquidity and dealing it out parsimoniously through bank credit failed thoroughly in producing economy-mindedness. The unquestionable priority given to physical plans resulted in carefree handling of funds, financial leniency, and quasi-automatic transfusions of funds from highly liquid enterprises to those in financial straights. The new arrangements will at least make the managers think of the marginal contributions of working capital to net sales, which is the beginning and also the essence of "capital husbandry."

The Price Reform

The proportionality of the value-added tax rate safeguards the role of net sales as the central financial objective, unlike the old profits tax which, when positive, drained most of the realized profits into the budget and became a subsidy if it was negative. The new value-added tax will be only positive, and its effect upon efficiency in production methods and in the choice of produced articles is supposed to work evenly throughout the economy. Here is where the price reform comes in. As long as the price system was not a price system, there was no point in applying one standard rate in taxing enterprises. It would have meant arbitrary discrimination in producing disposable revenue differentials without any link to efficiency. Also, during the past two years, levies on enterprise revenues — even those that switched to the new financial success indicators — had to be individually determined. After the first fundamental decisions on the new model had been adopted (January, 1965), it was soon recognized that the reforms will not be feasible unless prices are changed and knit into a coherent interlocking pattern. Financial returns of the enterprise can have meaning only if they follow from the internal cost-return structure of the price of every individual article. Therefore, it was decided to telescope the work on the price reform into about ten months of 1966 so that a new set of wholesale prices could

duced prices containing extremely comfortable profit margins. The level of industrial wholesale prices increased by 29–30 percent (compared to the anticipated 19 percent), and profits as percentage of wage cost reached 65 percent (compared to the anticipated 22 percent). As a result, enterprises earned enough in sales to be able to accumulate quickly a cushion of liquid working capital, softening the impact of many reform measures. See *Hospodářské noviny*, No. 41 (October 1967), 1.

be put into effect together with the new 1967 instructions for the financial management of enterprises.

The reconstruction of the wholesale-price system of 1966 deserves to be acknowledged as the crucial, most ambitious, and most sensible measure of the reform. Without it we would still be discussing money and finance in the old command-economy sense. This assessment holds, I believe, despite a curious theoretical confusion in the choice of the "price type" according to which prices are being recalculated, and despite the wide gap remaining between the reformed set of prices and that which would approximate true equilibrium market prices. The essence of the operation consists in accepting the average labor cost of each article at current wage rates as given, and then adding to it a profit markup according to some uniform rule. What this rule should be has been under discussion in both the Soviet Union and East Europe for almost ten years without any visible consensus emerging. The logic of the competitive model, whose allocative abilities the reformers plan to use, points to the principle of making the markup proportional to resources — or "capital" — invested in the enterprise, at least in constant cost situations. This corresponds to the Marxian concept of "production price." In Czechoslovakia this straightforward formula was rejected in favor of the so-called "double-channel" price type; that is to say, one where the markup is calculated in two parts: first, as a percentage on capital invested; and, second, as a percentage on labor cost. This hybrid type, it seems to me, lacks respectable theoretical justification. One wonders how Czech economists manage to convince themselves that they are dealing, after all, with a variant of the "production price" type unless they tacitly accept the slightly *esclavagiste* explanation propounded by the Hungarian Andras Brody who sees a portion of the markup as a return on human capital into which the state had invested its funds.[9]

Why the Czech technicians chose the particular percentages of markup they did — 6 percent on capital *stock* and 22 percent on the wage bill, i.e., a *flow* — is not clear. In choosing these values they did not reallocate the entire non-wage margin: there still remained enough room between the new wholesale prices and the retail prices (which, for the time being, are not prepared for a general overhaul) to accommodate the pe-

[9] András Bródy, "Three Types of Price Systems," *Economics of Planning*, V:3 (1965), 5.

rennial turnover tax. This outcome was not absolutely necessary. With the choice of different percentages, the total turnover tax might have been absorbed into the profit markup; but this would presumably have deprived the authorities of a cushion permitting another round of retail-price adjustments later. (In the next-round version of the model, the turnover tax is to be proportional to wholesale prices or serve as an instrument of specific consumption policies; the proportional rate will provide the linkage of production with consumer demand. In any case the percentages chosen for the profit markup raise anew the tantalizing question of the precise economic meaning of the distinction between indirect taxes and factor returns.)[10]

Whatever the demerits of the new price formula, at least it is consistent; and it may turn out to be just as useful as the creatures of market strategies and rule-of-thumb practices of capitalist businesses. There are two more serious deficiencies in the new price reform. As they come out from the computer, the new wholesale prices will be based on the average production costs of the industry; so that, with an increasing industry supply curve, there may appear excess demand and a renewed need to subsidize losses of marginal enterprises if shortages are to be eliminated. The other deficiency consists in the fact that the formula is not being applied to individual articles but serves only to bring the relative price levels of broad groups of commodities into a new consistent relationship. Prices of individual articles within an industrial group, scattered around the corrected partial price levels, will remain what they were before. This means that, at first, profitability may still vary arbitrarily from one article to another and that financial incentives may lead managers to push excessively articles with arbitrarily high markups.[11]

There is an awareness of these problems, and reformers hope that a long series of finer adjustments will bring order into the detail of the price structure to reflect users' preferences as well as relative cost con-

[10] Cf. Richard A. Musgrave, *The Theory of Public Finance* (New York: McGraw-Hill, 1959), p. 197.

[11] After the price reform was completed it appeared that a third deficiency of a practical sort had seriously vitiated the result of the ambitious price recomputations, i.e., the poor quality of primary cost data furnished by the firms. It seems that production costs were generally overstated. This may have been due to plain inadequacy of detailed cost accounting at the enterprise level. However, it may have been also due to deliberate cost padding on the part of enterprises, trying to counter in this way the imminent financial "crash diet," announced for 1967. (Cf. footnote 8).

ditions. However, the economic rationale of marginal cost pricing does not seem to have penetrated very far as yet.[12]

In practice, the state has deferred the necessity of dealing with pricing behavior of enterprises in strong monopolistic position by keeping, for the time being, the bulk of wholesale prices fixed — only 7 percent of the volume of commodities will have freely flexible prices. Under this constraint, enterprises will not be free to maximize revenues by price-and-output policies and will concentrate on expanding sales. As in the competitive model, or in Lange's old model, prices will be given to firms parametrically.[13]

Investment Finance

It is somewhat unfair to accept the insinuation that the capital charge is needed to stop enterprise managers from squandering fixed capital and making extravagant demands on investments. Demand for producers goods has simply been derived demand — derived from extravagant output plans — and in reality managers have been forced to make do with their existing equipment far beyond its economically useful life and to squander labor, not capital, on maintenance and capital repairs. The typical planners' attitude toward the need of capital replacement — pretend it does not exist — has always struck me as one of the features of command planning that went most *contra naturam*. Pooling capital consumption allowances, in addition to net financial accumulation and using it primarily for the establishment of new projects and only residually for organic replacement of the capital stock of old-time enterprises —

---

[12] The first article containing the familiar elementary exposition of the theory of the firm with the familiar set of basic diagrams, and hints concerning their applicability in the new model appeared — to the author's knowledge — in *Finance a úvěr*, No. 10 (1966), 622–31.

[13] Neither the authors, nor the commentators of the new rules seem very eager to face the problems posed by the vast amount of products — custom-made articles, new models, new products — which are individually priced and have traditionally been a source of uncontrollable inflationary price increases. Enterprises may be allowed to introduce a measure of flexibility into prices by means of rebates in bulk-buying, extra charges for extra short delivery terms, etc. The experience of 1966 taught the reformers some lessons on the absurdity of financial incentives as long as prices are not allowed to reflect demand conditions. Thus, for instance, under the pressure of interest charges on inventory, enterprises were led to keep their stocks of coal close to their current needs. This caused an extra strain in transportation during the fall months. A seasonal rebate on coal prices during the warm season might have evened out the deliveries, instead of letting coal mines bear the cost of summer stockpiling.

this practice negated the nature of the enterprise as a functioning living cell and turned it into a governmental bureau forever panting after forever uncertain appropriations. The new model is restoring a degree of reproductive functions and control over growth of assets to the enterprise. In the place of the old nonreturnable — but all too often nonobtainable — investment grants from the budget, enterprises will have equal access to a source of long-term investment credit with contractually binding repayment obligation and a price tag — interest.[14]

In reality, of course, government grants have always been subject to repayment — by the economy as a whole. The undifferentiated flow of sources of "finance" may have been dissimulating financial transfers between users of capital, the efficient ones repaying the grants and interest for the inefficient ones. The novelty of credit-financing under the new conditions will consist in making investible funds available in function of estimated prospective returns and repayable, with interest, from gross returns actually attained by the user himself. Responsibility of the user is, thus, becoming the obverse of his autonomy.

It may seem strange and incongruent to require from enterprises — as the new rules do — that they keep turning over depreciation allowances from their present capital stock to the budget instead of using them as part of their cash flow. The intention of this arrangement is to prevent discrimination in favor of enterprises which happen to enter the new era well endowed with capital stock from the past. The measure in question does not deprive them of replacement funds; it just makes sure that the replacement funds — merged with other investment credit — will from now on, in turn, pay for themselves and earn the minimum return.[15] An amusing detail: the practice of charging depreciation as long as an asset is in use, even though it may have been amortized several times over, will be discontinued. This practice might have encouraged enterprises (as it did in the experimental ones) to keep old and obsolete assets in operation just in order to increase the cumulative value of depreciation, since the capital charge is calculated from the depreciated value of capital assets.

The regime of depreciation allowances and of their use — keep the

[14] *Hospodářské noviny* (July 1966), p. 3.
[15] This measure is exactly parallel to the above-mentioned "confiscation" of working capital and its re-financing through credit, except that here the implementation is drawn out over the remaining useful life of the fixed-capital stock existing as of January 1, 1967.

capital of existing capacities intact or let them slowly finish their days while starting brand-new projects? — contains the crux of the problem of proper investment strategy. This regime also poses the problem of mobility of capital funds, structure of production of the individual enterprise, and structure of the economy as a whole. Should individual enterprises have the power to decide between investment alternatives at the rate at which the value of productive assets becomes liquid? Will an authentic capital market develop in due time? It would seem that this is the logic of the new model, but the issues are far from decided, if they are perceived by all. For the time being, the immediate task of the depreciation-replacement policy is the rejuvenation of the existing capital stock. In the consumer-goods branches, machinery and equipment have been depreciated close to 75 percent; more than half of it is over twenty-four years old; trucks and cutting and molding machine tools in use are twice or three times as old as in capitalist countries; annual replacement amounts to about 2 percent of installed assets.[16] The corollary of this policy has been increasing maintenance and capital repairs, operating costs, tying up of highly skilled workers in obsolete and senescent plants, and their shortage in new capacities. Furthermore, at present any overhaul of depreciation rules would make little sense without a fresh capital census appraising individual items at realistic current depreciated replacement values. The potential of "depreciation allowances as an instrument of active financial policy"[17] has come to the attention of Czechoslovak economists and officials and will probably occupy them more in the not-too-distant future.

The major weakness of the price system during the transitional period is the insulation of wage rates from the influence of market forces. This could hardly be otherwise as long as the economic position of individual firms under the new conditions is not clarified. Furthermore, in the reconstruction of the price system, wages and wage rates were accepted as the Archimedean "fixed point" — the set of prices which was assumed to deviate the least from equilibrium market prices. Whether an emotional or ideological distrust of forces of the labor market has been playing a significant role cannot be determined at this time, but it obviously exists. The authors of the new regulations stepped into the gap and tried to play the market gods by arranging for a steep increase

---

[16] *Plánované hospodářství*, XIX:5 (May 1966), 9.
[17] Title of an important article in *Finance a úvěr*, No. 6 (1966), 329–337.

in the cost of labor beyond a certain wage-bill ceiling. This is the meaning of the "payroll surtax" (item 3) which raises the effective wage rate by 30 percent once the enterprise wants to spend on labor more than what amounts to 90 percent of the 1966 planned rate. Together with the "decongestion tax" (item 10), which is also our own label, these discontinuities in the price of labor are expected to prevent the demand for labor from exceeding the present volumes too much. It seems to me that such a manipulation, in the absence of a market, necessarily introduces a new element of arbitrariness into the situation, thus reflecting a subjective estimate of relative factor scarcities.[18]

Nevertheless, the over-all impression given by the new rules points to a concerted effort to integrate the system of financing, investment decisions, and current operations with the normal circulation of enterprise funds. Long-range "business planning" — nonexistent under centralized command planning, weird as it may seem — is to be made possible by an official strong reassurance (though not a guarantee) that the principal tax rates will not be changed or at least by not more than one percentage point. Systematic management of the firm's liquidity, whether owned or borrowed, may thus be viewed as the unifying aspect of all economic functioning of the enterprise, just as the segmentation of funds in the old economic regime represented an outer interference with the natural unity of economic decisions. There will no longer be a special kind of "payroll money," "capital-repairs money," "material-purchases money," "small-purchases-in-retail-stores money," and so on, which managers could use only for those specific purposes and not for what was economically efficient. The emergence of money as a homogeneous, universal medium of exchange goes hand in hand with its reinstatement as a universal standard of value, the essential precondition of rational economic calculation. After the long years during which money was thought of as a punishment for original sins to be exorcized from the socialist economy, as one writer put it, it is understandable that economists can hardly conceal their exhilaration at the new vistas, despite the limitations we have already mentioned and those we have to deal with in the next section.

[18] Characteristically, lacking one good reason, the official interpreters of the measure have given three poor ones: (a) to obtain means for financing wage increases in the "non-productive" sector, (b) to release labor for an acceleration of economic development, and (c) to introduce an additional element of progressivity into the tax system so as to let the whole society share in the growth of revenues. See *Hospodářské noviny*, No. 30 (August 1966), Supplement, p. 6.

Trusts, Cartels, Holding Companies, and Investment Consortiums

Promoters of the market mechanism as a panacea for the ills of command-planning have concentrated on the role of active enterprise finances. The East European longing for an "invisible hand" has been contained in the search for incentives such that "what is good for an individual enterprise will be good for society." Therefore, it comes as an anticlimax to learn how little autonomy an individual firm will have in the management of its finances, at least at this juncture. The new model is being inaugurated in an organizational structure, which groups individual enterprises into formations vaguely resembling trusts, cartels, or perhaps holding companies. These "Economic Production Units" (VHJ, *výrobně hospodářské jednotky*), ruled by awe-inspiring executive organs, the Branch Boards of Directors (*oborová ředitelství*), overshadow single enterprises — their subjects rather than members — by the extent of discretionary powers in matters of finance, investment, production programs, and marketing.

As has already been hinted, setting the new price levels according to industrial averages of labor cost and capital intensity will result in the appearance of differential rents; that is, rate of profitability in differently outfitted enterprises. The question is: Should they be entitled to keep these rents? Obviously, the new incentive principles rely on differential rents to managerial ability, and to that extent they should not be touched. Furthermore, there may be good economic reasons for letting intramarginal enterprises use rents to unique factors for self-financed expansion. However, there may be a portion of rent which would be more efficiently used if it were spent at a different point of the economic system, where it would earn higher returns. The optimal allocation of rents is clearly a matter of delicate calculation. In the new model, the task has been entrusted to the branch Boards of Directors of the Economic Production Units. Boards of Directors will be levying from their subordinate enterprises a supplementary tax (*dodatkové odvody*), assessing them individually in absolute amounts. The proceeds of the supplementary tax will be used to subsidize less efficient enterprises, to renovate them, and generally to soften the impact of the new measures upon the weak units. The aim is to give the underprivileged firms a chance to recuperate from the consequences of previous policies which may have buried sources of efficiency still capable of recovery. Where the situation appears hopeless, the firm would be liquidated or merged with another one. In theory, the subsidizing enterprise is supposed to have a say — a sort of *Mitbestimmungsrecht* — in the affairs of the subsidized firm, but one can sense that the will of the Boards of Directors is expected to be overriding.

The funds may be given to the weaker enterprises in the form of a nonreturnable grant or credit. The Economic Production Unit thus becomes a true financial intermediary. It will, furthermore, serve as a broker in inter-enterprise loans and will organize pools of investible funds from free sources of individual enterprises for the financing of new investment projects. We may be witnessing, in the form of such "investment consortia," the beginnings of regular corporate finance and a further unlimbering of the flows of capital funds.

In the long run one foresees a gradual elimination of the supplementary tax and even the abolition of Economic Production Units which will prove useless. However, for an unspecified number of years they are here to stay, with the power of decision concentrated in the Boards of Directors. True, the Economic Production Units are supposed to perform a public service for their constituents in market research, technological research, and so on — all that is associated with their cartel functions. However, the features which really seem striking are those that limit the autonomy of individual firms: the decisive role of Boards of Directors in the appraisal of investment projects (hence, control over the allocation of investment credit); delimitation of competition by the control of marketing; powers over pricing policies and price setting; and powers over the proportions in which enterprises will be allowed to allocate their disposable revenue. It may be necessary to establish such controls for the period of transition in order to prevent irresponsible actions by individual managerial groups, but it also provides a new ground for possible lobbying, clique formation, and graft of the old style. Many Czechoslovak commentators have been expressing concern lest the degree of centralization of decisions in Boards of Directors "destroy the autonomy and material incentives of enterprises."[19] This concern is undoubtedly well justified. The full rehabilitation of the enterprise as the basic living cell of the economy, the establishment of objective conditions for long-range "business planning" by individual firms — all that still seems far off. For the moment it is hard to escape the impression that the new national eco-

---

[19] E.g., *Finance a úvěr*, No. 8 (1966), 460.

nomic model, with all its "market relationships," is made up of eighty-five miniaturized command economies.

The Banker as "Entrepreneurs' Entrepreneur"

In capitalistic economies, the banking industry — a profit-oriented business — is expected to play the role of an instrument of economic control. In the new economic model of Czechoslovakia, the banking official — a civil servant at the instruments of control — is supposed to act as a businesslike entrepreneur. It is one of the many paradoxes of the transitional period that the performance of the bank managers, who are expected to contribute to the financial success of their customer enterprises, are themselves exempt from the repercussions (*dopad*) of the new financial incentives.[20] Their professional conscience and ability are to be their sole guides.

However, if enterprise managers are suspected of being professionally ill-prepared for their new role, one can say the same of bank employees who are to be the judges of their applications for current operating credit and, especially for long-term investment credit. Since the latter will progressively eliminate direct budget grants,[21] and ploughed-back revenues cannot be expected to amount to any large sums, the bank becomes the most important arbiter in the allocation of investments. The training received by bank officials in the command system consisted in making them into inventory watchdogs. In the credit operations of command economies, one recognized a special version of the "real-bill" doctrine. This turned the bankers' attention mainly to the question of the specific purpose of the credit ("Is it covered by planned real-inventory collateral?") rather than to its financial quality. It would be interesting to know how much managerial know-how bankers acquired as warehouse inspectors and auditors of enterprise finances. The least they must have learned was a healthy respect for real economic processes. These processes have repeatedly resisted their verbal pressures and threat of financial sanctions, particularly during the inventory recession, which was an important part of the post-1962 crisis. In the new situation, bankers will be relieved

[20] In Yugoslavia, which in many ways has been a trailblazer of economic reforms, the banking system comprises commercial banks.

[21] During 1967, budget grants still represent 15 per cent of gross investment; depreciation allowances and retained disposable revenue, 24 percent; and credits, 60 percent.

of the necessity for continuously checking the enterprise operations and its use of credit funds. On the other hand, they will be required to evaluate long-term credit applications on the basis of unfamiliar data, without any precedent to guide them, in an atmosphere of a high degree of uncertainty concerning the ability of the borrower to fulfill the stipulations of the credit contract. Presumably, the risk will be somewhat reduced by the requirement of obtaining an approval of every investment project from a Branch Board of Directors and by the financial powers of the board which may be used in the future to bail out deficient borrowers.[22]

The new rules come to the assistance of bank officials by formulating rough criteria for the combined evaluation of the credit purpose and credit terms, if not of the applicant. The basic formula for grading credit applications takes into account the speed of repayment and the length of useful life of the durable productive asset. The speed of repayment depends on the efficiency of the investment project as reflected in the relative shares of depreciation allowances and current net revenue in the credit installments. Preference will be given to applications promising a higher share coming from the current net revenue.

The intention of the legislator here is to prevent further sinking of resources into large capital-intensive projects having a long gestation period and to stimulate small piecemeal investments and renovations which promise a quick return. In this connection, one should mention the problem of financial incentives in firms which do not produce for a mass market but for a single customer. This is typically true of large investment contractors. There has been no mention of competitive bidding as yet. The cartelized structure described above may present an obstacle. As a substitute for competition, various methods of staggered financial settlement have been considered, with short-term credit financing successive stages of the construction work and long-term investment-credit providing the customer enterprise with means of payment, and the contractor with means of repaying the short-term credit. Such an arrangement would link payment with the completion of a well-defined portion of the work and put pressure on the contractor to finish it within the foreseen period of time. This demonstrates the importance of such

---

[22] This may be the more necessary as the bank will be entitled to raise the interest rate up to 12 per cent for those enterprises unable to adhere to the conditions of the contract, which is somewhat reminiscent of the olden-time way of dealing with failing debtors by jailing or mutilating them, and making the repayment effectively impossible (*Finance a úvěr*, No. 2 [1966], 71).

prosaic matters as methods of billing and terms of settlement for the success of economic reform. The search for solutions in the construction of investment projects is just part of the general effort to strengthen the position of buyers. Not the least important aspect of the sellers' domination under command planning used to be the inability of buyers to inspect merchandise before accepting delivery and paying the bill: the state bank used to make the transfer of funds from the buyer's account automatically upon the seller's presentation of documents concerning shipment!

The old practices of "petty tutelage" of enterprises by bank organs may, to some extent, outlive the system of central command planning itself. During 1966, for instance, bank organs were enjoined to use credit terms in order to "improve the structure of inventories." The state found in 1965 that, in manufacturing, finished products made up only 14 percent of all inventories, and materials 60 percent (the proportions are about equal in the United States).[23] Banks began to grant enteprises interest-free credit on inventories of finished goods. This acted upon the speed of processing but not necessarily upon the total inventory turnover. A commentator rightly pointed out that "from the point of view of society it is the total volume of tied-up resources that matters, not their structure."[24] Similar attitudes continue to be noticed.[25] It will, thus, demand a profound change of institutional mentality to make banking officials relax about the specific use of their loans, as long as firms realize a return sufficient to allow them to fulfill the terms of the contract.

Credit and Monetary Policy

The truly great innovation in the thinking of banking authorities has been the discovery of the monetization of credit and the fading out of the "real-bills" doctrine: "From the point of view of the monetary function of credit," says a financial writer, "it is not of primary importance who are the subjects receiving and repaying credit; what is decisive is the final outcome of credit operations in relation to the money stock and to

[23] *Hospodářské noviny*, No. 47 (November 1965), 7.

[24] *Finance a úvěr*, No. 2 (1966), 103–104.

[25] For an example of a particularly obsessional attitude toward inventory control on the part of the bank's spokesmen, see L. Bakalář, "K zásadám úvěrové a úrokové politiky," *Finance a úvěr*, No. 2 (1966), 65–73. The experience of 1966 indicates that firms tended to increase their inventory level in order to achieve a smoother flow of production; cf. *Finance a úvěr*, No. 7 (1966), 423–424.

the behavior of effective demand in the national economy."[26] The concept of money is expanded: "Past conception of the money stock M is characterized by counting only cash held by the population. . . . Practical experiences have made our ingrained theorems obsolete and proven that individual forms of monetary circulation pass objectively one into the other."[27]

The comprehension of the credit-money connection sets the stage for an active monetary policy of the State Bank. Writes Otakar Pohl, the general director of the State Bank:

The conception of the credit-monetary policy of the State Bank respects, first of all, the requirement of supplying the national economy, via credit, with financial means in a quantity necessary for its maximum proportional development possible. This is why the bank's central organs have been working on the quantitative side of the credit supply and sharpening the instruments of monetary policy, among them the role of interest. This conception should make it possible for the bank to exercise influence upon the dimensions of investment activity and inventories by means of credit restriction, raising the interest rate, etc., or, under contrary conditions, to stimulate enterprises toward expansion of business activity through credit expansion, reduction of the interest rate, etc.[28]

These elementary-textbook verities represent the most significant breakthrough in the theoretical thinking of bank officials and economists. Such basic insights lead to the full range of problems and topics connected with stabilization and growth policies resting on manipulation of aggregate demand through money.

For a while during the discussion stage preceding the economic reforms, there seems to have been a conflict of opinion concerning the need to control the aggregate volume of credit. In March, 1966, the man second-in-command in the State Bank could still write: "The branch offices of the Bank have no limits in the supply of credits."[29] However, Evžen Löbl, one of the most outspoken spokesmen of the Bank, has argued forcefully in favor of regulating carefully the volume of credit

[26] Václav Beneš, "K některým teoretickým a praktickým otázkám peněžní funkce bankovního úvěru za socialismu," *Finance a úvěr*, No. 6 (1966), 359.

[27] V. Beneš, p. 366. (The author goes all the way to including in his concept of money time deposits as well; he finds support against the "erroneous traditional concept" not with Milton Friedman but in the French journal *Problèmes économiques*, No. 907 [1965], 18.)

[28] O. Pohl, "Nová úloha Státní banky československé," *Finance a úvěr*, No. 8 (1966), 452.

[29] *Nová mysl*, XX:6, p. 20.

and, thereby, the money supply: "Every branch office director performs to some extent the function of a bank of issue." [30] And further: "The lower limit of the credit supply required for the utilization of the productive potential is simultaneously just about its upper limit." [31]

It is the latter view which was adopted officially by the State Bank. With logical necessity it has also involved the bank in the general planning process itself. If gross aggregate demand — final and intermediate — is not going to have the form of physical production commands any longer, it will have to have the usual form of effective monetary demand. Planning the volume of output will mean planning the control of the volume of money expenditure. Controlling the volume of money supply will mean an influence over the general price movement, assuming a degree of price flexibility; in other words, control of inflation. Since relative prices can perform their signalizing tasks properly only under conditions of a reasonable price-level stability, the bank becomes indirectly responsible for the success of the reform in adapting the micro-structure of the economy to the structure of demand.

In full recognition of these responsibilities devolving upon the bank from the "activization" of money, Evžen Löbl has claimed for the bank a corresponding degree of power to exercise its own judgment and discretion. The accent is distinctly that of William McChesney Martin, Jr.: [32]

This is not a matter of some sharing of responsibility in the determination of the plan. . . . During the stage of plan construction, the bank has to have the right to influence the economic plan. This influence is precisely defined by the duties of the bank as an organ of issue. . . . Fundamental importance is attached to the demand that all investments should be credit-financed and returnable, and that the state budget itself must become part of the credit plan. . . . It is true, that, in principle, the bank cannot be superior to the state, but if the state entrusts the bank with the task of monetary stabilization the bank is not only entitled but has the duty to set up economic limits to the state's activity.[33]

The implementation of these strikingly novel principles seems well under way, judging by more recent declarations of the bank's general director

[30] Evžen Löbl, "K postaveniu banky v národnom hospodárstve," *Finance a úvěr*, No. 10 (1965), 595.

[31] E. Löbl, p. 598.

[32] Cf. W. M. Martin's declarations before the Senate Finance Committee in August 1957, cited in Andrew Schonfield, *Modern Capitalism* (New York: Oxford University Press, 1965), pp. 330–331, footnote.

[33] E. Löbl, p. 600.

on the "relative independence" of the credit plan and its flexibility.[34] The bank is getting ready to embark upon its own economic forecasting and business conditions analysis and to act "on the basis of its own assessment of the situation."[35]

If a value judgment is permitted at this point, then the stance of the bank cannot be praised highly enough, in contrast to planning centers which seem to find it hard to reconcile themselves to the principle of cutting the size of aggregate demand down to the real supply potential of the economy — with the new price system the second main pillar of the reform. The experience of the year 1966 should have driven home the lesson that excess monetary demand will give free rein to the monopolistic pricing powers of enterprises which even the regime of rigid price control will not be able to hold. If this situation were to continue, the beneficial effects of the price reform would be largely annulled.

Wage-price Guidelines Czech Style

Ota Šik, whose name the public keeps connecting with the economic reforms (it seems with less and less reason as time goes by), wrote on the subject of long-term price movements: "A planned progressive reduction of enterprise selling prices, based on the calculated trend of a feasible reduction of production costs, will stimulate the producer to actually reduce his production costs as fast as possible."[36] This view has been incorporated, to all appearances, in the new framework. In article 15, section 5, we read: "The system of uniform tax rates requires that unequal development of rentability in various sectors . . . be reflected in prices; in the long run the movement of price levels should not be detached from socially necessary costs."[37]

One is tempted to read into these and other statements the wish to pursue a deflationary price policy, especially since worries about inflation have been a constant theme of the two-year-old discussions about reforms. This principle would imply a policy of relatively stable wage rates and downward adjustments of price levels according to productivity increases. One may look upon this as one possible variant in the appli-

[34] O. Pohl, p. 452.
[35] O. Pohl, p. 453.
[36] Ota Šik, *K problematice socialistických zbožních vztahů* (Pregue, 1965), p. 170.
[37] *Hospodářské noviny*, No. 30 (August 1966), Supplement, p. 14.

cation of the principle of wage-price guidelines of the U.S. Council of Economic Advisors.[38]

Surprisingly, the authors of the Czechoslovak new rules do not commit themselves to this solution and leave the door wide open to intriguing possibilities by merely referring to some "optimal price stability." There are economists, for example, Bohumil Komenda, who are not afraid to accept a certain amount of inflation for the sake of effective pecuniary incentives: if an annual 5 percent increase of nominal wages is considered as the minimum consistent with workable incentives and productivity can hardly increase by more than 3 percent yearly, "one must rather expect a mildly rising tendency of wholesale prices."[39] The same author notes that price deflation may thwart technological progress and contends against Šik: "If we engineer a price movement such as is assumed to accompany a desirable economic trend, it is incorrect to think that we also create thereby conditions for the realization of such a trend."[40]

The discussions of the meaning of "optimum price stability" are not closed. In the meantime, price specialists are currently calculating projections of possible price trends on the basis of alternative assumptions concerning the behavior of the principal price-determining factors;[41] and preparations are being made for the collection of data needed in the calculation of honest and up-to-date price indexes. (In the past, pseudo-indexes based solely on official price lists were the rule.) One thing seems certain: regulation of price levels will be used as another active instrument in pursuit of a number of economic objectives: equalizing returns in branches with varying productivity; stimulating of promising export lines; repressing monopolistic tendencies, and so on.

Functional Finance?

In describing the system of "business taxation," we discussed the future major state budget revenues. In dealing with the new system of investment

[38] The guidelines aim at average price stability; but since they allow for wage rates to move in proportion with average productivity, and the unavowed objective is a stabilization of income shares, prices have to move down in lines with higher-than-average productivity increases and up in those with lower-than-average productivity increases. Cf. *Economic Report of the President* (Washington, 1966), pp. 89–90.

[39] *Plánované hospodářství*, XIX:7 (July 1966), 53.

[40] *Ibid.*, p. 47.

[41] O. Kýn, H. Kysilka, F. Nevařil, "Prognóza vývoje cen do roku 1970," *Plánované hospodářství*, XIX:8–9 (August–September 1966), 157–168.

finance and price reform, we were also saying something about the reduced importance of the budget item, "expenditures on national economy." As a consequence of all the changes, the total volume of the budget
is expected to fall short by more than a quarter of the total estimates
under the old conditions.[42] The budget, thus, will lose a great deal of its
traditional redistributive functions which, to the extent that they still
exist, pass into the competence of the Economic Production Units. There
remain a few remarks to make on the role of fiscality and fiscal policies
within the new framework.

As may have become clear by now, a perusal of Czechoslovak economic periodicals is bound to elicit a frequent "Hear, hear!" from the
reader, and such is the case in articles on the fiscal subset, for example:

Financial policy measures need not always have only a direct financial
effect accessible to calculation. They may contribute to the establishment of
certain economic interests and moods, brake or stimulate initiative, influence
the confidence in money, etc. Thus they have also an aspect of moral pressure
or stimulus, a psychological aspect which may enhance or weaken the direct
effects of financial measures.[43]

The important point is that the author does not imply — nor would the
Minister of Finance himself — that these positive psychological effects
are tied to budget balance.[44] The active role of fiscal policy will be made
felt by the policy of "business taxation," tax rates, tax relief, authentic
subsidization, and creation and utilization of fiscal reserves. A more relaxed attitude toward budget balance follows naturally from the fact
that revenues are losing their rigid, "to-be-counted-upon" character:
"Properly speaking, not a single item of the financial plan of an enterprise will have an obligatory character as far as its absolute level is concerned, and consequently no payment to the budget either."[45] Consequently, "government expenditures and revenues will become relatively
independent. . . . One has to count on a certain delay of the effect the
new system will have upon the state budget which may even produce a
considerable tension between revenues and expenditures."[46]

---

[42] *Hospodářské noviny*, No. 40 (October 1966).

[43] *Finance a úvěr*, No. 8 (1965), 451.

[44] In earlier days, the Minister of Finance would traditionally go through
the spiel of comparing socialist balanced budgets with the contemptible budget
deficits in capitalist countries. Today we may read: "An isolated treasury view may
befog economic relationships; it creates particular confusions around surpluses and
deficits of the state budget. . . . The economic essence of these categories is in
contradiction with accustomed notions." (*Finance a úvěr*, No. 8 (1965), 458).

[45] *Ibid.*, p. 453.

[46] R. Dvořák, Minister of Finance, *Finance a úvěr*, No. 6 (1966), 324.

It is interesting to detect the parallelism in the pronouncements of bank officials and fiscal authorities on the need for independent decisions, based upon their own economic forecasts and projections. However, the independence of the fiscal authorities is, in reality, limited by their adherence to the principle of long-run budget balance and the prospect of having to cover a possible deficit from bank credit. Such orthodoxy gives credence to the superior mien of the bank's spokesmen quoted earlier. Since the credit would be repayable, it means that the budget directors will become involved in public-debt management while the final and decisive word on financial policies will rest with the bank. The essence of the Czechoslovak monetary system may be that of "fiat money,"[47] but its outer form is bank deposits and bank bills, and its major source is the credit supply — which all effectively leave the "fiat" largely in the hands of the bank. Abba Lerner's words — "The purpose of taxation is never to raise money but to leave less in the hands of the taxpayer,"[48] or its reciprocal — have apparently not reached the coast of Bohemia as yet, so that budget deficits will remain, for the time being, a money inlet as little respected as in the West.

Among the new features of the role of finances in Czechoslovakia, the plurality of organs which will be influencing financial flows is particularly striking. The frictions between them that are already discernible may superficially appear as beauty defects. However, the prospect seems to be on the way to becoming accepted as a positive advantage. Thus, we read in the organ of the State Planning Commission:

In the old system there was only one center which was supposed to be the only source of all planned activity in the economy. In a decentralized system it is more appropriate to have in the economy a large number of centers acting as sources of planning activity, which supplement each other and can, up to a certain point, compete with each other.[49]

Polycentrism in monetary and financial matters, therefore, is a natural corollary of the new type of planning, which is moving toward an integration of conflict into the concept of planned equilibrium.

[47] George Garvy, "Banking and Credit in the Framework of New Economic Policies in Eastern Europe," *Banca Nazionale del Lavoro Quarterly Review*, No. 78 (Sept. 1966), 229.

[48] Abba P. Lerner, *The Economics of Control* (New York: Macmillan, 1946), p. 307.

[49] O. Kýn, H. Kysilka, F. Nevařil, p. 158.

BORIS P. PESEK

- •
- •
- •
- •
- •

The New Economic Model
in Czechoslovakia

My purpose in this contribution is not so much to focus on the specifically financial aspects of the Czechoslovak economic reform — this was ably done in Professor Holešovský's companion contribution — as to inquire into the "real" aspects of the reform (such as relative prices, interest rates, wages, and the mechanism of resource allocation) that set the stage for money flows.

THE OLD MODEL

Of all East European countries, only Czechoslovakia and Hungary are currently undertaking a thorough reorganization of their economic system. Other Communist countries, such as the USSR and Poland, are moving more cautiously; yet others still show little intention to change their economic institutions. Since my knowledge of the Hungarian situation is limited, I shall concentrate here on the Czechoslovak reform.

When we are told that an old economic model is being replaced with a new one, we want to know why. Professor Holešovský[1] provides an excellent brief summary of the troubles besetting Czechoslovakia in the past years. In contrast, Mr. Fekete devotes the first part of his essay in this volume to a description of how well the old model or models, about to be replaced, worked in Hungary in the past two decades. We are told that in 1944 his country lost an amount of capital equal to five annual

[1] See Václav Holešovský, "Financial Aspects of the Czechoslovak Economic Reform," in this book.

106

incomes[2] and that five years later the old economic model was able to bring national income back to its original level.[3] Assuming a constant capital-output ratio — not a bad rough approximation when we face short-run changes of such extreme magnitudes — this implies that the old model enabled Hungary to invest during these five years 100 percent of its income annually. I am sure that most Hungarians during those years felt just as if this implicaion were true, but I doubt these figures. With income restored to its old level in 1949 the Hungarian economy allegedly forged ahead but ultimately a reform became imperative.

The similarity between political economists and politicians is striking. In the United States, after years of disunity and economic mismanagement that left us with the expression "not worth a continental," the founding fathers, too, did not decide to replace the unworkable and failing with something new. Instead, they decided — in the words of our Constitution — "to form a more perfect union." Both in the United States at that time and in Hungary today, the old system was declared to be "perfect" and the new only one "more" so. A recently published Czech cartoon is worth, in this connection, a few thousand words:

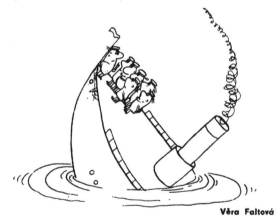

Věra Faltová

Analysis of the situation reveals that in the future we must
avoid similar errors.

(*Dikobraz*, Nov. 3, 1966)

If the world consisted only of Eastern Europe and the Western nations, it would be constructive to let bygones be bygones. Our East European

[2] János Fekete, "The Role of Monetary and Credit Policy in the Reform of Hungary's Economic Mechanism," in this book.
[3] Fekete, pp. 57–58.

colleagues face problems difficult enough and there would be little point in forcing them to dissipate their energy and influence on efforts to prove that their reform does not "actually mean the abolition of planned economy and the introduction or rather the 'rediscovery' of the market economy." [4] However, many new nations in Africa and Asia are now searching for a model to follow and we would do them a disservice if we would fail to challenge the argument that the old model is the natural starting ground for economic development and for a subsequent transition to the "more perfect" new model.

THE NEW MODEL

What is this new model that the Czechs and Hungarians are about to apply and towards which some other East European nations are groping more cautiously? I want to, first, try to establish the leitmotiv of the whole reform movement and then use implications of this leitmotiv for the economic organization as we now see it emerging in Eastern Europe.

The Leitmotiv

The key task of the new model is to end, once and for all, the *shortages* (as distinct from scarcities) *and surpluses* of both consumer and producers goods. Shortages which, on the consumer level, had to be resolved through long lines, favoritism by the sales personnel, rudeness of the sales personnel well aware that frequently by selling goods they are dispensing favors, repeated trips to the stores, and — in many cases — "resolved" simply through a failure to obtain badly needed goods or spare parts. On the level of enterprises, these shortages had to be resolved through bureaucratic allocations, rationing, quotas, and semilegal and costly bartering among enterprises. And, appearances to the contrary, both the consumer inventories and the enterprise inventories contained surpluses as well. The consumers, within the limit of the budget restraint, accumulated inventories of goods that happened to be currently available to guard against expected future shortages. On the enterprise level, surpluses accumulated partly for the same reason and partly because the budget restraint worked too imperfectly to prevent accumulation of unsalable goods in warehouses:

Products were not demanded because of their technical backwardness so that it was necessary to reduce their prices to sell them at all; yet, enterprises peace-

4 *Ibid.*, p. 69.

fully continued to produce them . . . because the reduction of retail prices was not matched by the reduction of wholesale prices but was matched by lower state receipts.[5]

The new system is to make sure of two things: First, all markets are to be cleared and just cleared. Second, not only on the consumer level but from now even on the enterprise level they are to be cleared, and just cleared, on the basis of rational economic calculus: on the basis of a budget constraint that both consumers and enterprises are to be free to shape by their own actions, unhampered by floors and ceilings. By now, the East Europeans are using fearlessly, even ostentatiously, concepts such as "exchange of goods," "supply and demand and the necessity to make them equal," "the market economy." These concepts are applied not only to bread and butter but to such "social services" as adult education. Recently I read a statement that it would be better to pay the market price for language courses and get them, than to have the warm feeling that one would pay very little for a course which one cannot get.

Thus the new economic model has a clear leitmotiv: to end the non-market allocation of factors of production and of consumer goods, to permit or force both consumers and enterprises to shape their own budget constraint, to restore the market economy, to let supply and demand reign. Of course, as in the West — and, as the East Europeans keep asserting, more so — social policy may and will require state intervention, but this intervention is to work through the market, not outside of it or against it. But if we do agree that the leitmotiv of the reform is to have markets (both product and factor markets) cleared, and just cleared, on the basis of rational economic calculus resting on the budget restraint, we should then have no difficulties in seeing the implications of this leitmotive for the way in which the new model is to function. My discussion of the specifics of the new model will be facilitated if I make use of the analytical framework provided by Frank H. Knight. According to him, every economic system has five basic tasks: fix standards; organize production; distribute output; provide for maintenance and progress; and adjust consumption to production in the short run.[6]

What may we say about the new model when we organize our discussion of it on this basis?

[5] *Rudé Právo*, Nov. 4, 1966, p. 2.
[6] Frank H. Knight, *The Economic Organization* (Chicago: University of Chicago Press, 1933), pp. 1–13.

Fixing of Standards

One of the major tasks of the reform has been well summarized as follows:

It constitutes an essential element of the reform to guide the undertakings by a more rational and elastic price system towards a better use of their resources, *towards the creation and maintenance of equilibruim between supply and demand* [emphasis mine] as well as towards rapid technical development.[7]

How well will the new model do this? Current prices are now being recalculated to provide enterprises with a more rational starting point. Two problems appear in this connection: first, how well will the starting prices reflect relative scarcities and, second, does not the mere fact that — once again — prices are being imposed from above and fixed indicate that the old ills will continue to exist?

Determination of starting relative prices

In both the Czech and the Hungarian cases, starting prices are to consist of factor costs plus markups for the use of labor and capital. There are two objections that one may raise: first, the factor costs are calculated on the basis of the rule that wage rates must not change and, second, the capital and labor markups are devoid of any economic rationale.

As for the key part of the prices, *the factor cost*, this does not appear serious. A starting point simply had to be provided. Subsequently, enterprises are to be guided in their factor-mix and product-mix policies by a rational economic calculus; selling prices are to clear the market. I am convinced that wherever such rational economic calculus leads, marginal cost-pricing — irrespective of the initial crude starting point — is bound to follow. Given the starting prices, enterprises surely will reorganize factor inputs (thus changing the factor costs initially assumed) and their outputs (thus changing the relative scarcities) and by all this, if markets are to be cleared, forcing changes in market prices. A process of successive approximations should, sooner or later, lead to rational factor costs to which the markups are to be added.

In contrast, the markups are and, presumably, will remain irrational. There is no reason why the capital markup should be, in Czechoslovakia, 6 percent on capital stock and 22 percent on the wage bill or, in Hungary, 5 and 25 percent, respectively. But, are the labor markups more arbitrary than our social-security taxes, unemployment-insurance contributions, progressive income taxes, and so on? Are the capital markups more ar-

[7] Fekete, pp. 73–74.

bitrary than our corporate taxes, state and local taxes on plant and equipment, tax incentives on new investments, fast write-offs, and interest rates manipulated by the Federal Reserve System? If nothing else, these constant percentage markups will be added to a factor cost base which, hopefully, will make more sense as finer adjustments in it are made.

By and large, it will be a mark of great progress when our East European colleagues will stop worrying about nonsensical prices and start worrying — along with us — about distorted relative prices.

Fixing of relative prices

The fact that a key element of factor cost, the labor cost, is to be held constant, and the fact that 80 percent of retail prices and 93 percent of wholesale prices are to be fixed might give rise to the conclusion that, even in the new model, enterprises will not be free to maximize profits by price-and-output policies. In view of the explicit determination "to create and maintain equilibrium between supply and demand" I wonder whether the fixing of prices is not more a matter of ideology and less of substance. Different nations have different sacred cows.

In the United States we are so devoted to the free-market mechanism that when we decide to give gifts to our fellow citizens, we cannot bear the thought of passing a law saying that the price of wheat is henceforth fixed at, say, $1.90 per bushel. Our dogma abhors fixed prices; if we want some specific price fixed nevertheless, we have the government fix it inconspicuously through purchases and sales. In Eastern Europe, the dogma is reversed and requires that all prices be fixed. If the planners want most of these prices flexible nevertheless — to make sure that the task of the reform is accomplished and that markets are cleared — all they need to do is to change fixed prices often enough. If the East Europeans had a dogma requiring the sun to shine only when permitted to do so by the state plan, there would now be a government official scanning the skies and signing a sunshine permit whenever the sun was about to come out. Some evidence indicates that the dogma of fixed prices will fare in just about the same way.

Clearing the Markets in the Short Run

The task of adjusting consumption to production in the short run Frank H. Knight lists as the last one and — *as long as the short run is really a short one* — rightly so: this is a relatively minor task. How minor it is may be best illustrated by the fact very few of us notice that even in the United States, so dedicated to the price system, this task is frequently not performed; markets in the *short* run are frequently not cleared. For instance, during 1966 deliveries of color TV set lagged behind orders, frequently by three to five weeks. Christmas after Christmas, airlines are booked solid weeks in advance; summer after summer, passenger traffic across the Atlantic is booked weeks, even months, in advance; IBM Selectrics take roughly from one to two months to reach a customer. Yet, we give such a small weight to the fifth Knightian task that surely the immediate reaction by most of us would be to say that our economic model does perform this task even though in our daily lives we frequently face cases of its failure to do so.

In Eastern Europe, the dedication to prices which are fixed by high-echelon bureaucrats may be expected to make the performance of this task still less efficient than ours is: it takes time for a price revision to run up and down the ladder of bureaucracy. However, here again there seems to be ground for the optimistic belief that the delay will not be too long. In the case of consumer goods, anger of the consumers with lines of waiting, store managers' favoritism, and just plain unavailability of many items forced price increases upon "the changers of fixed prices" even before the new model became operative. Bulging inventories in some items forced upon them all sorts of discount sales. Under the reform, enterprises are supposed to have a definite profit incentive and thus may be expected [8] to exert the same kind of pressure in favor of increased price flexibility of producer goods. If this belief is justified, then there may be even some merit in having the priestly class of "changers of fixed prices" — something like the keepers of eternal fire. Many powerful bureaucrats are unhappy these days as they see their jobs evaporate, and it might be a counsel of wisdom to let them do something since, as we all know, the devil makes work for idle hands.

Organizing production

Given rational standards — rational relative prices — we should expect rational organization of production if enterprises are permitted to change their factor-mix and output-mix, if they are given incentives to do so, and if they are blocked from maximizing merely profits (rather than profits and outputs) through monopolistic practices. These are big ifs.

---

[8] See the postscript following this contribution.

Freedom to determine factor and product mixes

Conceptually, the new model is supposed to transfer decision-making down to the enterprises, which are to bear the financial responsibility for and reap the fruits of their own output. But a careful reader of the East European discussions will note the determination shown by the bureaucrats in the central-planning offices and economic ministries to maintain their jobs and power by remaining in their offices. Individual Czech enterprises have been organized into groups, Sector Directorates (*odborová ředitelství*), called by the Czechs for brevity's sake "trusts" (*trusty*). These trusts, manned by the veterans of the old model, forced into the statutes governing the relationship between a trust and its enterprises the rule entitling the trust to impose obligatory deliveries "any time when the interest of the national economy or of the trust so requires."[9] As the Scientific Council of the Institute for Economic Laws of the State Arbitrator Court pointed out, this is a back door through which may pass the former method of organization of production by decrees. The same report states that many a management of enterprises enjoys this limit on its independence since this enables it to shift responsibility for decisions made upon someone else. One would expect, however, that when (or if) enterprises become the only ones which bear the financial burden or benefits of decisions made, their managers will become more anxious to assert their own independence. This brings us to the second "if" with which I started this section of my discussion.

Incentives to organize production rationally

The next "if" concerns the financial incentives given to enterprises. On paper, the enterprises will be free to reorganize their input-mix and output-mix so as to maximize disposable net revenue. Whatever the name, this excess of receipts over costs may be then used by the enterprises for wage bonuses or investments. However, in Czechoslovakia the trusts received the right to tap these profits and use them to subsidize deficit enterprises. The subsidies are supposed to be strictly a short-run measure. However, without enough incentives from the start, the enterprises will neither find it useful to assert their independence and combat the tendency of the trusts to hold on to the old command economy nor will they find it worthwhile to reorganize the input mix and the product mix. If the management of the trusts will tax successes too heavily and pamper

[9] *Rudé Právo*, Nov. 24, 1966, p. 2.

failures too generously, the essence of the new model will disappear. Even if markets will be cleared, they will not be cleared on the basis of rational economic calculus: we will face a shell of the new model with its content spirited away.

The 1966 Czech experience suggests that the managers of enterprises are confident that this will not happen. In a number of cases, these managers took unpopular measures only because they believed that they would receive the benefits of their courage. Some coal mines were closed; an unnamed enterprise in Pilsen discovered that it can buy steel and coke cheaper from outside, and closed a blast furnace and a coking plant (at the cost of 1,600 jobs). In Trinec, the management of a steel mill liquidated a brick factory, three blast furnaces and some other facilities and is planning to close nine more blast furnaces in the next two years. The managers also wanted to close a coking plant because of lack of demand for coke; however, this has been blocked by the State Planning Office.[10] Obviously, the managers are at the moment confident that they will be able to keep a major part of the profits resulting from the reorganization of production. Whether this optimism is justified, only future developments of the power relationship between the trust directorate and enterprise management will tell.

Monopoly power

The power of the trust directorates to reduce enterprises to command enterprises and to milk dry successful enterprises would destroy the foundations of the new model. In contrast with this fundamental issue, the problem of monopoly power appears minor to me even though it attracts much attention. Given a choice, surely both the consumers and the producers would prefer to face a profit-maximizing monopolist rather than the unpredictable "command enterprise." No rational organization of production or consumption is possible when one faces a command enterprise that may deliver a full loaf today, no loaf tomorrow, half a loaf the day after, and so on. In contrast, one may adjust (i.e., at least organize *one's own* consumption or production rationally) when faced with a profit-maximizing monopolist. Thus I would think that even if a sizable number of present command enterprises is converted into monopolistic enterprises, the organization of production (and of consumption) in Eastern Europe will improve. Our East European colleagues will

[10] *Rudé Právo*, Nov. 23, 1966, p. 3.

then be able to cease worrying about the utter irrationality of all command enterprises and start worrying — along with us — about the *relatively* harmless problem of some monopolistic enterprises.

Distribution

At present, output and income are admittedly not related. Educated people receive less than the average workers; the workers themselves face what is called "wage ceilings" so that "each worker makes sure that he does not exceed 'permissible' output and the management welcomes this 'self-discipline' of its labor force."[11] The daily press speaks about "the conspiracy of mediocrity." Equality of incomes — with departures in the wrong directions — and almost absolute job security is the order of the day. The new economic model is explicitly designed to change all this: the policymaker is aware that unless there is a drastic readjustment in incomes that people get and establishment of the radical principle that you get paid for *working* in a plant — not just for being there — the whole reform will fail. Indeed, the policymakers in Czechoslovakia are so aware of this that no other issue has been more thoroughly discussed in the newspapers and weeklies as the reform is being introduced.

The new model uses doubletalk on this sensitive issue. True enough, there is the rule that wage rates may not fall; however, there are several deliberate and explicitly stated weaknesses to this comforting rule. First, reorganization of input and output mixes will bring with it reassignments within enterprises, and there is no rule that blocks reassignment of people to jobs yielding lower rates of pay. Thus, even with fixed wage rates and labor force, individual incomes will be affected. Second, the planners stress that there is "overemployment" in many enterprises.[12] It is foreseen that many enterprises will release some workers for other tasks — as the papers delicately put it; the service industries and construction are frequently mentioned as two fields in which underemployment exists. Even the most pampered group of Czech workers, the miners, were told that some of them — in view of declining demand for coal — will have to seek other, less rewarding, occupation. The Pilsen steel plant I discussed earlier already announced "the release" of 1,600 workers. Thus, in the case of "releases," fixed hourly wage rate becomes multiplied with zero hours

[11] *Ibid.*, Nov. 4, 1966, p. 2.
[12] Cf., e.g., *Rudé Právo*, Nov. 4, 1966, p. 2.

worked, existing income drops to zero, and a new and a different income will have to be sought by the worker.

The public is shocked by all this. How much so is demonstrated by the fact that the weekly of the Czech Communist Party had to answer charges that this was an attempt to introduce capitalism.[13] Indeed, the president of Czechoslovakia was placed in the absurd postion of giving assurances that the aim of the Communist party was not to make the nation worse off: "The goal of the Communist party is not a continuing reduction of the standard of living; on the contrary . . ." and "Therefore, comrades, I shall close by emphasizing again that it could not be a Communist party which would put into its program the reduction of cultural and material standards of the population."[14] Obviously, the reintroduction of the labor market, "denivelization," reintroduction of income inequalities, and the firing of some workers promises to be an infinitely painful process in a nation in which it became customary to pay "irrespective of merit, importance, and quality of work but by the number of children"[15] and which became accustomed to almost absolute job security from "enterprises viewed as social-security institutions."[16] The screams of outrage that a reorganization of distribution of income brings about and will keep bringing about, will be due to both subjective and objective reasons.

Subjectively, the population is said to be dedicated to the notion that "we all have the same stomachs" and that justice demands innumerable types of hidden and open subsidies; job security is taken for granted. Any income differentiation (which is not made economically meaningless through offsetting subsidies) will bring home to the mediocre, incompetent, or simply superfluous that they are mediocre, incompetent, or superfluous; a cultural shock of the first magnitude. At the same time, the drop in income will force upon this part of the public decreases in consumption of the innumerable items which it has been told "justice" demands that it gets. Of course, given the size of income, for every loser there will be a gainer. However, recent surveys indicate that many Czechs have an exaggerated notion as to how much any extra effort that they might supply is worth. The conclusion has been reached that any wage bonus smaller than 300 crowns — 20 percent of the average monthly

[13] *Kulturní Tvorba*, Nov. 17, 1966, p. 5.
[14] *Rudé Právo*, Dec. 21, 1966, p. 4.
[15] *Kulturní Tvorba*, Nov. 17, 1966, p. 5.
[16] *Rudé Právo*, Nov. 24, 1966, p. 3.

wage — fails to furnish incentive to an extra effort. Thus, it appears possible that if one person loses and another gains, say, 300 crowns, the loser will be outraged with his loss and the gainer contemptuous of his gain. At the outset, before the new economic model brings fruits and increase incomes of everybody, the public in general may be expected to feel exploited.

Objectively, there are at least three problems. First, in Eastern Europe no unemployment exists and thus no unemployment insurance. Unless new measures are taken, the cost of employment reallocation will fall, entirely, upon those "released for other tasks." Second, the punitive 30 percent wage-bill tax on wage bills exceeding (in 1967), nine-tenths of the planned totals for 1966 will act as a strong brake against the hiring of those fired by other firms short of labor. Third, the reallocation of the labor force inevitably brings up the housing problem which the planners, fearless as they in general appear, did not have the courage to tackle. The planners keep giving assurances that everybody "released" will find a job — perhaps paying less, perhaps in a different city, but a job nevertheless. It is pointed out that service industries and construction are seriously understaffed. This is cold comfort to those fired in any society, including ours. In Eastern Europe, the housing situation makes this even worse. In the daily press, both those seeking and offering labor frequently demand or offer provision of housing. Unless a free market in housing is reestablished — and nobody as yet dared to make this proposal to the public accustomed to pay some 3 percent of income as rent — the resistance to the reallocation of the labor force in accordance with rational economic calculus by the enterprises is bound to be tremendous.

The new economic model has received the huge task of cleaning up the debris left by the old one. As for distribution, this task appears really formidable since here it is sure to meet resistance, which the crucial housing problem will make only more fierce than it would be otherwise.

Provisions for Maintenance and Progress

The last task that an economic model must, or should, perform is to provide for maintenance of physical capital and for progress. The concept of maintenance is unambiguous; in contrast, there are so many concepts of "progress" in the discussions emanating from Eastern Europe that it appears worthwhile to pin down at least the three basic ones and then attempt to establish in what manner the new economic model provides for them.

For expository purposes, take any simple production function, such as $Q = a\, C^\alpha\, L^\beta$.

Progress A: If there is misallocation of resources, actual output Q_A will be smaller than output Q which may be obtained by the use of a given capital and labor in a manner given by presently available technology and the state of arts. Thus, Progress A may be achieved through reallocation of resources; through changes in the factor and product mixes.

Progress B: Given technology and the state of arts, an increase in output Q_A *or* Q will result from an increase in capital or labor: ΔL or ΔC.

Progress C: Finally, inventions, innovations, education, etc. shift the entire production function upwards and cause an increase in output (from Q or Q_A to Q' or Q'_A), even with given L and C, as a result of changes in productivities: Δa, $\Delta \alpha$, $\Delta \beta$.

Although in any actual economy it would be hard to find examples of "pure" progress A or B or C unaccompanied by associated progress in some other category, there is — I believe — a merit in this classification. By and large, with some notable exceptions, the East European countries in the past two decades concentrated on Progress B: huge investment programs and sizable increases in the labor force. The stagnation in the recent years is interpreted by the economists in the West and in the East — after we strip away the terminological differences — in the same way: Progress B became offset, and in a few years more than offset, by a negative progress A. The misallocation of resources started to swallow, and even more than swallow, increases in output resulting from scraping the bottom of the labor barrel and from the investment program:

Despite the encouraging results it became clearer in recent years that the methods of economic management applied up to now — the detailed plan instructions decreed from above, the allocation system, and the high degree of centralization in respect to management — which rendered good services in the liquidation of an economy characterized by shortages — do no longer ensure an adequate rate of development. More is needed than a simple modification and improvement of some details of an otherwise unchanged method of management by centralized plan instructions. A major change was rendered urgent also by the fact that the manpower reserves necessary for large-scale development are becoming exhausted. It is for this reason that we have to find ways and means for the transition from extensive to intensive methods of development.[17]

[17] Fekete, pp. 67–68.

Progress A

Thus, there seems to be general agreement in the East and the West that the key task of the new economic model is to bring about Progress A. Rational standards (relative prices) leading to rational distribution and — in association with profit incentives to enterprises — to rational organization of production are expected to yield dividends rich enough to outweigh the obvious ideological sacrifices and the no less obvious initial outrage of the public.

Progress B

The new model has little to say about Progress B: about the manner of accomplishing changes in capital and labor that would lead to optimum increases in output. In addition — and in contrast to sound provisions that are being made for Progress A — the little that the new model does have to say about Progress B seems to make little sense. The guiding light of the model builders seems to be an effort to force the enterprises to economize with labor; this is to be accomplished through (1) fairly heavy taxes on the use of existing quantities of labor, (2) punitive, perhaps even prohibitive, taxes on the use of additional labor, (3) in contrast, very low charges (relatively to labor) on the use of existing fixed capital and extremely low charges on the use of variable capital, and (4) low charges on the use of additional fixed capital and, again, extremely low charges on the use of additional variable capital. Progress B is to be accomplished, the new rules seem to say, through negligible increases or even decreases in labor and through heavy increases in fixed capital and even heavier increases in variable capital. Discussion of the capital charges I shall leave for the next section of this contribution, dealing with money and credit. What can we say, however, about the rules that the new model sets up for the use of labor?

As pointed out in the discussion of relative prices, the new model imposes a 22 percent tax on labor inputs and a 6 percent tax on capital inputs (the figures are only slightly different for Hungary). In addition, the new model imposes an extremely heavy — perhaps even prohibitive — surtax on labor inputs exceeding nine-tenths of the labor inputs planned for 1966. This surtax amounts to 30 percent so that the total tax on the upper 10 percent of existing labor inputs and on any additions to the existing labor inputs — leading to progress B through ΔL — increases to 52 percent.

These rules reveal a gross confusion of the planners between the requirements of Progress A and Progress B. If Progress A were impossible
because of correct allocation of existing resources and if enterprises in
the past became accustomed to wasting labor inputs, there might be
some merit in jolting managements out of their slothful habits by reinforc-
ing the market commands through punitive taxes and almost prohibitive
surtaxes. The trouble is that although the second condition is true, the
first one is not. The planners themselves insist that although some sectors — especially industry and administration — are wasting labor inputs
on a major scale, other sectors — especially services and construction —
are grossly short handed; the planners expect substantial Progress A from
a reallocation of labor inputs. But when they become immersed in their
notion of desirable Progress B, and impose a punitive surtax on all new
hirings by all sectors except administration and farming. This makes reallocation of labor, which even when left to the market would be painful,
even more painful. Overstaffed industry, guided by profit incentives, presumably will — as the planners euphemistically put it — "release labor
for other tasks" but the understaffed services and construction will face
a 30 percent labor tax on new hirings and will have very small incentive
to employ these fired workers. Instead of positive Progress A resulting
from reallocation of labor inputs one would expect negative Progress B
resulting from an absolute reduction of labor inputs (assuming, of course,
that the marginal product of labor is non-negative).

Thus, it is hard to avoid the conclusion that the labor tax and surtax
(which I can explain only by assuming that the planners strangely forgot
the requirements of Progress A and became prisoners of their notions
as to the desirable type of Progress B) is a major blunder of the new
model. Since in all other respects this model appears soundly conceived,
I am led even to wonder if I am not missing some special rule or set of
exceptions. However, even if a blunder did occur, it is not a blunder in
design of the new model but merely one in specifications. Should the difficulties I am visualizing actually obtain and endanger positive Progress A
and cause negative Progress B, it should be simple enough for the planners to reduce the basic labor tax and — especially — the apparently
prohibitive and thus apparently extremely low-yielding surtax. One might
even hope that after two decades of such poor experiences with interfer-
ences with the working of the market the planners will resist the temptation
to reduce it on a selective basis.

A question also appears with respect to capital changes which bring about Progress B. According to the present rules, changes in capital are to be financed (a) by bank credit, (b) from the fixed 2 percent reserve fund, and (c) optionally, from the profits of enterprises which may be used either for investment or for wage bonuses. About the intended size of the first type of investment nothing is being said; the size of the optional investments I would expect to be below the optimum. The Czechs seem to share this opinion since they are already worrying whether in the new model enterprises will make the "right" choice between wage bonuses and investments.[18] If the existing labor force owned the enterprises outright, there would be no problem. However, there is no such direct ownership, and the current labor force surely realizes that in the case of wage bonuses *they* will benefit where as in the case of investment decisions some future labor force — of which the current decision maker may or may not be a member — will benefit. This, it is easy to show by elementary analysis, imparts a definite anti-investment bias to the current decision makers. Thus, the East European decision to invest ownership of factories in the continuing labor body — not in individual workers — is bound to create investment problems. Unless counteracted through government fiat, there is bound to be a misallocation of income in favor of present consumption: Progress B will be smaller.

Progress C

The new model has next to nothing to say about Progress C. Here, I believe, the significant question to be asked concerns the problem as to who, in Eastern Europe, will become the risk taker: who will accept the risks inherent in the attempts to change a, a, and β in the production function with which I started. As Professor Jacob Schmookler has shown, we know little about conditions for innovations and inventions that shift existing investment function up, that make for progress, but we know that there must be somebody who takes risks. Unless the decision makers bet their own resources in case of failure, and unless they get a big chunk of the gain in case of success, risk-taking is likely to be irresponsible. In the Hungarian case, one mention of conditions facing Progress C sounded ominous: "the reserve funds . . . enable the enterprises to assume — with adequate circumspection — rational risks."[19] About the second

---

[18] *Rudé Právo*, Nov. 4, 1966, p. 2: "Conflicts will appear . . . even where there will be profits, especially with respect to decisions . . . how much to devote to wages, how much to investments, and how much to social or cultural needs."
[19] Fekete, p. 72.

source of investment into Progress C, bank credit, the Czechs have even less encouraging things to say: "The banks — advised by the trusts — will select those actions [i.e., investments] which will be sufficiently reliable; that is, in the case of which there is no risk of a failure to repay."[20] Thus it would appear that both the Czechs and the Hungarians seem to want to court Progress C by assuming only riskless risks; a futile rule in love and war and economic development.

Money and Credit in the New Model

With respect to monetary policy, I get the distinct impression that we are going to be as much in the dark as we were in the old model. The reason for this is that data itself are still treated as secrets, and that the policy criteria — since the need-to-know principle is limited to a small group of top-level bureaucrats — receive scant discussion in the professional literature.

There are some peculiar features in the new model as far as the credit charges and tax policies are concerned. First, enterprises will be charged rental payments to the state on all resources used in production irrespective of whether they are leased from others (labor from the workers), whether they are in possession of enterprises at the start of the new system (fixed and variable capital), or whether they are purchased for cash or on credit by the enterprises after the start of the new system (column 1 of the table). Next, enterprises are also going to be charged a tax (essentially, in lieu of interest payments) or interest payments for the resources that they use but do not "own" (column 2 of the table). Next, in the case of two inputs, labor and variable capital, enterprises will be charged a surtax (essentially, a penalty interest rate) if the use of these resources exceeds a norm: (a) nine-tenths of the wage bill planned for 1966 in the case of labor and (b) discretionary norm in the case of variable capital. Finally, the demand for credit — given the budget constraint — depends not only on current cost of it but also on amortization payments required. (By amortization I mean repayments of loans.) Since labor inputs cannot be purchased outright, the issue does not come up; for comparative purposes, I entered "no amortization" in column 4. In the case of capital, purchases of fixed capital on credit require amortization whereas purchases of inventories (that are being constantly renewed) do not require amortization.

[20] *Rudé Právo*, Nov. 3, 1966, p. 3.

SCHEMA OF INPUT CHARGES AND CREDIT (OR QUASI-CREDIT) COSTS

Input	Rental payments on all resources used	Interest or quasi-interest on resources rented	Surtax on "excess" inputs	Amortization
Labor	Wage bill	22% of rental	30% of rental	No
Fixed capital	6% of value	6% of value	None	Yes
Inventories	2% of value	4% of value	Exists but level not known	No

Out of the items listed in the table, the banking system administers, of course, only the allocation of credits to finance fixed capital and inventories, sets the volume of these credits, and has the right to change the interest rates charged to credit users. What are we able to say about the performance of these three tasks? Since price stability is being pursued vigorously both by the Czechs and by the Hungarians, one surmises that the *volume* of credit will be set by the banks so as to make the supply of new capital equal to the volume of credit granted. However, as far as the *allocation* of this given volume is concerned, the banking system and the Treasury will impart to the enterprises some peculiar information about the costs of resources which are being used up. Let us translate into words the economic message sent by the banks and the Treasury, as specified in the table:

As far as the resources that enterprises "own" are concerned (by "resources owned" I mean resources which the enterprises held in possession at the start of the reform, which they purchased for cash afterward, or which they purchased on credit after this credit is repaid), the management is being told that fixed capital is three times as expensive to hold than inventories (column 1); as far as the resources purchased on credit are concerned, fixed capital is twice as expensive as inventories (the sum of columns 1 and 2). This message is only reinforced by the amortization rules: credit on fixed capital is to be allocated by the banking system to enterprises which will offer the fastest amortization of loans.[21] In contrast, in the case of inventories credit is extended on a given level of inventories and thus is, essentially, nonrepayable as long as the enterprise does not reduce this level. Why the planners decided to make inventories so cheap in general, and to have differences in the extent of

[21] *Ibid.*

the cheapness depending on whether this capital is "owned" or purchased on credit I find myself unable even to guess. My puzzlement is only heightened by the fact that there were, and still are, persistent complaints that enterprises maintain excessive inventories. Just recently the Czech president complained that, in 1966, "increased production was to a great extent immobilized in inventories. The state plan expected in 1966 an increase of 1.8 billion crowns while the actual increase will exceed 5 billion crowns." [22]

At the same time, the planners seem to realize that by making the relative cost of using variable capital (both owned and borrowed) lower than that of fixed capital they will face strong demand for this type of credit and will be forced, once again, to make administrative allocations of it. Banks were told to charge penalty rates on credit furnished to enterprises experiencing "excessive growth of inventories." Also, this part of banking policy (i.e., credit on variable capital) has been declared to be a tool of "state economic policy. The credit policy of the state will be aimed at restrictions and will guide enterprises to maintain only essential inventories (of variable capital) and to finance any increases out of their own funds." [23]

While analytically messy, the effects of the combined rent and interest policy may be expected to be mitigated somewhat by the fact that enterprises will find it profitable to borrow as much as possible — even if the purpose is to be a purchase of fixed capital — on their inventories: so far as they are successful, this will reduce the distortion in this part of the cost of using fixed and variable capital. Also, we would expect inventories to be bigger than they would be in the absence of this distortion of the relative prices of fixed and variable capital. Unmeasurable cost, finally, is to be found in the fact that rationing of credit on inventories, administered by apparently the least professionally competent group of bureaucrats, will perpetuate at least one element of the command economy.

CONCLUSION

I would conclude that the new economic model about to be applied in Czechoslovakia and Hungary appears, on paper, a sound one. It offers a promise that it will tackle rationally three of the five basic tasks of any economic model: fixing standards, organizing production, and distribution of the final product. The next task, adjusting consumption to pro-

---

[22] *Ibid.*, Dec. 21, 1966, p. 4.   [23] *Ibid.*, Nov. 3, 1966, p. 3.

duction in the short run, it is unlikely to perform well; however, as long as the short run will be kept short, this is relatively a minor blemish. Innumerable problems appear in the case of the last and extremely important task of providing for maintenance and progress. Here, both the labor policies and investment and credit policies appear badly conceived. Yet, this may be less serious than it would appear at first sight. Merely to bring about Progress A through reallocation of the present input-mixes and output-mixes may yield progress enough in the next decade. The planners, therefore, may have made a sensible decision of tackling first things first and they may have left the problems of Progresses B and C for a later date.

Whether the new model will succeed in bringing significant Progress A is one of the most fascinating economic issues of this decade. Much depends on the political leadership in Eastern Europe. Will it be able to override the resistance now forming among the high echelons of the civil service who see both their ideological orthodoxy and their jobs in danger? Will the leadership be able to withstand the heat generated by the enraged public which, at first, will face only the sacrifices but not the rewards? Much depends also on the economy itself: how fast will a price system be able to bear fruit? If the fruits come fast, the conservative element in the upper civil service will be discredited, and popular resistance weaken and possibly be converted into support. Thus, absurdly enough, the only hope of the new economic model is that those Western economists who believe the price system to be a slow and ponderous machinery be proved wrong and those — like Milton Friedman — who believe that the price system is one of the most sensitive instruments ever devised by man be proved right. The West German upsurge following the monetary reform and restoration of the market economy in the middle of 1948 gave to the believers in inherent flexibility of the market-directed economy the first round; we shall all wait most anxiously, I am sure, to see who will win the no less important second round about to start in Eastern Europe.

POSTSCRIPT

The rapid pace of political developments in Czechoslovakia has prompted the preparation of this postscript as the book is about to go to the printer. The postscript brings our account of the events to the beginning of May 1968.

First Year of the New Model. — As already indicated, 1967 was the first year of the New Model. Economically, it was not a good year. Most Czechoslovak newspapers spoke of "an economic crisis," said that "Czechoslovakia is passing through serious economic difficulties," and the like. At first glance, statistical evidence as reported by the Planning Office does not support this. According to the official report on the year 1967, national income rose by 8 percent or by 15 billion crowns; surely, a very encouraging result. However, one discovers that from 11 to 12 billion crowns of this increment went into inventories. Past experience indicates that inventories — before they are converted into sales — are next to impossible to evaluate: they may be worth the amount stated, or they may be worth half of the amount. In any case, deduct the increment to output that the public did not get, and the rate of growth falls to some 2–1.5 percent; deflate this by the reported cost-of-living increase of 1.5 percent, and nothing is left.

However, it is not the New Model that is getting the blame. Institutionally, the *ancien régime* imposed upon the economy a policy of small steps, all of them leading back to the Old Model. One example must suffice. In January 1967, *binding* economic plans for enterprises were abolished. However, the Planning Office was permitted to work out "guide numbers" for the various sectors. Next, the sectors allocated these "guide numbers" to the mentioned trust directorates. The trust directorates allocated these, still merely advisory, guide numbers to the individual enterprises. And then came the squeeze back toward the Old Model: unless the enterprises fulfilled the quotas assigned by the supposedly advisory "guide numbers" they could not pay management bonuses, wage premiums, and so on. At least in one important respect, by December 1967 Czech economic organization was precisely where it has been during the past 20 years.

Post-January 1968 New Model. — The new Czechoslovak government includes, as one of two vice premiers, Professor Ota Šik who, in the popular mind, is the pioneer of the New Model. This, by itself, is significant. Also, the Communist party published a massive *Action Program* for the new government. This program, if acted upon, will bring about a fundamental reorganization of Czechoslovak economic and political life. It is unfortunate that the American press has a tendency to concentrate on the showy froth while missing the fine points. One such point is the decision to convert Czechoslovakia into a *confederacy* of the Czech countries and of Slovakia. If this happens — and steps in this direction have been already taken — this is likely to have some startling consequences. Since caution in everything we in the West print at this critical juncture seems imperative, let me put it delicately: To lock in the reforms desired by the public and to prevent retrogression as happened in Poland a decade earlier, is it necessary to have a political democracy with a two- or multi-party system, or is it sufficient to have a one-party system, composed of two territorially confederated parts? Turning to the economic sections of the *Action Program* we find:

1. *Enterprise management.* — Management is to be responsible to an "organ" elected by and from the employees of the enterprise and which, however, will also contain members charged with protecting the interests of society as a whole.

2. *Trust directorates.* — I have seen in these directorates the major danger to the New Model. Now they are to be made purely voluntary associations, with enterprises having the right to decide which directorate to join and the right not to join any.

3. *Cartels and monopolies.* — The dangers of voluntary associations acting in restraint of trade and monopolies did not escape the writers of the *Action Program*. One suspects that the experience accumulated in 1967 helped in this respect. In any case, the program states that "an indispensable part of the economic activity of the state consists of effective measures that would protect the consumer against the misuse of monopoly power and of economic power of industry and trade." "The basic incentive must become economic competition, especially competition with highly developed [current euphemism for Western] foreign competitors."

4. *Subsidies.* — "It is impossible to blunt our economic policy forever by taking away from those who work well and giving to those who work poorly." "Economic reform will increasingly put enterprises into situations in which they feel the consequences of good as well as bad management."

5. *Market forces.* — "Instead of a systematic effort to institute market criteria, which would reveal backwardness and deformations and which would keep eliminating these two, there are still at work attempts to deform these market criteria, to fit them to the existing conditions, and to create a comfortable situation in which backwardness and distortions can survive and be parasites at the expense of all of us."

6. *Cooperative and Private enterprise.* — "In connection with the development of cooperatives it appears useful to work out in detail co-ownership rights of the members of the cooperative in relation to the cooperative." "Small, personally owned, enterprises have their place in the service sector."

Needless to say, the *Action Program* (published by the newspapers in Czechoslovakia on April 10, 1968) restates and amplifies with vigor the principles of the New Model which, previously, have been stated with much greater circumspection. Indeed, some wits in Prague are said to have suggested that the surplus statues of Stalin could be put to good use: just replace the familiar *visage* with that of Adam Smith.

ADDENDUM IN PROOF

The occupation of Czechoslovakia in August of 1968 may invalidate much that has been said above. To make predictions now (September 1968) appears impossible. Professor Evžen Löbl, a prominent government official, is reported to have said that two major parts of the New Model cannot be implemented: (1) elimination of several thousand of incompetent planners and managers and (2) emasculation of the trusts which form the power base of these people. I, myself, would suspect that the plight is even more serious than that. *Any* reorganization of the economy — for reasons which I attempted to outline — was bound to be unpopular in the early stages. It appears to me doubtful that the current government, faced by its desperate need to maintain its broad national support, will find it advisable to proceed even if permitted to do so. Finally, the permission itself appears to be in doubt. Vigorous Soviet attacks on the New Model, on Vice-Premier Šik, and his inability to return to Czechoslovakia all give rise to a suspicion that — for the time being — the New Model is dead.

EUGENE BABITCHEV

•

•

•

•

•

The International Bank
for Economic Cooperation

Dissatisfaction with limited payments agreements and associated bilateralism has prompted countries in the Soviet bloc to set up machinery that would facilitate multilateral settlements and promote an increased volume of trade. The decision to organize an international bank for this purpose was loudly advertised by the Council of Mutual Economic Assistance (COMECON) at the end of 1962. By mid-1963 the Foreign Trade Commission of COMECON announced that January 1, 1964, had been set as the target date for the bank to start operations. On October 22, 1963, an agreement was signed in Moscow by the eight members — Bulgaria, Czechoslovakia, East Germany, Hungary, Mongolia, Poland, Rumania, and the USSR [1] — creating the International Bank for Economic Cooperation (IBEC).[2] This agreement represented the culmination of extensive top-level negotiations for achieving a multilateral system of payments for COMECON countries. Originally, it was intended to name the new institution the International Bank of the Socialist Countries, but because of various considerations — perhaps predominantly a desire to attract noncommunist countries as members of the bank — a less tendentious name was chosen.

[1] At the 22nd Congress of the Communist party of the USSR in October 1961, Albania, which had joined COMECON in 1949, was officially denounced for, among many other things, "provocative actions against the USSR," and shortly thereafter it was banned from participating in COMECON activities. Curiously enough, Albania still considers itself a member with equal rights.

[2] The text of the agreement and the statutes of the IBEC (both in Russian) appeared in *Vneshniaia torgovlia*, No. 8 (1964), 47–55.

COMECON PRICES AND EXCHANGE RATES

The movement toward multilateralism in the COMECON countries must be viewed first against the background of those countries' pricing and exchange-rate practices. Soviet propaganda likes to depict the ruble as a widely accepted international currency, the only one in the world with a hard, gold content. In practice, however, the ruble is not a gold currency in any sense of the term, because it is not convertible into gold internally and because ruble balances held by foreigners cannot be freely converted into gold; as a matter of fact the ruble is not even "international." It does not approach the international status of the currencies of the industrial countries of the West, which are convertible against one another and are relatively free of exchange controls. For the ruble to be international, two conditions would have to exist. First, it would have to be used in making and receiving payments to and from other countries for the whole range of international transactions. In reality, however, this condition is fulfilled only within the COMECON area. Second, the ruble prices of USSR commodities moving in international trade would have to be related to internal prices, as would also — through established exchange rates — prices expressed in terms of foreign currencies. This condition is far from being realized.

But the USSR is not the only country within the COMECON whose prices are out of line with the world market. Indeed, domestic prices in all Communist countries have little connection with relative scarcities or with utility considerations, but are controlled according to other criteria; some are subsidized while others, through the levy of a "turnover tax," yield substantial profits to the government. In the absence of a system of linked market economies such as exist in the West, where prices are determined largely in response to supply and demand forces, each COMECON country has its own set of prices. The various internal pricing principles differ so widely that the adoption of a single price pattern now in effect in any one country would not solve the problem, as it would benefit some countries and be detrimental to others.

Consequently, prices in intrabloc trade are determined on the basis of "world prices," defined as an approximation of the price a COMECON country would have to pay if it bought a given item from a capitalist country. To remove the influences of seasonal and cyclical fluctuations, average prices have been taken over a period of several years.[3] These prices, once

---

[3] G. L. Shagalov, *Ekonomicheskaia effektivnost' tovarnogo obmena mezhdu sotsialisticheskimi stranami* (Moscow, 1966), pp. 71–74.

arrived at, remain valid for some time, with the result that they consistently tend to reflect prices prevailing on the world market a few years earlier. During the first two years of the bank's operations the world price level of 1957–1958 was used; in 1966 the prices were changed to represent average main world market prices during 1960–1964. Such pricing practices have been harshly criticized within COMECON, especially when the trend of world prices was unfavorable for a particular country.[4]

The existing price system is not too rigid, however. It frequently happens that one COMECON country, in the process of negotiating a bilateral trade agreement with another, demands an increase in the price of some of its export commodities — claiming, for example, that they are of better quality. In return, the reciprocal-trade partner seeks to increase the price of some of its own goods, and the outcome is a tendency for many prices to rise. According to the calculations made by Hungarian economists, machinery prices in intra-COMECON trade deviate by more than 25 percent from world prices, and those of raw materials by as much as 15 percent.[5] To make things more complex, intrabloc commerce includes some goods for which no world prices can readily be established (ships, electronic equipment, complex machinery, and the like). The practice is to trade such items on the cost-plus basis,[6] but inability to calculate actual costs (taking into account all factors of production) may have the result that export of a given good is not profitable, or even advantageous for the producing country.

It is difficult to visualize how the COMECON countries can make major economic decisions about foreign trade on the basis of prices that prevailed some time ago in the capitalist markets and are at variance with the prices used in guiding their internal decisions regarding output and investment. This problem is sufficiently recognized in all the countries.[7] Clearly, a common system of prices must be devised that will be accepted by every member country and be applied to national planning as well as to foreign trade.

As regards exchange rates, those for "commercial transactions" among

[4] Pricing problems within COMECON have been well described in Michael Kaser's COMECON — *Integration Problems of the Planned Economies* (London: Oxford University Press, 1965), pp. 140–157.

[5] V. D'iachenko, "Osnovnye napravleniia sovershenstvovaniia tsen vo vzaimnoi torgovle stran-chlenov SEV," *Voprosy ekonomiki*, No. 12 (1967), 67.

[6] A. D. Stupov, ed., *Ekonomicheskoe sotrudnichestvo i vzaimopomoshch' sotsialisticheskikh stran* (Moscow, 1962), p. 63.

[7] See for example, A. Probst, "Ob opredelenii ekonomicheskogo effekta vneshnei torgovli," *Planovoe khoziaistvo*, No. 11 (1965), 39–44.

the bloc's currencies are determined on the basis of gold parities. For "noncommercial transactions" the conversion rates are adjusted to reflect purchasing-power differences.[8]

The gold parities of the individual currencies are artificial, however; they have nothing to do with gold content, or with the relative purchasing power of the national currency units. Problems associated with exchange-rate determination are discussed in Communist economic literature in an extremely vague way, and it is still a mystery how these rates were actually set. In all likelihood, the motives for linking gold with national currencies were largely political and psychological, calculated to increase the prestige of Communist money and confidence in its value; moreover, homage to the gold standard is consistent with the teachings of Karl Marx. The fact is, however, that under present practices, the gold parities and exchange rates have little significance because the transactions are carried out in prices irrelevant to domestic economies. Prices are expressed in a commonly agreed-upon conventional unit, which happens to be the ruble but could be any other accounting unit, including the dollar or sterling.

The degree to which the commercial exchange rates are out of line with the purchasing power of the different countries is indicated by the disparity between established commercial and noncommercial rates, which in some cases is substantial. For example, 100 Polish zlotys are exchangeable under the commercial schedule for 22.50 rubles, but under the noncommercial schedule for only 6.67 rubles. On the other hand, for 100 Bulgarian leva the commercial rate is 76.92 rubles, but the noncommercial rate is 112.36 rubles.

In addition to commercial and noncommercial exchange rates, other methods of conversion are used. Thus in constructing joint COMECON projects (including scientific research institutes), the costs of building materials and equipment, transportation charges, amortization of fixed

[8] Commercial transactions are those that involve "commodities and services exchanged with someone outside the country," and "include the international purchases and sales of commodities and commodity transport." Noncommercial transactions involve "goods and services sold to and consumed by a foreigner within the country's borders," and "include receipts and expenditures by international tourists and by embassies, receipts and expenditures for passenger transportation and international telephone and telegraph services, and individual and institutional remittances." (Definitions are from P. H. Thunberg, "The Soviet Union in the World Economy," in *Dimensions of Soviet Economic Power,* Joint Economic Committee, Congress of the United States, 87th Congress, 2nd Session, 1962, pp. 422–23.)

capital, and other associated expenses, as expressed in a given national currency, are converted into rubles with the help of "coefficients," which supposedly account for the differences between domestic and foreign prices. These coefficients are computed for major basic materials and for various types of equipment by comparing the domestic prices with the established prices in intrabloc trade. To convert into rubles the costs of some materials for which no separate coefficients are available, the weighted average coefficient for several representative inputs is used. Labor costs (including fringe benefits) connected with the projects are converted into rubles in accordance with the noncommercial exchange-rate schedule.[9] Judging from an account of the proceedings of the COMECON's Standing Commission on Foreign-Exchange and Finance the practical application of these conversion rules is too cumbersome and in need of considerable simplification.[10]

THE MOVEMENT TOWARD
MULTILATERALISM

Problems arising from intrabloc trade became evident soon after the end of World War II. When reconstruction of the devastated economies began, badly damaged production facilities could not satisfy the demand for goods, and in a world of shortages there was little to spare for exports, with the exception of goods that could be traded for essential imports.[11] Economic relations with the West, including participation in the Marshall Plan, were effectively opposed by the dominating Soviet Union, because of political considerations. In that state of isolation there was no choice but to negotiate bilateral trade and payments agreements within the bloc. These usually amounted to nothing more than arrangements for barters of equal value, even though precise balancing of trade within the year was not always possible. Each country, practically without exception, was confronted with two related problems: first, it was unable to earn enough by exporting to pay for imports necessary for the

[9] For a fuller discussion, see K. Larionov and N. Obolenskii, "Plodotvornoe sotrudnichestvo valiutno-finansovykh otnoshenii," *Finansy SSSR*, No. 1 (1965), 35–39.

[10] "V Postoiannoi Komissii SEV po valiutno-finansovym voprosam," *Finansy SSSR*, No. 12 (1966), 90 and No. 12 (1967), 88.

[11] To make things even worse, the Soviet Union demanded (and received, of course) large reparations — mostly in the form of industrial installations — from several of its satellites which had fought on the side of the Axis.

development of its economy; second, it often could not use the proceeds earned by exporting to one country for purchases in another. These difficulties were not easy to eliminate; they continued for a long time and are present, to a varying extent, even in current intra-bloc trade relations.

It was widely recognized that the bilateral trade arrangements and limited payments agreements were hampering integration within the bloc, and in fact were a contradiction of the "Basic Principles of the International Socialist Division of Labor"[12] adopted in 1962 at COMECON's 15th session. Although the foreign trade turnover among bloc members grew by 360 percent during 1950–1964, it was evident that balancing payments on a bilateral basis was becoming increasingly difficult, necessitating frequent resort to reexporting operations; that is, some countries were forced to accept unwanted goods in exchange for exports and then try to reexport these goods to other bloc countries. Also, it was not uncommon for, say, country A to receive goods from country B without being able to supply B with the commodities it needed; in such cases, A was compelled to reduce its imports from B or to make arrangements with a third country to ship goods to B in exchange for imports from A.[13] Thus foreign trade was not yielding its maximum benefits, and in some countries the production of some commodities was held below capacity, despite an obvious need for the same commodities in neighboring countries. To overcome such difficulties — and in the absence of any hope of achieving complete convertibility — the only feasible solution was to multilateralize intrabloc trade.

An experiment with multilateral clearing was first attempted in 1957, with some COMECON members given the prerogative of transferring credit balances from bilateral to trilateral accounts, by mutual consent. The effort was not successful. Under the concluded agreements, the settle-

---

[12] *Osnovnye printsipy mezhdunarodnogo sotsialisticheskogo razdeleniia truda* (Moscow, 1964), p. 31. The relevant passage here reads: "The multilateral coordination of plans and ensuing recommendations concerning the specialization and cooperation of production should insure the balancing of payments relations of each socialist country, specifically through wider use of multilateral settlements. It should be noted that by bringing the balance of payments into equilibrium, it is not intended to counterbalance mutual payments of separate categories of merchandise and products. Rather the fulfillment of obligations incorporated in trade and other agreements, particularly in regard to agreed volumes, quality of goods, and delivery dates, should be considered the primary responsibility of the socialist countries."

[13] M. N. Sveshnikov, *Sistema raschetov mezhdu stranami sotsialisticheskogo sodruzhestva* (Moscow, 1964), p. 17.

ments essentially retained the bilateral pattern; moreover, they were applicable only to some goods and could be effected only on the basis of special arrangements, not automatically. As a result, the volume of multilateral settlements was small, and no further efforts were made to introduce improvements until the present system went into operation.[14]

IBEC FUNCTIONS, ORGANIZATION, AND CAPITALIZATION

The IBEC, located in Moscow, apparently operates not as a policy-making institution but as a technical agency to facilitate clearance of payments arising mostly from trade among the Soviet-bloc nations. Although the statutes do not indicate as much, it seems to function as an organ of COMECON. As stated in the agreement, the bank was established to promote economic cooperation, the development of the national economies of member nations, and cooperation between the members and other countries. To attain these goals it was authorized to effect multilateral clearing in transferable rubles; advance credits for financing foreign trade and other transactions of member countries; solicit from the members and from other countries, and accept for deposit, transferable rubles, convertible and other currencies, and gold, and perform various financial operations with these funds; finance the construction, reconstruction, and operation of joint industrial projects and other enterprises within COMECON; and perform other banking operations consistent with the stated aims and tasks.

The Bank Council is charged with the determination of the IBEC's general policy. It is composed of three representatives from each participating country, appointed by their respective governments. Chairmanship of the periodic council meetings is alternated among the representatives. The council adopts its own rules of procedure, and all its decisions must be unanimous. The council approves credit and other plans; decides on the disposition of profits; issues instructions and rules governing financial, credit, and currency operations; establishes interest rates for credits and for deposits on current and time accounts; approves the organization and personnel arrangements; has the final word on the size of the bank's budget; and confirms the annual report and the balance sheet.

[14] V. P. Komissarov and A. N. Popov, *Mezhdunarodnye valiutnye i kreditnye otnosheniia* (Moscow, 1965), pp. 385–387.

Responsibility for execution of the council's directives, for the direction of the bank's activities, and day-to-day operations (as well as for its representation before official national and international organizations) lies with a managing board. This board and its chairman are appointed by the council from nationals of member countries for a period of up to 5 years, and its size is determined by the council. At present the board consists of one representive from each member country, under the chairmanship of K. I. Nazarkin, a high official of the State Bank of the USSR and vice president of the Foreign Trade Bank of the USSR.

As the bank is now constituted, it consists of three major departments. The *Operational Department* is responsible for the organization and functioning of the bank's clearing and other activities. It performs the actual settlement and credit operations, maintains the bookkeeping apparatus and produces statistical data as a by-product of its routine operations. The *Foreign-Exchange and Economic Research Department* studies monetary conditions in the world's major countries, foreign-exchange fluctuations and developments in the principal markets, conditions governing the sale and purchase of gold, and problems associated with arbitrage, conversion, and other foreign-exchange operations. This department is also charged with establishing correspondent relationships with central and commercial banks throughout the world. The *Credit Planning Department* is charged with the preparation of various economic projections and credit plans. It also deals with the technical problems of credit extension and repayment and with the organizational aspect of multilateral settlements. Apart from these major departments, there are supplementary units concerned with internal administration, personnel, and legal matters, and also a secretariat. The staff consists mostly of economists and financial experts recruited from employees of member countries' official banks.

The authorized capital of the IBEC was set at 300 million rubles ($333 million at the official exchange rate). Shares of individual member countries were determined in accordance with the proportion of each nation's volume of foreign trade within the bloc, as shown in the accompanying figures. Member contributions to the authorized capital were to be made in transferable rubles or in gold or convertible foreign exchange.[15] Each

[15] Transferable rubles, however, can be acquired only by exporting goods to another member country. But this implies that every country would be in surplus vis-à-vis the rest of the bloc, which is arithmetically impossible because net positions of all members combined should add up to zero. Among countless possibili-

member country was obligated to pay in at least 20 percent of its share of capital during the first year of operation,[16] the remaining payments to be made later in accordance with a schedule determined by the Council. Furthermore, a provision in Article II of the agreement reads: "The Council of the Bank shall at the end of the first year of operation examine the question of establishing a part of its statutory capital in gold and freely convertible currencies, and also decide the question of possible convertibility of transferable rubles into gold and freely convertible foreign exchange." The first part of this provision was carried out in the autumn of 1965, when the Council ruled that the second instalment to the Bank's capital, amounting to the equivalent of 30 million rubles, be contributed during 1966 in gold or convertible currencies.

The agreement also provided for the establishment of reserve and special funds, of a size and purpose to be determined later by the Bank Council. The profit for the first two years of operation of 852,000 rubles was transferred to the reserve capital; the disposition of the profit for 1966, which amounted to 1,265,000 rubles, has not been made known, but will probably be identical.

IBEC 1964–1966 OPERATIONS

Undoubtedly, the bank's main objective and its main present activity is the maintenance of a mechanism for clearing and settling current accounts among members on a multilateral basis. The clearing operations are similar to those followed by the now defunct European Payments Union, which greatly facilitated Western European trade in the early 1950s, when postwar currency restrictions were in effect.

ties, the likeliest one would be that the Soviet Union is underwriting the whole scheme by being in deficit vis-à-vis the other countries combined.

	Millions of rubles	Share of total capital (in percent)
USSR	116	38.7
East Germany	55	18.3
Czechoslovakia	45	15.0
Poland	27	9.0
Hungary	21	7.0
Bulgaria	17	5.7
Rumania	16	5.3
Outer Mongolia	3	1.0
TOTAL	300	100.0

[16] Curiously, the bank's balance sheet as of December 31, 1964, shows paid-in statutory capital of 59,711,359 rubles — 288,641 rubles short of the required 60 million.

Clearing is conducted in transferable rubles, which have the same nominal gold content as the Soviet domestic ruble (0.987412 grams). The actual mechanics of clearing operations may be summarized as follows: All reported transactions among member countries are recorded by the bank at the end of each working day, and the accounting surplus or deficit for each country is determined. This is calculated as the sum of a member's bilateral surpluses and deficits— that is, as its net position vis-à-vis all other members combined. Its various bilateral positions with other members are thus eliminated and replaced by a net position with the bank. Member countries whose foreign trade is in surplus have no other alternative but to keep their export earnings with the bank, either in current or in time deposits. The funds deposited on current account earn 0.25 percent; the interest rate on time deposits ranges from 0.5 to 1.5 percent, depending on the duration of deposit.

As a means of speeding up the multilateral settlements, the bank administration has selected, among the settlement procedures used for domestic payments in the COMECON countries, the so-called "subsequent-acceptance" form.[17] The subsequent-acceptance procedure makes it possible to accelerate clearings by two or three days, and in view of the volume of settlements, this time-saving frees substantial amounts of financial resources. Refusals to accept account for a negligible amount of the total value of transactions (in 1964 for only about 1 percent) and, according to the bank's chairman, are due mainly to accounting errors in supporting trade documents.[18]

During the first three years of the bank's operations, economic conditions favored the trade of the COMECON countries with one another. Intra-COMECON trade increased by 8.3 percent in 1964, by 4.5 percent in 1965, and by 6 percent in 1966.[19] A prominent feature of the members' economic development during these years was the accelerated rate of in-

---

[17] Other techniques for transferring funds are the "prior acceptance" and "akkreditiv" methods, but they are of subordinated importance. Under the subsequent acceptance method the bank debits the payer's account immediately, giving him the opportunity to refuse later to accept the debit. Under the prior-acceptance method the bank must wait for a given period, usually three days, to give the payer-country time to decide whether to accept or not. The *akkreditiv* method resembles letter-of-credit financing of international trade.

[18] K. Nazarkin, "Mnogostoronnee sotrudnichestvo i mnogostoronnie raschety," *Voprosy ekonomiki,* No. 10 (1964), 64.

[19] Derived from statistical data published in *Vestnik statistiki,* No. 5 (1966), 89, and K. Nazarkin, "Segodnia i zavtra Mezhdunarodnogo banka sotsialisticheskikh stran," *Vneshniaia torgovlia,* No. 6 (1967), 51.

dustrial expansion. In addition, gains in personal and social consumption, generally on a modest scale, were discernible in most of the countries. As a result, original import targets were raised in many cases; in fact, a direct inducement to surpass the planned volume of imports originating in COMECON territory was provided by the practice of entering into additional compensatory agreements for imports in excess of the originally planned levels. A further important factor influencing the foreign-trade policies of several COMECON countries, and contributing to increases in their imports, was the Soviet Union's large-scale purchases of grain in the West. This development forced the Soviet Union to reorient its trade by reducing imports from other convertible-currency areas while enlarging purchases (particularly of machinery and equipment) from COMECON countries and in return increasing its own fuel and raw-material shipments to them.

Reflecting these intra-COMECON foreign-trade activities, the bank's multilateral clearings in 1964, its first year of operation, amounted to 22.9 billion rubles. About 88 percent of these settlements were offset with available funds, and this, according to a Soviet source, represented almost a 50 percent reduction in the need for trade credits.[20]

To overcome seasonal and other temporary shortages of means of payment, the bank grants revolving short-term credits. The charge for this facility is 1.5 to 2.0 percent per year, depending on the purpose of the credit. The penalty rate for overdue credits is 3 percent. Up to a limit, however, all member countries are exempted from paying any interest charges. These limits are not the same for each country in absolute magnitudes; they are rather determined in terms of a percentage of the total volume of payments projected for a given country for the year as a whole. In 1964 and 1965 (and presumably in later years) the interest-free credit limit for each country was established at 2½ percent of that country's total foreign trade turnover in the preceding year.[21]

In 1964 the bank extended short-term credits totaling more than 1.5 billion rubles. By far the largest proportion of credits — 72.6 percent — was in the form of settlement credits (at 2 percent per year), designed to ensure availability of funds for imports by countries whose payments

[20] K. Nazarkin, "Vzaimovygodnoe sotrudnichestvo ravnykh," *Mezhdunarodnaia zhizn'*, No. 5 (1965), 98–99.

[21] K. Nazarkin, "Raschety v usloviiakh sotsialisticheskogo sodruzhestva stran," *Den'gi i kredit*, No. 10 (1964), 15 and L. Suliaeva, "Valiutnofinansovoe sotrudnichestvo stran-chlenov SEV," *Planovoe khoziaistvo*, No. 5 (1967), 81.

temporarily exceeded receipts. In the first half of 1964 the average duration of such credits was 17 days; in the second half the repayment of loans slowed down, making the average duration for the year as a whole 25 days. Most remaining short-term credits (at 1.5 percent per year) were granted for seasonal needs, for the alleviation of temporary balance-of-payments difficulties, and for the expansion of trade.

More significant, perhaps, are credits for the expansion of intra-COMECON trade. Such credits, unlike the settlement and seasonal credits, do not have to be repaid within the year. Their maximum duration is two years, and they enable a member to ship to or receive from the other COMECON countries goods in excess of those envisioned in the existing foreign-trade agreements, because the acceptance of goods under this arrangement does not obligate the receiving country to export goods in an equivalent amount within the same year. Bank credit permits immediate payment for the increment in imported goods, with the proviso that increased exports in the second year be used to repay the credit. Available evidence suggests that in 1964 East Germany and Outer Mongolia availed themselves most of this facility.

The bank's credit activity is guided by a plan that is essentially a detailed projection of sources and uses of funds. On the one side, projections are made of the capital resources, including both statutory and reserve capital and also special funds; of member and nonmember current and time deposits; and of funds to be contributed for the construction and operation of COMECON joint enterprises. On the uses side are projections of the various types of credit to be extended, including credits for the development of joint projects; operations with nonmembers; and the managing board's contingency fund. The plan is drawn up quarterly and must be approved by the Bank Council.

In 1964 the bank's credit projections reflected accurately the requirements for seasonal credits so that it was seldom necessary to resort to the managing board's contingency fund. There were some deficiencies, however, in the utilization of credits and export proceeds. Thus, in some cases, settlement credits were used for seasonal and other purposes. Frequently, the proceeds from exports were used not to pay for imports but to settle inter-governmental credits or to pay for other indebtedness incurred before the formation of the bank. There were also difficulties in establishing the repayment schedules for seasonal credits, though these may have been due to a lack of experience on the part of the IBEC and member banks, and also to the fact that the agreements between trading partners stipulated deliveries during the quarter, rather than on a definite date. As a result, the credit plan was altered in the second half of 1964 to allow for the extension or shortening of outstanding credits for which the previously established repayment dates did not coincide with the deliveries of the goods. It was expected that in the coming years the experience acquired by the bank in 1964, combined with changes that would be introduced in regard to contractual delivery dates, would improve the planning procedure.

In the second year of operations the volume of multilateral clearings increased by more than 5 percent, to 24.1 billion rubles. Quarterly settlements effected in 1965 followed a pattern established in 1964: starting at approximately 5 billion rubles in the first three months of the year, they leveled off at about 5.5 billion in the two middle quarters, and finally reached their peak, near 7 billion, in the last quarter. In each quarter in 1965 the volume of settlements was higher than in the corresponding period of 1964.

Bank financing in 1965 was required for 13 percent of the payments cleared, a negligible increase of one percentage point over the preceding year. Nevertheless, short-term credits granted by the bank increased nearly 20 percent over 1964 to 1.8 billion rubles, of which more than half were granted free of interest. The need for seasonal credit declined and the proportion of the settlement credit increased to 85.3 percent of the total credits extended. But the rise in the share of interest-free credits had further reduced the average interest rate charged by the bank from 0.81 percent in 1964 to 0.64 percent in 1965. The total amount of credit outstanding rose from 160 million rubles early in 1965 to more than 350 million rubles in May, and then declined to 204 million rubles at the year's end — a general pattern that prevailed also during 1964, except that then the peak (of about the same magnitude) was reached later in the year and the accelerated repayments in the fourth quarter resulted in a more precipitous decline, to 126 million rubles at the end of the year.

During 1965 the total amount of deposits with the bank, resulting from temporary surpluses arising mostly from differences in delivery dates, increased by 38.3 percent over the corresponding figure of 1964. In addition, the time structure of deposits had the tendency to shift toward longer maturity, with the average interest paid on deposits rising from 0.55 percent in 1964 to 0.64 percent in 1965, thus exactly equaling the average rate charged by the bank on its credit operations. At the end of 1965, member bank deposits stood at 215 million rubles, against 109 million rubles the year before.

In 1966, the latest year for which the data are available, the bank's clearings amounted to 23.9 billion rubles, a decline of 0.2 billion from 1965. In comparison with the previous two years, the flow of shipments in intrabloc trade was more evenly spaced, with the result that the seasonal pattern of payments was considerably smoother. The member countries were able to offset most of the clearings with available resources, thus diminishing the need for seasonal credits, and requiring bank-financing for less than 12 percent of total transactions. The amount of credits extended totaled 1.6 billion rubles, with settlement (revolving) credits again predominating at 84 percent of the total. An increase during 1966 in credits for the expansion of intra-COMECON trade — not due for repayment before the end of 1967 — brought the member banks' indebtedness as of December 31, 1966, to 224 million rubles, against 204 million rubles a year earlier.

In the first three years of operation, progress toward other goals envisioned at the time the bank was established was meager. Extensive preparations for financing joint COMECON projects through the creation of a 250–500 million ruble investment fund, to be administered by the IBEC, remained largely on paper. Nothing was heard of the plan to channel COMECON aid to underdeveloped countries through the IBEC. It was originally intended to supply investment funds to the developing Asian and African nations by merging into a single IBEC account the long-term credits hitherto granted them by each member country. To most COMECON members the economic advantages of this aspect of the bank's functions simply do not exist or are insignificant in relation to the political advantages of direct financing. Indeed, in most bloc countries suppressed but considerable opposition exists to the whole principle of foreign aid, although the principle continues to be officially accepted. An even more general ground for opposition to the idea that aid should be handled by the bank is that the most obvious beneficiary, in political terms, is thought to be the Soviet Union.

Under the statutes it is possible for non-COMECON countries to acquire membership in the bank, provided they contribute to the capital in a manner prescribed by the council and agree to "share the aims and principles and assume the commitments stemming from the statutes." This provision was apparently included with the intention of enticing the less-developed and other "nonaligned" countries into bank membership. Presumably, the lure is that credits would be granted them from the bank's resources for stabilizing and perhaps even increasing their trade with the COMECON countries. Since the latter part of 1965, efforts to attract non-COMECON countries into financial relations with the IBEC have intensified. Indications are that the rules concerning affiliation have been considerably relaxed and that the bank, apparently for prestige reasons, is striving to promote settlements in transferable rubles between its members and the outside world. Communist countries not affiliated with the COMECON are offered low-cost credits on the same terms as members, provided they join the mutual clearing system. Less developed, and even Western industrialized countries, can similarly avail themselves of the same benefits, without formally joining the bank, if their entire foreign-trade activities with the COMECON are channeled through the IBEC as intermediary. Should their foreign-trade transactions with the COMECON area be carried out through the IBEC only in part, or only with some countries, they still may be eligible to receive short-term trade credits upon the request of interested members.[22] So far, the invitation to participate in the activities of the Bank has remained unheeded by outside countries, even by Cuba and Yugoslavia.

Furthermore, a member country may now be authorized to swap transferable rubles accumulated on its account at the IBEC against convertible currencies, or against credit balances in clearing accounts maintained with third countries. Outside countries that acquire transferable rubles in such a way will be free to use them for purchase of goods in any of the COMECON countries.[23]

The hopes that the bank would become a link between the currencies of its members and the convertible currencies of the West have not materialized. However, efforts in this direction are continuing, as witnessed by the report that the bank council at its October 1965 meeting in Sofia had authorized the establishment of business relations with the Bank for International Settlements in Basel.[24] Although the bank has established a number of correspondent relationships with commercial banks in the

[22] K. Nazarkin, "Mezhdunarodnyi bank ekonomicheskogo sotrudnichestva," *Den'gi i kredit*, No. 12 (1966), 41–42.

[23] *Ibid.*

[24] "O zasedanii Soveta Mezdunarodnogo banka ekonomicheskogo sotrudni-chestva," *Den'gi i kredit* (December 1965), 92.

West and exchanged with them reciprocal balances in convertible currencies, including dollars and sterling, it appears that the level of such balances is relatively low. The figures are not published. It is merely stated that the number of convertible-currency accounts opened with the IBEC by other banks in 1965 more than doubled, and that the operations in these accounts exceeded the level of 1964 by 120 percent. In 1966 the number of such accounts increased further by 27 percent, with operations rising 200 percent over the preceding year. Between 1964 and 1965 the number of convertible currency accounts opened by the IBEC with other banks doubled, with operations on them increasing by 250 percent. In the third year of the IBEC's existence the number of such accounts rose by 37 percent and operations expanded by 130 percent. All in all, the bank's operations in convertible currencies reached an amount equivalent to some 2 billion rubles in 1965 and 3.8 billion rubles in 1966. But the word "operations" in this context is ambiguous, and without knowing its exact meaning the indicated total is merely an accounting figure and signifies little about the actual amount of business. Nevertheless, the bank's profit of almost 1.3 billion rubles in 1966 had been achieved, according to a newspaper report, in large measure due to the expansion in convertible foreign-exchange operations.[25]

PROBLEMS OF MULTILATERIZATION

The achievements of the IBEC are inevitably influenced by the environment in which it operates. Several aspects of this environment are particularly relevant to an appraisal of the problems that COMECON is confronting in its efforts to achieve multilateralism of trade settlements.

As already stated, one of the most serious difficulties arises from the irrational domestic price structures in the countries. The extensive application of indirect taxes and subsidies, designed to implement specific internal economic policies, prevents prices from reflecting accurately relative scarcities. Furthermore, failure to include fully interest, rent, and depreciation in calculating costs of production exerts an undesirable effect on the supply function, which in turn causes economic decisions to veer from rational norms and creates numerous planning difficulties. So long as this muddled state of affairs continues, the disequilibrium of

[25] "MBES: itogi 1966 goda," *Ekonomicheskaia gazeta*, No. 25 (June 1967), 42–43.

exchange rates — otherwise so serious a factor — is of little practical importance. To be sure, it distorts the relationship between domestic and foreign price levels, but those levels themselves have only arbitrary significance in intrabloc trade.

A new system of COMECON prices that went into effect in 1966 has somewhat improved the terms of trade for the other Eastern European countries vis-à-vis the USSR, through reducing the prices of raw materials and increasing those for finished goods. Consequently, the existing price patterns tend to encourage exports of finished goods rather than foodstuffs, fuels, and primary commodities. This policy has led to an expansion of manufacturing capacity geared to the export market and a neglect of investments in agriculture and basic industries. In some countries the pursuit of such policies may be justified on economic grounds, and is even desirable, but in others it is not.

There are signs that the more recent revisions in price structures, introduced in some of the countries in connection with the current economic reforms, are bringing domestic prices more closely into line with prices prevailing in the world markets. But the measures so far adopted are inadequate. A more thorough approach to the problem is needed. In the absence of a rational price system the possibilities for meaningful international comparisons of comparative advantages are limited, and decisions already taken in regard to the specialization and division of labor within COMECON can be only tentative. A complete overhaul of pricing practices and consequent exchange-rate adjustments are almost mandatory if the existing multilateral payments system is to function smoothly and effectively. The problem of price formation in intra-COMECON trade occupies the minds of the best economists in the bloc.[26] Work toward devising a transition to "socialist world prices," which would more closely reflect the specific regional costs of production and transportation, is in process in various economic research institutes of COMECON. The task, originally scheduled to be completed in 1965, is still unfinished. To judge from articles in Soviet economic journals, there are a number of theoretical and methodological problems for which no acceptable solution is in sight.[27]

[26] See for instance "Tseny na mirovom sotsialisticheskom rynke," *Vneshniaia torgovlia*, No. 11 (1966), 19–22.

[27] Some of the obstacles, along with the proposals for overcoming them, are discussed in A. Alekseev, "Nekotorye voprosy dal'neishego sovershenstvovaniia tsen v torgovle mezhdu stranami SEV," *Vneshniaia torgovlia*, No. 9 (1967), 22–23,

A second, and related, consideration is the nature of over-all central planning. The external trade of a Communist country does not operate independently of its central economic plan. On the contrary, its over-all import and export program — formulated in advance each year by the planning authorities, who try to balance imports with expected exports — is geared into the whole complex of planned production. But planning the volume and nature of foreign trade in advance is extraordinarily difficult. The possibility of error increases when it is attempted to project not only the country's foreign trade in general, but its precise interchange of goods with particular countries. When the exchanges to be planned involve a wide range of goods — some scarce, others less so, with the prices of some goods subsidized in one country and pushed high by government policies in another — the situation becomes a planners' nightmare.

Another important constraint relevant to the IBEC goals is the tendency for bloc countries to strive for some autarky. The economic advantages arising from international division of labor are sacrificed in favor of the security advantages of maximal domestic production of all goods considered essential. The ineffective cooperation and thus inadequate integration within the COMECON framework is predominantly the result of the centralized system of economic management and national planning. This is primarily because in a highly centralized economy it is administratively more convenient to rely on internal sources of supply and to plan accordingly. Any meaningful calculation of comparative advantage is prevented not only by the irrational price structures and arbitrarily set foreign-exchange rates, but also by the tendency for each country in the bloc to conceive its industrialization in the image of Soviet economic development; hence producer-goods industries receive priorities and are planned to develop at a faster rate than the consumer-goods industries, which, indeed, is one of the main reasons for the slow increase in the domestic standard of living.

A third problem that affects the bank's operations is the member countries' continued practice to follow bilateral instead of multilateral patterns in negotiating trade agreements. Much of the initial enthusiasm for the IBEC came from a belief that it would help get intra-COMECON trade out of the shackles of bilateralism. But the available evidence suggests that practically the same forces that pushed the Communist coun-

and in O. Tarnovskii, "Regional'naia stoimost' i rynok SEV," *Voprosy ekonomiki,* No. 10 (1967), 81–92.

tries into the bilateral system after World War II are operating to keep them there. Even though multilateral clearing through the IBEC makes possible a greater volume of trade than bilateral clearing, the cumbersome method of concluding trade agreements prevents the potential increase from being realized.

The actual procedure has been to engage in two steps of negotiations: first, purely bilateral trade talks between two members; and second, a general negotiation in which these two members try to offset surpluses and deficits with each other by taking account of credits and debits with other member countries.[28] Thus the eight members must conclude twenty-eight different bilateral trade agreements among themselves, and these must be painstakingly coordinated, since the old procedure of listing the specific goods to be sold and bought in detail still persists. Given this lack of flexibility in negotiating trade agreements, any improvements in the method of making financial settlements are clearly only of marginal effectiveness. This point of view is shared by the Czechoslovak Deputy Minister of Finance Miroslav Dluhos, who stated at the IBEC Council meeting in October 1966 that the method of multilateral settlements had not had any actual significance on the development of the intra-COMECON trade because this trade is still based on bilateral and not on multilateral agreements.[29]

Still another problem that is directly connected with the bank's operations is the insufficient differentiation of interest rates charged by the IBEC. The main defect here is that credits are extended without interest or at a relatively low rate of interest and without any regard to the length of time the credits are used. This practice does not provide sufficient incentive to repay outstanding credits on time and, furthermore, inevitably results in that deliveries of goods (in lieu of repayments) are not always made on schedule. It is known that Poles are particularly dissatisfied with the existing arrangements and have made numerous proposals to alter the system in favor of charging higher rates for longer term credits. The acceptance of such a scheme would undoubtedly induce member countries to adhere more closely to their export plans by exerting pressure on them to repay credits on time, thus reducing to a minimum the volume of unplanned and overdue loans.

[28] P. Nosko, "Novaia sistema raschetov," *Vneshniaia torgovlia*, No. 7 (1964), 30.
[29] "O dzialalnosci Miedzynarodowego Banku Współpracy Gospodarczej," *Trybuna Ludu*, October 9, 1966, p. 6.

A Polish economist went as far as to suggest the feasibility of complete abrogation of interest-free settlement credit and its replacement with credit whose cost will rise sharply with the duration for which it is outstanding.[30] A proposal to this effect was put forward at the October 1966 IBEC council meeting by Stanislaw Majewski, the president of the Polish National Bank and Poland's representative on the council. Later it was reported in the press that this problem has not been resolved and will be put on the agenda of the future council meetings.[31] It seems that the Russians are not too favorably disposed toward this proposition. They constantly emphasize that to promote a greater volume of foreign trade the IBEC credit, in contrast to capitalist banks who charge 5 or more percent for short-term credit, should be cheap or even free.[32]

Finally, intrabloc trade, and thus the bank's operations, are hampered by the difficulties in making the transferable ruble convertible and acquiring deposits in gold or convertible currencies. Hungary proposed as far back as 1958 that the ruble used in bloc trade should be made convertible. In October 1963, the concept — strongly supported by Henryk Kotlicki, the Polish delegate to the bank and director general of Poland's Ministry of Finance — was incorporated in the agreement establishing the bank. It was reiterated by Piotr Jaroszewicz, the Polish member of the COMECON executive, and by the Hungarian member Antal Apro in March 1964.

Criticism of the inconvertibility of transferable rubles erupted forcefully in the Polish press in the spring of 1965, with Kotlicki again the chief critic. Poland's attack appeared to be deliberately timed, as it came just before the members were scheduled to contribute another 60 million rubles to the bank's capital, in the second of the five annual installments that are required to raise the total capital to the authorized 300 million rubles. Kotlicki stated that the already paid-in capital of 60 million transferable rubles was sufficient for the bank's clearing and credit operations at the current level of trade, and declared that the next installment should be made in gold or convertible currencies to be used for loans to member countries and for making the transferable rubles partly convertible. Furthermore, Poland proposed that countries chroni-

[30] Adam Zwass, "System kredytowy Międzynarodowego Banku Współpracy Gospodarczej," *Finanse*, No. 9 (1966), 47.
[31] *Trybuna Ludu*, October 9, 1966, p. 6.
[32] See for example K. Nazarkin, "Mnogostoronnee sotrudnichestvo i mnogostoronnie raschety," *Voprosy ekonomiki*, No. 10 (1964), 66.

cally in surplus with other members should be permitted to convert part of their surplus into gold, and conversely that members in deficit should pay equivalent parts of their debt in gold or convertible currencies; this proposal called for the initial conversion of only 10 percent of surpluses, but the proposition was to be raised gradually over five or ten years to 100 percent, that is, complete convertibility.

In the opinion of Kotlicki, implementation of the Polish proposals would give the IBEC an instrument for influencing all trade among member countries, and the prospect of even partial convertibility would be a major incentive to increase COMECON trade. It would also, he held, have considerable importance in improving the quality of traded goods, because the importer who knows he may have to pay in gold for even a part of his purchases will insist on highest quality. Kotlicki dismissed the argument that the possibility of having to pay in gold could result in unwillingness to make major purchases. He conceded that individual importing countries might refuse to buy for some time, but he held that importers would not definitely refuse to buy goods they need; furthermore, "they have the right to, and they should — just as Poland does — refuse to import unessential goods and goods that are of poor quality. Good and needed products will always find willing buyers."[33]

Poland's position is understandable. Its trade with the rest of the bloc, though showing a small deficit in early 1964, climbed by the end of that year to a surplus of 50 million rubles. As long as surpluses held at the IBEC represent nothing more than entries on its ledger, they can be used only to buy goods from other COMECON countries. However, goods which the other bloc countries are in a position to deliver Poland regarded as unneeded or of inferior quality. Moreover the Polish government will undoubtedly require a sharp increase in convertible foreign-exchange earnings, given that, according to newspaper report,[34] it will have to begin in 1967 the conversion into dollars of the equivalent of $500 million in zlotys — held by the United States in counterpart funds — and arising from payments for agricultural commodities.

The Polish proposals received support from the other countries with only the Soviet Union taking a cautious, if not a negative, attitude. They were extensively discussed at the sixth meeting of the COMECON's Stand-

[33] "Kotlicki's Interview on the International Bank for Economic Cooperation," *Trybuna Ludu,* April 27, 1965.
[34] "U.S. to Push Drive to Cut Soft Money," *Journal of Commerce,* July 21, 1965.

ing Commission on Foreign-Exchange and Finance, held in Kiev in May 1965. The committee decided "to examine this matter in detail, and to prepare and submit concrete conclusions for the creation and use of part of the capital in gold and freely convertible currencies."[35] It is understood that the Poles raised the problem again a month later in Leningrad at the COMECON's Eighteenth Executive Committee meeting, but the communique issued after the meeting made no mention of action taken.

Finally, in October 1965 the bank council decided that the members' next contribution to the bank's capital — the equivalent of 30 million transferable rubles — was to be paid in gold and convertible currencies, in proportion to the members' shares in total statutory capital. This decision made no reference, however, to the other Polish proposal — provision for partial settlement of surpluses in gold or hard currencies. The bank's report for 1965 merely states that "the establishment of a part of the bank's nominal capital in gold and convertible currencies will enable the IBEC to widen considerably credit and other foreign-exchange operations in these currencies." The deputy premier of Poland regarded this decision as "a modest but constructive step in the desired direction." He cautioned, however, "that this is not a step that can produce a tangible improvement in the system of multilateral settlements. It does not as yet indicate that we have embarked upon the road leading to convertibility of the transferable ruble."[36]

The desire to make the transferable ruble at least partly convertible into gold or Western currencies is still much alive in the minds of most IBEC members. At the October 1966 bank council meeting, several representatives of Eastern European countries stressed the importance of attaining convertibility, and some even intimated that this is the only way whereby the use of the ruble could be extended to the sphere of non-COMECON countries.[37] The Russians are apparently in agreement with this view. As stated in a recently published theoretical monograph on the role of money in the Communist society, "the convertibility of the transferable ruble is the requisite condition for its appearance on the international scene and the gradual displacement of the dollar as world currency."[38] However, convertibility cannot be simply proclaimed by

[35] *Finansy SSSR*, No. 8 (1965), 93.
[36] Piotr Jaroszewicz in *Trybuna Ludu*, December 5, 1965.
[37] *Trybuna Ludu*, October 9, 1966, p. 6.
[38] I. I. Konnik, *Den'gi v period stroitel'stva kommunisticheskogo obshchestva* (Moscow, 1966), p. 145.

the decree of the Communist party. Its introduction would require extensive reforms and the setting up of necessary economic conditions.[39]

The idea of making the ruble convertible must be appealing to the Soviet Union for prestige reasons, but acceptance of it would carry various risks. Above all, and Kotlicki's statements notwithstanding, convertibility could conceivably lead to a contraction of intrabloc trade. If deficits incurred in intra-COMECON multilateral trade became gold or hard-currency liabilities, each country would have to be just as careful in its dealings with bank members as it is in its trade relations with the convertible-currency areas. The logical corollary of this is that if surpluses were to become convertible (as well as transferable), their holders might tend not to use them for imports from the other members but to demand gold or hard currency instead, for the purchase of needed goods from the West. Thus the distinction between Eastern (soft) and Western (hard) currencies could become less meaningful, with the bloc countries becoming less protected from Western competition. Since members would have strong incentives to dump into the COMECON market products that were unsalable in the West there could be a deterioration in the quality of goods traded in intrabloc commerce.

The unfavorable implication for the Soviet Union is not only that the COMECON countries could obtain a further degree of freedom in their trade relations with the West, but also that they could diminish their purchases from the USSR. After all, the COMECON countries account for approximately 60 percent of the Soviet Union's total foreign trade turnover, and once Western competition appeared in an area over which the USSR had long exercised economic domination, it would certainly lead to disastrous consequences from the Soviet point of view. Furthermore, the Soviet Union, as the only gold-producing nation in the bloc, would be expected to carry the brunt of financing the deficits in intra-COMECON trade — a responsibility that would tend to represent an increasing drain on its gold reserves.

One cannot deny that the existing multilateral clearing system operated by the IBEC has produced some tangible advantages for the participating countries — if for no other reason than that no member has to worry about its bilateral position with any other member, but only about its over-all position with the bank; perhaps the system has had some beneficial

[39] These, by the way, are examined in detail in Marcin R. Wyczalkowski's "Communist Economics and Currency Convertibility," *IMF Staff Papers*, XIII:2 (July 1966), 155–197.

indirect effects as well. On the other hand, and mostly through no fault of its own, the bank has not been able to achieve some of its planned ob‑ jectives. Most limitations were recognized from the beginning, but loudly heralded announcements surrounding the creation of the IBEC and its proposed activities magnified the expectations of many individuals, espe‑ cially in the West.

It should not be expected that any clearing device would correct the distortions characteristic of centrally planned economies and their trade relations. To be sure, the clearing system should not impede correction, preferably should help it, and certainly should not enlarge the distortion. In this regard no complaints can be lodged against the IBEC, which seems to conduct its routine clearing and credit transactions efficiently. The problems lie elsewhere. They are essentially in the way the plans are drawn, the costs calculated, the prices formed, and the trade agreements negotiated. And no major improvement in the volume and efficiency of intrabloc trade can be realized before improvements are brought about in these fundamental aspects of economic policy in the COMECON countries.

GEORGE GARVY

•

•

•

•

•

East European Credit and Finance in Transition

The contributions included in this volume as well as the related comments and oral discussion at the Workshop covered a much broader range
of topics than "money and finance in Communist Countries." Indeed,
the financial reforms now being introduced from the Oder to the Sea of
Japan are embedded in a complex process of change that encompasses
many aspects of life in the countries of Eastern Europe; an attempt to
assess their significance thus becomes a true exercise in political economy.
We are confronted with considerably more than a package of stopgap
measures designed to meet or avert one of the recurrent difficulties. Whatever the official label attached to the new economic policies in the individual countries of Eastern Europe, it is clear that we are looking at a
major change in their economic policies and institutions. Their main
traits and underlying philosophy are sufficiently similar — though not
necessarily made explicit in all cases — and add up to such a significant
change that we shall refer to them as the Reform, with a capital "R," a
term proudly used in some of the smaller countries and ultimately accepted in the Soviet Union.

* Dr. Garvy's contribution stems from his extensive summing-up remarks at the
conclusion of the Workshop. This explains the many references to observations
by participants other than the authors represented in the present volume. It was
felt that the references not only express the flavor of the exchange of opinions at
the Workshop but also bring out the complexities of the problem treated. Hence,
it was decided to retain them in this volume. However, the individuals whose
observations are mentioned have had no opportunity to review them and therefore
should not be held responsible for them. — Ed.

153

NATURE OF THE REFORM

The financial aspects of the Reform cannot be understood and evaluated separately; as Professor Pesek rightly points out, it is impossible to separate the "monetary" and "financial" aspects of the Reform from the others. Therefore, Workshop papers and comments naturally broadened to questions of resource allocation, role of the price system, functioning of markets, degree of independence of enterprises, redirection of investment flows, and the relation of credit to budgetary policy.

Centralized command economies were shaped by conditions of over-all scarcity; they could not cope with incipient abundance. But what precise constellation of economic and social factors caused the various countries of Eastern Europe to embark upon a "reform of economic steering"? No simple answer that would be valid for all countries of that area will ever be possible. Speculation about the extent to which past economic successes and failures, increasing breakdown of intellectual isolation, and the growing inability of yesterday's ideologies to solve (or even to identify) today's problems have contributed to the Reform would lead to one of the most fascinating explorations of the dynamics of change in human affairs.[1] This certainly is not the place to probe into the Reform's origins and longer-run potential.

The objective, scope, and timing of the Reform have been for several years a central issue of Communist party debates in the individual countries of Eastern Europe. There are considerable differences in the institutional and policy changes which constitute "the" Reform in the various countries.

Arguments to show the need for a reform involved a varying degree of criticism of past policies, institutional arrangements and achievements. Yet, in no country has the struggle for reform led to explosive intra-party conflicts. It does not need to; it easily could, as the road still to be traveled is long and arduous.[2]

---

[1] At least one Soviet economist has been willing to raise the question whether, granted the achievement of the five-year plans, the over-all performance of the Soviet economy might not have been even better if the market mechanism had been used. See G. S. Lisichkin, *Plan i rynok* (Moscow, 1966), p. 50.

[2] The first significant ideological cleavage and differentiation in the Communist party of the USSR occurred in 1921, at the time the New Economic Policy (NEP) was under discussion. It seems that it is recognized now in the Soviet Union that the insurrection of the sailors of Kronstadt against the Lenin government — a startling blow coming from one of the mainstays of the Bolshevik revolution — was not the work of "foreign agents" or domestic "counterrevolutionaries," but the

Even a provisional appraisal of the scope and significance of the Reform, and in particular of its financial aspects, is difficult because of the frankly experimental nature of some changes and the prevalence of transitional arrangements. In all countries some of the essential steps are still to be put into effect at some later time. In many cases it is not easy to determine what are hard facts and what merely ambitious plans; temptation to interpolate and to extrapolate must be resisted. Any attempt to appraise the Reform involves promise, not reality; and rhetoric must be distinguished from substance.

The fact that in individual countries, and most importantly in the Soviet Union, experimentation involves alternatives is of considerable significance by itself: the road to progress is no longer sought in revelations by leaders or correct interpretation of texts. Some of the new measures appear to be reactions to past irrationality rather than rational solutions of current problems. Others have all the hallmarks of a political compromise and appear to be watered-down versions of more ambitious reforms. Clearly, the full significance of the Reform lies not in its present scope, but in its promise for the future.

Because of scarcity of overt theorizing surrounding the introduction of the Reform, its meaning must be frequently extracted from a maze of technical regulations and instructions. Yet the important fact is that, as Professor Edward Ames of Purdue University remarked at one of the Workshop sessions, policy discussions (in the main in Hungary, Czechoslovakia, and East Germany) are conducted in terms more familiar to Western economists. Some of the remaining terminological and conceptual differences are essentially ideological — both sides pay heavily for the burden of dogmas.

But are the problems really new, or only the discussion, as Ames implies? And indeed, even some of the discussion is not so new, as the recent exhumations and rehabilitation of the early discussion in the Soviet Union (say, in the works of Professors Evsey D. Domar, Alexander Erlich, Nicolas Spulber, and others) shows. However, even if they are not new — and some of the discussion is merely old wine in new casks — these problems are increasingly being tackled with solutions which have heretofore not been open to socialist economies. Perhaps the ultimate reason lies in the similarity of problems mankind has to resolve, irrespec-

result of the failure of the first economic policy of the Soviet government, known as War Communism.

tive of the location of its individual tribes on the crust of this earth and of tribal mores and taboos.

There is certainly a tendency this side of the Atlantic to be more relaxed in examining the unfolding picture in Eastern Europe. However, we still tend to look at policy choices in Eastern Europe as a valid counterpart of those open in the West (such as deliberate trade-off between slower growth and price stability) without fully acknowledging basic differences in starting points and constraints. Our propensity to rationalize different economic, social, and political structures in our own terms remains overwhelming. But one does not have to accept the "convergence hypothesis" to believe that the process of which the Reform is both evidence and an essential element has its own logic. One is tempted to hope that the break with the belief that a centrally directed economy is the only and final answer has started a process in which rationality is bound to win over dogma.

In view of all this, the variety and range of interpretations reflected in the papers and comments of this volume is not surprising. Not merely differences in appraisal and temperament are involved: there are considerable differences in actual developments in individual countries, in spite of broad similarities. They are rooted in resources structure, economic potential, divergence of recent experience, and willingness to write Reform with a capital "R". It is hardly surprising that the last country to introduce reforms (following fairly closely the cautious approach of the Soviet Union) was the one which in recent years had the most favorable record of uninterrupted and impressive gains in real income under conditions of considerable monetary stability — Rumania. On the other hand, Professor Holešovský's conclusion that the appearance of a large number of malfunctions of different types which caused a protracted economic recession was a crucial causal factor in Czechoslovakia, cannot be extended to the other countries. It is now clearly more fruitful to analyze policies of individual countries of Eastern Europe than to focus on the common characteristics of "Soviet-type" or "centrally planned command economies" and to make daring generalizations about the emerging socialist market economy. Indeed, too frequently, the tendency of economists and political scientists to categorize interferes with their ability to understand.

Yugoslavia presented us with the first challenge to appraise an emerged socialist economy in definite relationship with its geography, heritage, possibilities, and heresies. For a long time, the other Eastern European countries practiced something like a conspiracy of silence with regard to Yugoslavia's efforts to find its own way; proponents of the Reform in other countries generally avoided identification of their proposals with Yugoslavia's pioneering efforts. But even in the Soviet Union, which has sinned more in this respect than the smaller countries of Eastern Europe, there is now considerable reporting on Yugoslavia's economic policies and even some guarded analysis. It is not within the scope of my assignment to trace the Reform to Yugoslavia's path-breaking; it would be a lack of perspective not to pay homage to the country which started it all.

Things are in flux — and this is the cardinal fact. We know where the movement comes from, not where it leads. Broadly, we can describe this as a move toward a socialist market economy, but we have no clear idea how (through which institutional arrangements and constraints) the rationality of the market mechanism can be reconciled with social (political) priorities of the various countries. One important (but not the only) significant aspect of the new policies is the intention to use consumer preferences and the market mechanism for the allocation of resources, for deriving the pattern of production of final products (in the sector where strategic decisions from the center do not apply), and for achieving the required transfer of resources. It is also intended to achieve a better structure of foreign trade based on comparative costs (hopefully by gradually diminishing the historically and politically determined preference for intrabloc trade).

If the Reform is to succeed, considerable ideological and organizational underbrush will have to be cleared away. More importantly, it must overcome numerous political, environmental, and economic obstacles, whose respective significance must be assessed for each individual country, but whose combined weight is heavy in each case. Among them the rigid price system, which does not recognize certain factor costs, does not reflect relative scarcities, and which embodies certain social (or call them economically-strategic) preferences, occupies a central place. The view that the success of the Reform, and the real significance of new policies in the area of banking, money, and credit hinge on the future role of the price system and of market adjustments, is general on both sides of the Shredded Curtain. It therefore seems proper to address ourselves to this problem before turning to finance.

PRICES

In the centrally planned economy, the government and not the producing unit is the price maker and price adjuster. As in the capitalist economy, the consumer is essentially a price taker and quantity adjuster. His reactions to the price system are only imperfectly transmitted to production planners, if at all. Long-term price stability of prices facilitates planning, and administrative changes in prices are undertaken reluctantly. Adjustments are made by planners typically to cope with shortages of specific goods (and in some cases — with popular dissatisfaction) rather than as a systematic reaction to economic impulses received through the market. Under conditions of pervasive shortages there was for producers no penalty for nonadjusting.

There is no need to document the fact that the price structure of each socialist country is badly distorted. This has been long recognized by planners and economists of Eastern Europe. As Professor Ragnar Frisch reminds us with regard to pricing: "There has been no single problem in economics about which one has talked about so much in theory (in the Soviet Union) and done so little in practice to solve efficiently."[3] More realistic and pragmatic discussions, however, have emerged elsewhere, in particular from Czechoslovakia and Hungary, where it is also widely recognized that the price structures of Eastern Europe are inimical to an optimum international allocation of resources. Even when corrected in each country through a complex system of dual pricing and multiple exchange rates, it remains an inadequate guide for a rational allocation of resources between domestic use and export and for determining the pattern of imports. This conclusion is illustrated by numerous concrete examples cited in internal discussions of the role of the price system now under way in the countries of Eastern Europe.

[3] "Rational Price Fixing in a Socialistic Society," *Economics of Planning*, VI:2 (1966), 97. For a review of the Soviet discussion on the "law of value," the Marxist password for price theory, see A. Zauberman, "The Soviet Debate on the Law of Value and Price Formation" *in* G. Grossman, ed., *Value and Plan* (Berkeley and Los Angeles, University of California Press, 1960), pp. 17–36. See also Morris Bornstein, "Soviet Price Theory and Policy," in *New Directions in the Soviet Economy*, Joint Economic Committee, U.S. Congress, 1966, pp. 63–98. Eugène Zaleski, *Planning Reforms in the Soviet Union, 1962–1966* (Chapel Hill, N.C., 1967), chaps. 4–8, and Jere L. Felker, *Soviet Economic Controversies* (Cambridge, 1967). For a useful bibliography on economic debates in Eastern Europe up to the beginning of 1963 see Jan S. Prybyla, "The Quest for Economic Rationality in the Soviet Bloc," *Social Research* (August 1963), p. 343. Much of the recent discussion on this topic in the Soviet Union is mentioned in V. G. Lopatkin, *Tovarnye otnosheniia i zakon stoimosti pri sotsializme* (Moscow, 1966).

Hungary and Czechoslovakia at least, envisage a socialist market economy as the goal of the Reform.[4] Yet the real function of a free market, its ingredients and logic, and, even more, the atmosphere are still a mystery to most economic officials of Eastern Europe who are painfully emerging from the protective cocoon of communist "dirigisme."[5]

The badly distorted price system is, perhaps, the worst legacy of centrally directed systems to burden the economic system of the brave new world sketched out at the Communist party congresses of recent years. But it can be claimed that a socialist market economy will not work unless it embodies all the characteristics of a perfect competitive market? Surely not. In discussing the role of prices envisaged by the Reform, there is a definite danger of pushing purism to the point of hypocrisy.[6]

The "free market system" has its own nonmarket constraints, priorities, and significant oligopolistic and monopolistic elements. The perfect competitive market never existed, and the price system nowhere functioned to satisfy conditions laid down in textbooks.[7] Yet, in spite of market imperfections, we in the West have a dynamic growth economy and enjoy unprecedented levels of material well-being. In the United States, there is no completely free market allocation of investment funds, and yet we have built a most efficient and dynamic industrial system. Our

[4] In the Soviet Union, in contrast, considerable effort is being made to present the Reform merely as a means of improving the efficiency of central planning. Several Soviet economists have been pointing out that Lenin never considered the use of the market, the introduction of *khozraschet*, and the use of profit criteria as a temporary concession at the time of the NEP retreat, but rather as a proper basis for building a socialist economy (see for instance, G. S. Lisichkin, chap. ii). "What is more, Lenin regarded NEP as an economic policy which all countries would have to adopt when they chose socialism," writes V. Dmitrenko in "The New Economic Policy," *Soviet Life* (March 1967).

[5] In specific cases, their views of the actual functioning of markets in the capitalist world range from naïve faith in the omnipotence of competition (as in the case of some pioneers of a socialist market economy in Poland immediately after 1956) to the repetition of boilerplate notions about monopolistic exploitation.

[6] It would be irrelevant if the purist could be simply ignored as a hypocrite, an ignoramus, or a "specialist" familiar with the characteristics of a specific economic system but somehow unaware of the fact that some of its shortcomings might also exist elsewhere and thus possibly be due to more general causes and not endemic to the system studied. The matter becomes serious only when the criteria and standards applied in judging the nature and prospects of the reform interfere with a realistic appraisal of potentialities and problems of change in Eastern Europe.

[7] It might be worth recalling that the lead sentences in two successive paragraphs in one of the most prestigious textbooks by an outstanding champion of free markets read as follows: "In our society, the *basic* method of organizing production is through the price system. . . . Our society does not rely *exclusively* on private efforts directed by prices to organize production. (Italics supplied.) George Stigler, *The Theory of Prices*, 3rd ed. (New York, 1966), p. 16.

economy is not free of interference with free access to skilled jobs, discriminatory employment practices, protective tariff policies, and counterproductive farm subsidies. There are numerous other types of interference with optimum allocation of resources here and in other Western economies. Should we emulate some economists of Eastern Europe by claiming that our system, as it actually operates, is identical with its pure theoretical model and actually results in optimum allocation of resources?

The real question, then, is: Can the functioning of the economic systems of the countries of Eastern Europe be substantially improved and a more rational allocation of resources be achieved by developing the dynamic characteristics typically linked to price and profit incentives? Will the continuing preemption by the central government of a range of decisions as to feasible rate and desirable patterns of growth preclude an essentially market-directed allocation of a large portion of investment funds? The Reform will not create a self-regulating market system, but it will permit judging more objectively the results of economic activity by substituting more rational and uniform criteria. It will, as Professor Pesek points out, end the nonmarket allocation of factors of production and of consumer goods. A mixed system may emerge in which central decision on the level and pattern of socialized consumption, direction, and scope of technological effort, and key investment continue to be centralized, while the output of consumer goods and services and the flow of raw materials and intermediate products are determined by market forces. It is likely to be more efficient and more conducive to a rational integration of the economies of Eastern Europe into the network of world trade than the present system.

The current approach to the restructuring of prices, which clearly is one of the key aspects of the Reform, raises a number of questions in the minds of the contributors to this volume. But would it not be enormous progress if prices became more meaningful than now? If a more meaningful system emerged as a result of progressive approximation? Removal of subsidies (even if, as Dr. Gert Leptin suggested at the Workshop, a piecemeal reform should require temporary new subsidies in certain cases), introduction of capital as an explicit factor cost, coupled with a realistic revaluation of fixed assets, and a revamping of the wage structure alone would permit considerable progress. To amplify Pesek's remark, it would be a sign of great progress when our East European colleagues will stop worrying about nonsensical prices and start worrying — together with us — about distorted relative prices, but, also, when Western economists will recognize the potency of halfway solutions. One does not need to go so far as to argue, with Pesek, that marginal pricing is bound to ultimately emerge from the changes now being undertaken.

The countries of Eastern Europe are unlikely to achieve in the near future freely operating markets for all resources, but they are definitely becoming market-oriented. The old system was static and the infrequent changes were made by administrative decision. The new system contains elements of adjustment, but not a complete mechanism that would automatically lead the economy toward an equilibrium position. Greater reliance on market mechanisms (for products, and personal services, since no financial markets exist or are envisaged) does not mean establishment of *perfect* markets (as Professor Herbert S. Levine pointed out at the Workshop). But does use of quasi- (or pseudo-) market techniques lead only to "arbitrary results," as Professor Donald R. Hodgman claimed in the discussion? And, if they yielded results less arbitrary than those achieved by central planners, without precluding still better results as prices move closer to factor costs and production patterns become increasingly influenced by consumer preferences and external (world market) prices? A quasi market will not allocate resources optimally, but it will emit signals. The old system did not even flash clear signals; it kept planners ignorant, and thus did not provide the elements for approaching optimum production by successive approximations.

What matters is not the ability of Eastern European countries to achieve markets with perfect price flexibility, but the recognition of the market process as a most efficient allocator of resources (as an alternative to central direction) in response to preferences expressed by final users (rather than planners). Price flexibility does not require daily fluctuations of prices. Even centrally determined, but frequently changed prices may adequately approximate market equilibrium prices. Profit maximization may become an adequate guide for establishing and changing production patterns (and production functions) even when prices do not embody all factor costs and do not adequately reflect scarcity; indeed, as Pesek points out, fairly arbitrary labor markups are not necessarily more arbitrary than our social security taxes and some other elements of price structures in capitalist countries. It remains to be seen whether the new price-fixing and output-determining policies will become flexible enough to permit individual enterprises to maximize profits by price-output policies.

The socialist firm cannot be expected to behave as though maximizing profits were its sole goal, for neither do firms in the West.[8] In both areas the objective of profit maximization in the long run may dictate decisions inconsistent with maximization in the short run. Growth strategy involves investment decisions for which *future* (foreign as well as domestic) prices and price relations are relevant. Current market demand is not a perfect guide for future demand patterns which are crucial for investment planning, as stressed by Professor Raymond P. Powell in the discussion.

Ragnar Frisch has recently pointed out[9] that in a socialist country a price system based on the concept of optimal prices is only a necessary, but far from a sufficient means of implementation for steering the economy in a direction which conforms with the intentions of the responsible political authority, and that the postulate of marginal pricing and clearing the market may be inadequate for the purpose. His further point that "the problems of rational price fixing can only be handled in a really rational and fruitful way by considering it as a part of the general problem of decision making for the economy as a whole" is well taken.[10] The Reform raises the broad problem of the decision-making authority and process in a society groping for workable (polycentric?) alternatives to central command. If the price of achieving at least Pesek's "Progress A" model is perfunctory for a — hopefully aging — sacred cow,[11] as he implies, I would consider it negligible.

RENAISSANCE OF MONEY?

Clearly, the financial aspects of the Reform are an important part, and perhaps even its core, as Holešovský claims, even though, in East Germany at least, significant changes in banking and credit antedated its official advent. He certainly is right in claiming that the emergence of uni-

[8] See R. W. Davies, "Planning in the Mature Economy of the USSR," *Economics of Planning*, VI:2 (1966), 151.

[9] *Ibid.*, p. 100.

[10] *Ibid.*, p. 108.

[11] The ideological obstacle to accepting the market as an allocator of resources and flexible prices should not be underestimated, even against the background of the gradual fading of Lenin's writings as a source of wisdom. Did not Lenin write shortly before his death: "Only children might not understand the importance of price regulation and why it is necessary for the Soviet economy." (*Ekonomicheskaia zhizn'*, May 24, 1924).

fied money will contribute greatly to the "objectivization" (p. 83) of economic relationships. It certainly will greatly facilitate analysis of the performance of the economies of Eastern Europe.

The Workshop papers and discussion expressed an increasing interest in the rationale of financial aspects of the economies of Eastern Europe,[12] and in casting financial relationships in terms of a flow model which could be contrasted with that of capitalist economies. But there remains considerable disagreement with regard to several aspects of the function of money in command economies and the role assigned to it by the Reform.

Does money matter as long as the economy is managed essentially through material balances? How meaningful is credit policy as long as loans are automatically available for the sake of plan fulfillments? Assessments also differ with regard to the significance of the partial substitution of credit for budgetary financing, which is an important and, in each country of Eastern Europe, much discussed aspect of the Reform. Will the rechanneling of financing result in a significantly different pattern of investment? Does it really matter if in the future part of the surplus product reaches the budget under the guise of a standard capital charge? Will the new arrangements diminish the centrally administrative nature of financial controls? Will economic adjustment ("steering") mechanisms replace administrative controls?

The — still limited — move toward "unification of money" has many theoretical as well as practical aspects.[13] I am not sure, however, whether the changes made so far — even in the countries which have gone furthest

[12] Compare also the major endeavor along these lines by E. Ames in his recent *Soviet Economic Processes* (Homewood, Ill., 1965), and R. W. Davies, "The Soviet Planning Process for Rapid Industrialization," *Economics of Planning*, VI:1 (1966), in particular the scheme on p. 63.

[13] The need for a "uniform economic equivalent the actual volume of which would not depend on the particular sphere in which it is used" is recognized by the more enlightened economists in Eastern Europe. See József Bognár, "Overall Direction and Operation of the Economy,"*The New Hungarian Quarterly* (Spring 1966), p. 13. He goes on to say that since in the pre-Reform system "money does not fulfill the role of equivalent on the macroeconomic level, it is not possible to select the growth variant correctly" (p. 18). On the history of views on the role of money in centrally planned economies, see P. J. D. Wiles, "The Political and Social Prerequisites for a Soviet-Type Economy," *Economica* (February 1967).

The following inside view on the shortcomings of the present state of monetary theory in the Communist countries, is refreshing: "Marxist economic theory up till now merely noted the existence of money under socialism and recounted, in a formal way, the monetary functions that had already been discovered by Marx. But it was unable to explain why these general theoretical statements differed from the operation of money in socialist economic practice, nor the reason for the specific changes in these functions brought about in the present-day economies." Ota Šik, *Plan and Market Under Socialism* (Prague, 1967), p. 351.

in this direction — permit us to speak of the end of segmentation of money balances and of compartmentalization of financial flows.

Centrally planned economies are money-using, but quantity-maximizing economies. They require money to avoid the cumbersomeness of barter, but not a financial system beyond an elementary transfer mechanism for investment funds. Holding of money makes sense only in a world of uncertainty; an adequately functioning planned economy needs no money balances, except as required by the specific payments mechanism in use. There may be some similarity between the neoclassical view of money and the role assigned to it in the pre-Reform economies of Eastern Europe. The first saw the function of money to be merely to facilitate the market process by serving as a standard of value and a medium of exchange rather than to regulate the economic system, while in command economies it facilitated planning by making different activities comparable; it did not regulate — it controlled.

To the extent that the Reform requires a shift from tied to discretionary money, it will increase the "moneyness" of money, even if, for the time being, the separation of money flows into two circuits is to be preserved. Many monetary processes and financial phenomena will assume a form more similar to corresponding processes in Western countries (as Holešovský points out). This will not necessarily help the analyst to separate appearance from substance and to identify the functional meaning of legal and procedural changes. Indeed, the temptation is great to interpret the new attitudes toward credit and interest as the Eastern counterpart of the "rediscovery of money."[14] It may save us from illusions and disillusionment to recognize the probable limitations of the propulsion of money and credit into the role of a key "economic lever" of the Reform. Will the invisible hand of the cost of money replace the mailed fist of the central planner? Only if Holešovský's hopes are fulfilled[15] and money is permitted to become the "binding agent" of the new economic system; only if, to some significant degree at least, compliance with long-run plan guidelines will be sought through manipulating financial variables (such as cost and availability of credit). Two developments

[14] Limitations of fiscal policy, which the Great Depression and Keynes have propelled into the position of a key tool of economic policy, were widely recognized in the United States and elsewhere in the early fifties. See for instance, Howard S. Ellis, "The Rediscovery of Money" in *Money, Trade, and Economic Growth* (New York, 1951) and Robert V. Roosa, "The Revival of Monetary Policy," *Review of Economics and Statistics* (February 1951).

[15] See the first paragraph of his essay.

will be of particular significance as evidence of the possible evolution toward active money and the use of credit as an agent of economic policy and as a means of profit maximization ("economic lever" in the current terminology of Eastern Europe): the role which the State Bank will assume in the hierarchy of "economic organs," and the extent to which financial tutelage will continue as a form of administrative control.

Under the centrally planned system, a number of detailed decisions were shifted from state to bank bureaucracy,[16] but the range of alternatives and the scope of discretion were severely circumscribed by the plan and by minute regulations regarding form and terms of payments and credit. In the words of the former head of the National Bank of Hungary: "The principal function of the banks under such circumstances is to check the execution of the plan and to notify the superior organs of any departure from the plan, so that these should be able to take the necessary measures."[17] No wonder the monobank does not rank high among policy organs of centrally planned economies, though its contribution apparently ranges in individual countries from active participation in the formulation of plans to their mechanical translation into appropriate financial magnitudes.

The role played by state banks in originating and formulating the Reform also differed from country to country. There is a striking contrast between the Gosbank of the USSR, which as late as the beginning of 1967 still saw its role in the new circumstances as one of improving the quality of detailed financial plans and of policing their execution,[18] and the claim for quasi-independent framing of credit policies in Czechoslovakia, so forcefully stated in the article by one of the leading officials of the *Státní Banka*, quoted by Holešovský.[19]

The precise role assigned to banks in the new system remains uncertain.

[16] Compare Rudolf Bićanić, "Economics of Socialism in a Developed Country," *Foreign Affairs* (July 1966).

[17] Bela Sulyok, "The Socialist Banking System and the Hungarian Banks," *The New Hungarian Quarterly* (Summer 1966), p. 29. Compare the following criticism by two staff economists of the Gosbank: "The basic shortcomings of the [present] system is that it requires from the offices of the Gosbank nothing more than merely meticulous following of instructions and, in effect, does not stimulate them to seek out possibilities for increasing the efficiency of the credit granted. In fact, the local offices of the bank have been transformed into technical implementors of directives and instructions given by higher level offices; they can merely signal existing conditions in the economy, instead of actively utilizing credit for improving its performance" (*Izvestiia*, February 5, 1967).

[18] For official Gosbank views, see for instance, *Den'gi i kredit* (January 1967).

[19] See quotation from E. Löbl, p. 101.

Yet, under any reasonable interpretation of the Reform it is bound to grow, even though official documents and some of the surrounding discussion leave room for doubt. Presuming that they are given greater latitude, will State Bank officials be able to undergo the mutation from inventory checkers to risk appraisers? The significant question, however, is not whether the role of credit (or banks) is to be enlarged, but whether its functional relationship to resource allocation and profit maximization is being changed.

FINANCIAL CONTROLS

If the Reform is to be more than a substitution of control mechanisms, financial processes must acquire a new and independent function. The entire activity of the Gosbank ever since it stepped into the economic chaos of 1930 / 31 has been focused on implementary controls. The same is true for the other countries after they had taken over and assimilated the structure and functions of the "standard system." [20] Leptin is certainly right in arguing at the Workshop that the analysis of the New Economic System in East Germany should be approached from the point of view of changes which the control and supervisory functions of the financial system are now undergoing.

The notion of "control" is crucial, indeed, for the interpretation of the functional role of the banking system in the old as well as in the new systems. A number of related questions are involved, ranging from the actual effectiveness of the old system to the degree of possible substitution of price for quantity controls under the new arrangements. The financial and administrative coercive dimensions of controls are closely integrated in the Soviet Union, but there is some question about the extent to which this prototype was actually and fully implemented in the other countries. Professor A. Brzeski's discussion of inflation in Poland suggests that it was possible only because in that country financial controls were much more permissive than in the Soviet Union (or only intermittently effective). Other countries of Eastern Europe, however,

---

[20] See George Garvy, *Money, Banking, and Credit in Eastern Europe* (New York: Federal Reserve Bank of New York, 1966), chap. 2. For a fairly sophisticated statement from a planner from Eastern Europe, see Ottó Gadó, "The Role of Socialist Finance in Securing a Balanced Development of National Economy," *Public Finance Policy and Techniques for Economic Stability and Balanced Economic Growth* (Report of the Budapest Congress, 1964), published by the International Institute of Public Finance (The Hague, 1966), and contributions by Julius Branik, Zdzislaw Fedorowicz, and Erhart Knauthe in the same volume.

seem to have achieved a closer approximation of the Soviet pattern in which all financial processes, including methods of account settlement and payments discipline become a part of coercive surveillance, as Holešovský points out.

Under the old system, in spite of continuous surveillance and petty tutelage, financial controls were negative and therefore passive. Their objective was formal compliance with norms and plans, not optimum deployment of resources.[21] Mr. Paul Gekker rightly asked in the Workshop discussion whether routine and formal controls are necessarily the most effective ones even from the point of view of a command economy. No doubt, disenchantment with their effectiveness, even as a means of achieving plan fulfillment, was one reason for their downgrading and dismissal in Hungary even before the embracing of the Reform (János Fekete, p. 66). But Professor Leonard D. Goldberg observed in the Workshop discussion that no evidence of relaxation or refocusing of financial controls was as yet apparent in the Soviet Union.

The degree to which administrative interference will be reduced and its exercise shifted from the center toward organizations in closer touch with the production process (intermediary organizations of enterprises, bank branches, specialized banks, and so on) will be indicative of the true significance of the Reform. So will the role assigned to particular control mechanisms, including financial and banking controls. In the Soviet Union, controls continue to be enforced by administrative rather than economic sanctions, but there is considerable evidence that financial sanctions and incentives are being increasingly used in the other countries.

It remains to be seen to what extent the new "economic levers" will operate through the market rather than merely as substitutes for orders from the center. An interest-free loan (or a loan proffered at a preferential rate) may be a sugar-coated order: Can the manager afford not to take it without having to face up to "public criticism?" A number of elements in the new financial arrangements in various countries of Eastern Europe provide a potential mechanism for continuing administrative interference, such as the setting of depreciation rates, employment taxes, and so on. The actual experience, as the Reform moves on, will have to

---

[21] Again, in the words of the man who under the old system was head of Fekete's bank: "It is through supervision rather than through direct credit policy that the National Bank fulfills its tasks of implementing economic policy" (B. Sulyok, p. 31).

be analyzed carefully to assess the degree of survival of administrative controls and of their interference with the market process.

INFLATION

The effectiveness of direct controls inherent in the command economy must be assessed against the performance record of each country of Eastern Europe which, in each case, involves trade-offs between growth and stability. Of particular interest to those focusing on the financial aspects of socialist economies is the way in which they have dealt with the problem of inflation.

Like all rapidly growing economies, the economies of Eastern Europe have been exposed to inflationary pressures. The degree of success in containing these pressures has varied from country to country, and from period to period. In each case, the outcome depended more on the success in balancing, through direct controls, the flow of purchasing power to the population against the limited volume of available consumer goods than on the indirect influence of monetary policy operating through availability and cost of credit or on the inducements to save rather than to spend. Under such circumstances, adjustments occur, in the last analysis, as a result of the planners' reaction to observable disequilibria, including those between controlled and any existing free markets. The contribution of the banking system to containing inflation was largely passive and inherent in its implementary nature and dependence for efficiency on the ability of controllers to keep the underlying flows within the framework of plans.

Because of the tight system of material controls, inflationary processes in Eastern European economies took usually the form of consumer-price rather than producer-price inflation. In most cases, below-equilibrium consumer prices resulted in long waiting lines and bare shelves, and in conspicuous price differentials for identical or closely related products in controlled and free markets. Examples of overt inflation were more frequent than those of repressed inflation (both not necessarily nearly adequately reflected in official price indexes) since consumers were usually reluctant to accumulate cash and savings balances (the only two forms of financial assets available to them, not counting government loans usually placed under pressure as an anti-inflationary policy measure). Disproportionately large price increases tended to occur in the free markets for farm products (*kolkhoz* markets) and in other areas, including services, escaping official price fixing. Some countries, like Hungary, have been more successful in matching the flow of disposable consumer income with the output of goods and services available to them, while in others inflationary pressures persisted chronically, or occurred in spurts, through the late fifties, with Poland as a conspicuous example.

Whether, given the historical circumstances, inflation was the unavoidable price to be paid for rapid growth is a question which still awaits a thorough country-by-country exploration.[22] Similarly, a clear relationship between the rate of output growth and the rate of inflation is as difficult to establish for command economies as for the lopsided capitalist economies grafted on the semifeudal subsistence economies of Latin America. But, as Brzeski claims in this volume, in Poland at least inflation might have been a deliberate policy, or at least the deliberately accepted result of the managers' endeavor to increase output or productivity (or both) by escaping, flouting, or circumventing the constraints of inept planning and of stifling controls. Indeed, under arrangements where credit is almost automatically forthcoming once the underlying real transactions are consummated, at least when the chips are down, the ability to bid for (labor or material) resources at higher than planners' prices depends on the tightness of controls, the effectiveness and connivance of the economic administration, and the rewards and penalties involved.

Clearly, in Poland, at least through 1957, the structure of economic administration gave sufficient scope to endeavors to meet physical targets at the easily validated cost of bidding for resources at prices set above; inflation was the obvious consequence. The dynamic aspects of the inflationary process were, however, largely blunted as the resulting rearrangement of resource use, final output composition, and price relationships were limited and did not always occur in the direction of optimum. Some reallocation of resources took place in response to price increases (in particular in the allocation of skilled, and therefore scarce labor), but by and large the various parts of the economic system did not respond to the stimulus of higher prices. Professor Montias, however, arrives at a much less pessimistic conclusion than Brzeski. He points out that the monetary and financial authorities have considerable scope for

[22] See, however, J. M. Montias, "Inflation and Growth: the Experience of Eastern Europe" *in* W. Baer and I. Kerstenetsky, eds., *Inflation and Growth in Latin America* (Homewood, Ill.: Irwin, 1964).

taking measures, by manipulating real as well as financial variables, to offset *post factum* the inflationary consequences of their collective mistakes — and perhaps even of disruptive actions by plant managers.

Looking into the future, it seems clear that several aspects of the Reform have inflationary potentials, as demonstrated by the Yugoslavian experience. One of the most complex problems which the proponents of the Reform in the individual countries have yet to solve is how to minimize potential inflationary pressures when the shift takes place from a command to a demand economy under conditions in which the working of market-guided adjustment processes are deficient for various reasons, including continuing tendencies to resolve emerging difficulties through interference from the center.

INTEREST RATES

We are confronted with the perplexing problem of what precise role the interest rate might play in a socialist market economy; this role does not need to be small merely because by no stretch of imagination can it be construed to be a market-determined equilibrium rate. But even though such concepts as time preference and risk premium cannot be expected to play a significant role in determining the level or pattern of rates in the new system, must we conclude that we are confronted merely with just another accounting artifice without precise economic meaning? Or should we envisage it as a subtle and flexible, and to some degree impersonal, tool for expressing and implementing social priorities by using the market and price mechanism in preference to direct allocations and subsidies?

In a socialist economy, the interest rate does not need to clear the market for loanable funds, as long as (a) the demand for real resources is not dependent on availability of financial resources (including credit) alone, and (b) a rate which is not an equilibrium rate can be maintained through nonprice rationing by controlling the supply of loanable funds as well as the demand for them. Nonprice rationing in financial markets is not unknown in Western economies. The effectiveness of interest charges (in somes cases disguised as a "production tax" to give it a right of citizenship in the family of factor costs in a socialist economy) as a level will depend, in part, on the way they affect retained profits; in particular, the part available for staff (managerial) remuneration.

Relatively little is as yet known about the precise way in which interest rates will be set and manipulated and how much flexibility there will be in credit procedures.[23] Clearly, there is no uniformity on this among the various countries, and the first steps are necessarily tentative. We have some information on rates, but little explicit reasoning as to the desirable term structure and differentiation.[24]

So far, we have little evidence of rate flexibility as contrasted with rate differentiation. Even in the pre-Reform system, different rates usually applied to specific kinds of credit. Every specific end-use, or type of borrower, however, commanded one definite rate, determined at the center and uniformly applied without regard to the financial position of the borrower. The lending officer had no latitude for varying terms according to the performance and prospects of the individual borrower. Mr. János Fekete's contribution suggests that this is to change, at least in Hungary.

There should be generally little trouble in developing a rate structure ranging from subsidy to penalty levels: The question is to what extent interest is to be used as the allocator of resources rather than as an alternative to purely administrative sanctions — as a cost rather than a fine. Will the rate include a risk premium? And what precisely is the nature of risks in a society in which the state is the ultimate owner of all nonpersonal assets and the source of all macroeconomic decision-making? This does not deny the legitimacy of a risk premium in a socialist economy — but merely raises the question of the proper determination of what must be regarded in essence as a risk of nonperformance rather than of insolvency.

Another financial cost in the new system of economic steering is variably known as a production tax or a capital levy on fixed assets[25] (and

[23] In the Soviet Union three alternatives are being offered, on an experimental basis, for the crediting of collective farms, each reflecting the preferences of a different administration: Gosbank, Ministry of Agriculture, and State Planning Commission. Given the choice, borrowers overwhelmingly opted for one of them. "Priamoe bankovskoe kreditovanie" in *Ekonomicheskaia gazeta*, No. 49 (December 1966), 29–32.

[24] See, for instance, E. Mitel'man's questioning of the rationale of the newly introduced structure of interest charges for short-term loans in the Soviet Union, ranging from 1 to 6 percent. He also criticizes the new system of penalty rates and opposes differentiation of rates within individual industries in favor of low profit enterprises which would defeat the role of interest as an allocator of resources ("economic lever"). See "Pribyl', rentabel'nost, protsenty za kredit," *Den'gi i kredit* (February 1967).

[25] Its ancestry can be traced to the NEP. A proposal was made by the *Komissariat* of Finances in 1922–23 to introduce a capital tax for all government-owned

in some countries, on working capital as well). It is intended as a check against excessive use of fixed capital in a system in which there are no capital markets. Among the various possible interpretations of this novel attempt to introduce the cost of capital into the cost structure of the socialist economy, its treatment as a property tax or as a minimum socially acceptable rate of return on productive assets (being at the same time the minimum share of government in total profits), as suggested by Holešovský and others, seems the most logical.[26] Again, we are led to the question: How much does it matter for the performance of the system if from here on part of the surplus product is to be earmarked for government use and covered into the budget under a different label? The introduction of the capital tax, furthermore, must be regarded as only one aspect of broader changes in the system of financial flows.

PROFITS

It is not surprising that the authors of the Workshop papers have not given the same prominence to profit and the profit motive as many of the less well informed commentators of the current Eastern European scene. Profit has long been an integral part of the economic calculus of the countries of Eastern Europe. The Reform has not elevated profits to a new crucial role; it has merely shifted much of the responsibility for profit maximization from the central planner to the enterprise manager. The stress on profits neither moves the economies of Eastern Europe in the direction of capitalism, nor does it guarantee the success of the Reform.

Capitalism is not only a money-using and profit-seeking system. It is, among other things, also a system of incentives and rewards related to risk taking. One question on which the present contributions were not able to shed much light is the link between profits and incentives in the new system, and the intriguing question at what point risk-taking will affect significantly the scope of responsibilities of the manager (Pesek, p. 113).

The enterprise manager will operate under numerous restraints — but the actual profit will depend increasingly on his decisions, not on the

enterprises as a means of improving the use of fixed and working capital; a rate of 4 to 5 percent was discussed at that time. See E. Mitel'man, p. 42.

[26] This was, according to G. S. Lisichkin, p. 33, the role envisaged for the interest rate by one of the earliest Soviet planners, A. M. Ginzburg.

proper execution of detailed plans handed down from above. A price system that reflects relative scarcities is essential for the new system: without it, profits cannot serve as a guide to enterprise behavior to maximize profits.

I am not certain to what extent discussion of the new role of profits in the various papers reflects differences of interpretation rather than country differences. The role of profits in the socialist economy is currently the subject of a lively and embarrassed debate in the Soviet Union and in the other Eastern European countries. It would be well if at least Western students of these economies kept in mind that profit maximization is an economic technique, not a characteristic of a specific economic system. Only the conditions under which maximization take place and the distribution of profits add up to significant characterization.

What is really new is the role assigned to profits as a key criterion for the distribution of rewards and for channeling investments. As Gekker pointed out at the Workshop, "the notion that investment decisions, except for some limited types, should be dependent upon enterprise profits is entirely novel to the whole working concept of the Soviet system." No wonder that a lively discussion is under way in the Soviet Union and in some of the other countries about the proper way of calculating prices to establish a proper profit ratio (the Marxian $\frac{m}{c+v}$) to be maximized. Should it be related to labor inputs, to fixed capital, or to total production costs? At this stage, it seems quite possible that the individual countries of Eastern Europe might adopt, or begin experimenting with, different solutions. The specific choice does not matter much; what matters more is the reorganization of the entire economic process around a criterion that, among other things, will permit meaningful comparisons of interfirm performance.

The purpose of higher profit retention, which is a uniform characteristic of the Reform in all the countries[27] is to make feasible schemes designed to offer meaningful material incentives for management and staff, as well as to enlarge enterprise investment independence. The actual use made of the larger share of enterprise and intermediate units in total profits will be one of the most significant indicators of the real significance of the Reform to watch.

[27] In the Soviet Union, however, the bulk of profits of the first groups of enterprises shifted to the new system continued to be channeled into the budget.

FINANCIAL FLOWS

How will changes in financial flows affect the operating characteristics of the system? Ames reminded Workshop participants that the — so far limited — steps in this direction are the only significant changes to occur in the financial sphere in the Soviet Union in forty years, except for credit financing of small-scale mechanization.[28] But Leptin remarked that in the other countries of Eastern Europe, the shift to what he called a "three-channel system" was one of the most widely discussed financial aspects of the Reform.

Changes in the flow of investment (including depreciation) funds and credit will affect patterns of real investment, inventory behavior and producers' price structure. As Powell pointed out at the Workshop, their main importance will be for users of capital, but these changes are bound to affect the whole performance of the economy, and thus consumer welfare. The broad question is, indeed, as Powell rightly stressed, whether reforms in finance will tend to raise efficiency of investment and the rate of real growth of output. Experience is evidently too short for even a tentative answer, and Pesek's suggestion (p. 123) that other aspects of the Reform have an anti-investment bias may well be justified to some extent.

The redirection of financial flows, with increased retention by profit-generating units (though tempered by quasi-automatic transfusion of funds to enterprises in financial straits through intermediate units; see Holešovský p. 95) and greater emphasis on decentralizing investment decisions are significant aspects of the Reform, but by themselves can hardly be taken as convincing evidence of "convergence of the two systems." But will increased use of credit result in greater latitude for enterprise managers, or will it merely represent an alternative means of channeling socialized profits into capital formation?

Availability of financial (internal or credit) resources is a necessary, but not sufficient condition for decentralizing investment decisions. As long as centralized control over real resources is maintained and administrative assent is necessary, the individual enterprise's autonomy in matters of investment will remain severely limited. Even if allocation of part of the investment funds is to be guided by marginal productivity, the bulk

---

[28] Specific terms and the scope of such credit varies from country to country but similar financing became available in all countries of Eastern Europe some time after 1956.

could continue to be channeled through planners' direction, not market guidance. As Ames pointed out at the Workshop, the real problem of socialist economies is not to raise enough investment finance, but to use it properly; the ability of enterprises and intermediate units to improve the patterns of investment will be a touchstone of the new system.

It is clear that the Reform will result in a greater diversification of financial flows (compare Holešovský, p. 92) and — hopefully — in a greater part of profits being invested by the generating unit itself or by the intermediate organization to which it belongs. Making loans and grants dependent on profit prospects will introduce new rationality into the economic process of the countries of Eastern Europe.

No doubt, use of credit for capital formation can become a powerful means of increasing the efficient use of inputs. It is by no means sure, however, as Powell reminded us, that in the past loan-financed inventories have typically been managed more economically than grant financed investment. A good deal is expected of the new system to speed up completion of new construction projects, in particular those involving a major investment in plant and equipment. Special arrangements involving interest and other incentives have been introduced as part of the Reform in several countries (for instance in Czechoslovakia; see Holešovský, p. 91ff) in order to reduce the huge amount of investment funds tied up in projects the completion of which is delayed by faulty planning and performance shortfalls. This is an area where financial levers are widely expected to work miracles.

Will significant modification in the area of finance add up to a new system? asked Gekker at the Workshop. Dr. Erich Klinkmüller suggested that if the essence of the Reform in the financial field consists mostly in adjusting economic command to the realities of the already existing situation the immediate economic significance of financial changes will remain negligible, whatever sociological and political interest they might have. Several other commentators were also skeptical. Others, including the present writer, tended to take a more sanguine view.

AN ENTERPRISE ECONOMY?

One of the significant — and in the long run perhaps crucial — elements of the Reform is the enlarged autonomy of enterprises.[29] But are we not run-

[29] This is, indeed, recognized by the partisans of the Reform. Thus, József Bognár writes that "the success, rationality and efficiency of the [new] system of

ning a bit ahead in speaking, as Holešovský does, of an emerging "enterprise economy"? In the Soviet Union Professor E. Liberman's "no more petty tutelage of enterprises" is still a battle cry, but in some countries, and perhaps most conspicuously in East Germany, enterprise management is being given more freedom of action and more encouragement to use it. But what is the scope of this freedom? To choose the best means for achieving plan targets passed down from the center? Will enterprise managers be free to make adjustments at the margin, or will they have merely more flexibility in dealing with marginal matters? To what extent will the "basic assortment" of goods to be produced continue to be centrally determined, and what will be the scope of individual enterprises to determine their structure of outputs and inputs?

Fekete's essay suggests that in Hungary enterprises will have considerable authority to make such decisions. Even in those countries of Eastern Europe in which this is not the case, one does not need to belittle the fact that under the new system authority is limited to the organization of production, as pointed out by Goldberg at the Workshop. There is considerable scope for improving performance by policies for which the old system offered little incentives — such as economizing on fixed capital and inventories, better capital maintenance, and minor improvements in materials handling.[30] Even if the road for enterprises to become "basic living cells" of the economy (see Holešovský's contribution, p. 84) may still be long, much could be achieved by merely effectively shielding enterprise managers from administrative interference. Old soldiers may fade away, but there is little evidence that old bureaucrats look with equanimity toward any diminution of their supervisory functions. Earlier examples of economic reorganization in the Soviet Union and elsewhere show a great propensity of bureaucrats to come out on top of every restructuring of institutions.

Therefore one tends to look with suspicion at the new types of industry-wide and regional groupings of firms. Yet, the emphasis of the new intermediate units is on financing, product specialization, and their service function in research and development, training, and marketing — all relatively new functions in socialist economies. With the present pace of

direction depend on how the central economico-political decisions can be transferred to the microeconomic plane, i.e., the enterprises" ("Overall Direction . . . ," p. 6).

[30] Boris Pesek's "Progress A." I would hope that this would be accompanied by simultaneous stimulation of movement along the lines of Progress "B" and "C."

technological progress, and in view of the considerable change in requirements and preferences of consumers, the optimal use of the flow of depreciation funds and retained earnings commends the use of such intermediate units as an alternative to extreme centralization of such flows which characterized the old system. Leptin rightly pointed out at the Workshop that the greater flexibility of financial flows facilitating resources transfers within industry branches is the main function of the VVB's (*Vereinigung Volkseigener Betriebe*) in East Germany. Even sharing between enterprises and intermediate units of responsibility for choosing between investment alternatives would be progress as compared with existing arrangements. But is the prospect that from now on several different organs will influence financial flows a sufficient reason to anticipate, as Holešovský does (p. 105), the emergence of "polycentrism" in monetary and financial flows?

The new multichannel system of investment flows represents a limited system of financial intermediation, and one wonders whether at some later stage it might evolve, at least in the smaller countries, into some kind of a socialist counterpart of nationwide capital markets. In this direction, again, Yugoslavia has made some important pioneering steps. In the meantime, we must agree with Gekker's remark that "the Soviet economy will tend toward a system in which different economic patterns and operating rules will prove to be sensible." Differentiation of organizational forms and processes has now become feasible in the Soviet Union and the other countries of Eastern Europe, as a result of political evolution. This, indeed, is important for the organizational structure of their economies, and also for the future character of their societies.

Interestingly enough, economists in socialist countries are becoming aware of the enterprise nature of banks. The question is being raised whether profit maximization might not also be considered as a guiding principle for their activities. The paradox, pointed out by Holešovský, that banks, the "enterprises' entrepreneurs," are to be exempt from the play of new financial incentives may be temporary only.[31] To make bank credit extension dependent on profit expectation would, presumably,

---

[31] In an article which appeared in the Moscow *Pravda* on the very day of the Berkeley meeting, two Gosbank economists came forward with the suggestion that "material stimulation of bank employees should be tied to its profits, as in production enterprises shifted to the new system of economic administration" (V. Belkin and B. Ivanter, "The Reform and the bank," *Pravda*, December 29, 1966).

require at least splitting the monobank into central-bank and credit-bank components, or even creating a network of competing commercial banks, as has been done in Yugoslavia. Indeed, the profit criterion can serve as a guide for commercial-bank activities, but not for those of a central bank.

PROBLEMS OF TRANSITION

Several papers and comments discussed problems of the changeover to the new system. The point was made that efforts to minimize problems of transition (for instance, through subsidies or reduced interest rates, and capital taxes favoring the less efficient units and those operating at a loss) might deprive the economy of the full benefits inherent in a market-oriented economy. Piecemeal introduction of the Reform, beginning with selected groups of enterprises, tends to create its own difficulties without achieving the full benefits of market allocation. As Holešovský remarked, in reforming economic systems "rehearsals are not possible." He was impressed by the difficulties of partial introduction of market processes and incentives while for the bulk of the economy the command system is retained and the price system remains essentially unchanged. Similarly, Pesek feared that attempts to smooth transition by temporary subsidies might sufficiently undermine incentives for a rational redeployment of resources so that "we will face the shell of the new model, with its content spirited away." More fundamental, perhaps, is the fact, pointed out by Holešovský, that an important category of prices — wages — will not be exposed to the play of market forces. No doubt this list can be expanded.

Policy-makers in the various countries are aware of at least some of these problems; their timetables recognize at least some prerequisites and priorities. For instance, a basic revision of wholesale prices is under way in most countries, including the Soviet Union. This is likely to be a long process, but it has already resulted in considerable increases in some categories of prices, and thus in the cost structure of industry. The general objective of minimizing the effects of such revisions on the general level of consumer prices by absorbing net cost increases, mainly through reduced turnover taxes and other levies, requires complex budgetary offsets.

The greatest obstacles to overcome, however, are likely to be overt or passive resistance of the bureaucracy at all layers of economic administration,[32] and the inability of the men on the firing line to cope with the new problems. Of the two, unpreparedness of the plant manager — the newly appointed carrier of progress — looms as a major problem. I wish I could share Pesek's cautious optimism that if the success of the Reform is demonstrated fairly rapidly, the resistance or even sabotage by the bureaucracy (which he charitably calls civil service) will be broken. Still, nothing succeeds like success. But will the target fulfiller be able to become a decision maker?

Although in the longer run the future of the price system is crucial, in the short run the ability of the plant managers to stand on their own feet will make or break the Reform. Because of their age alone, many of them are unfamiliar with the working of markets. The greatest obstacle to achieving a profit-motivated (rather than a profit-calculating) economy is a management accustomed to operating under a centrally directed system, with targets stipulated in real terms, and sources of inputs and outlets for output rigidly prescribed. They are distrustful of changes which require adaptation to the unfamiliar and largely unknown. Many of them are still clamoring for better instructions, updated in conformity with the new policies, rather than for greater freedom for decision-making.

There are indications that in the smaller countries of Eastern Europe plant managers are better equipped to deal with the new situation, and many are willing and eager to show what they can do, once freed from the fetters of material balances and complex success indicators. In some (for instance in Czechoslovakia) plant managers and senior staff have been among the most enthusiastic proponents of the Reform.[33] But in the Soviet Union at least, in spite of the usual spate of public grassroots endorsements of the new policies, the shift of gears may cause real problems.

[32] The following comment by the vice chairman of Gosplan of the USSR is a typical example of rearguard action: "The question of the necessity of centralized planned direction of the Soviet economy has long been resolved, definitely and irreversibly, by Marxist-Leninist theory as well as by actual experience." A. Bachurin, "Contemporary Stage of Development of the Soviet Economy and Bourgeois Critics" (being, in effect, a review of *New Directions in the Soviet Economy* (as cited in n.3, above) in *Mirovaia ekonomika i mezhdunarodnye otnosheniia* (March 1967).

[33] In Communist societies, once the die is cast, the placing of new men in key positions and instinctive recognition by opportunists of which side of the bread is buttered tend to put considerable momentum behind any change of policy. However, in the present case, the problem for the plant manager is not to execute properly new policies handed down, but to formulate proper policies for his unit.

But this is not the first time that the managers of the Soviet economy are being confronted with radically new problems. A contemporary writer in the official Soviet publications aimed at United States audiences recalls the reaction of managers to Lenin's New Economic Policy: "They now had to find their own working capital, cut production costs, search out wider markets, increase profits, all this in an atmosphere of conflict, since many 'Red Administrators' could not psychologically face up to the requirements of the new policy."[34] Read "enterprise managers" instead of "Red Administrators," and you have, forty-five years later, one of the key problems of the Reform. An important difference is that in the earlier situation, the Red Administrator was perplexed to be told to follow some of the principles commonly associated with the regime which he had just helped to overthrow. His successor, nearly half a century later, whatever his ideological reactions, simply does not know how to operate in and for a market. He has to learn and — what is even more difficult — to unlearn. Here, the contrast between the historical experience of the Soviet Union and that of the other countries of Eastern Europe, where the thread was never completely broken, emerges with full force.

EAST-WEST CONVERGENCE

The Reform can be contrasted with the state of affairs it has been called upon to improve. Alternatively, it can be assessed in terms of the ways in which it is supposed to solve the basic tasks of the economic system. Other approaches are also possible. The first approach is likely to lead to a positive appraisal. Pesek, following the second, concludes that the Reform is sound on paper, thus reserving judgment until it can be observed in full operation. On the whole, however, and understandably, the contributors to this volume are more inclined to raise questions than to express judgments about a reform so young in years and so full of promise. But a number succumbed to the temptation to react to the convergency hypothesis.

Logically, convergence implies movement from both sides toward some middle ground. Leaving aside the question of evidence on our part,[35]

---

[34] Dmitrenko, "The New Economic Policy."

[35] Convergence is one of the main themes of J. K. Galbraith's *The New Industrial State* (New York, 1967). At one point he concludes: "Thus convergence between the two ostensibly different industrial systems occurs at all fundamental points" (p. 391). Another main theme is to deny that the typical textbook discus-

espousal of the convergence hypothesis necessarily hinges on the interpretation of the substance of the Reform and on the standards applied. If one accepts Professor Alexander Eckstein's oral comments in the discussion that the substitution of consumers' for planners' preferences is more important than ownership of the means of production, any movement toward a socialist market economy will appear as convergence. But I see little advantage in being entrapped by a terminology which is heavy with political overtones but adds little to the understanding of the economic process.

What is widely interpreted as "convergence" may be nothing more than the recognition of the basic identity of economic problems to be resolved even when radically different sets of socioeconomic objectives are pursued. Economists now also seem to be more ready to realize that different institutional arrangements and policies can generate the required flows of inputs, optimize the distribution of outputs, and achieve desired intermediate and financial flows. Focusing on the command features of Soviet-type economies tends to disregard the fact that both economic systems must find workable solutions for a wide range of similar problems. Even before the Reform, the resulting solutions — although, in most cases, radically different with regard to institutional arrangements and decision-making processes — show in some areas considerable similarities with regard to flows, including financial flows.[36] If the promise of the Reform with regard to pricing, the new role of profits, and enterprise autonomy is carried out, similarities, including those of a superficial and formal character, are bound to increase.

Once the similarity of the basic problems of all developing countries, irrespective of political regime and historical heritage, is recognized, comparisons invite themselves. A common need is to obtain adequate financing for investment. Deprived of the essential source of such finance open to other developing countries — foreign or international — the Soviet Union devised (and the other countries of Eastern Europe took over) a unique system designed to maximize domestic finance for investment and to control its use. It was easy for Western critics to show that it was

sion of the price system is relevant in assessing the actual performance of our economic system. Cf. above, section on prices.

[36] The contrast between arrangements existing in Eastern Europe and those in France or the United Kingdom with regard, for instance, to investment flows is less striking than when they are compared with those in the United States, which are at one extreme of the institutional scale.

rigid, wasteful, and bureaucratic, and that it did not prevent inflation from rearing its head from time to time. But how has it performed to meet the challenge of development, in comparison to other forms of response to this challenge in other developing countries? Have the successive development programs in Brazil, Colombia, or Chile — just to name a few — been more effective? Has a combination of local talent, foreign advice, and international tutelage created superior mechanisms for obtaining development finance and achieving higher real growth rates and a higher standard of living in non-Communist developing countries? Most students will give differentiated and qualified answers.

Some of the aspects of "convergence" are merely the natural result of the fact that having reached in a relatively short period a level of industrialization and urbanization comparable to the Western World, the countries of Eastern Europe are now confronted with a host of similar problems, including rapid technological obsolescence, computerized business management, increased importance of research and development, urban congestion, and juvenile delinquency. Is closing of the industrialization gap "convergence"?

With war damages repaired, the initial push toward industrialization achieved, and the organization of agriculture no longer the dominant political-economic problem it was for a generation in the Soviet Union, the East will find, as the West has found, the growth-stability dilemma to be central for the economic policy process. Greater (though in many respects only superficial) similarity between the two systems may open a new chapter in comparative economics in which identical standards of performance are applied and the analytical focus is on the suitability of institutions to reach set goals and on the interplay of goals, policies, and institutions. From such a vantage point, we may want to reexamine the financial system of Soviet-type economies as one variant of combining fiscal and monetary processes and policies to achieve rapid growth. Such reexamination will probably show how the administrative and coercive aspects of the system tended to reduce its effectiveness. Yet the monobank-monobudget system was one possible rational answer to the problem of an optimal financial structure for growth under conditions of reasonable monetary equilibrium.

The financial system designed to facilitate forced industrialization at the expense of the consumer has outlived its usefulness. To some degree it has become the victim of its own success as well as of its shortcomings and limitations.

The fact that the decisive pressure for change seems to have come from consumers rather than from producers may have significant implications for future social and political developments in the countries of Eastern Europe. One can see why reforms were overdue and how the specific variant of the Reform devised in each country could be led to success. But will these reforms be carried out as sketched out by their proponents? The checkered history of economic policies of the Soviet Union suggests that the fate of the Reform depends to a considerable degree on internal political factors.

Index

Accounting practice, 49n
Action Program (Czechoslovakia), 128
Albrecht, J., 20n
Alekseev, A., 145n
Ames, Edward, 155, 163n, 175
Apro, A., 148

Babitchev, Eugene, 11
Bachurin, A., 179n
Bakalář, L., 99n
Bank for International Settlements (Basel), 143
Banks: nationalization of, in Hungary, 59; role of, 97–99, 165–166. *See also* Credit policy, interest, *and under name of country*
Belkin, V., 177
Beneš, V., 100n
Berliner, Joseph S., 10n, 34n
Bićanić, Rudolf, 165n
Bognár, J., 163n, 175n
Bornstein, Morris, 158n
Branik, J., 166n
Bródy, A., 89n
Bronfenbrenner, M., 35n
Brzeski, Andrzej, 10, 18n, 33n, 38, 55, 169
Budget surplus, 40, 52, 56

Cambridge-type coefficient, 27
Chernov, I., 13n
Choice: freedom of, 4, 51
Clearing, multilateral. *See* Multilateral clearing
Coefficient: Cambridge-type, 27; currency conversion, 133
COMECON. *See* Council of Mutual Economic Assistance

COMECON Bank. *See* International Bank for Economic Cooperation
Command economy, 5
Command principle, 8
Control, 5, 6, 7, 9, 10, 13, 19, 166, 167
Convergence, 156, 174, 180–182
Convertibility. *See* Rubles, transferable
Convertible currencies. *See* Gold and convertible currencies
Coordination, 8
Council of Mutual Economic Assistance, 129–152 *passim*; exchange rates in, 130–133; prices in, 130–133
Credit policy, 76–78, 91–102, 121
Currency conversion coefficients, 133
Czechoslovakia: price reform, 88–91; reform, 11, 13, 80–128 *passim*; wages, 14

Dalton, George, 16
Davies, R. W., 162n, 163n
Delivery contracts, 66
Demonetization, 11, 12
Deposits: enterprise, 39, 43, 55
D'iachenko, V., 131n
Division of labor, international socialist, 134
Dluhos, Miroslav, 147
Dmitrenko, V., 159n, 180n
Domar, Evsey D., 155
Drewnowski, J., 26n
Durgin, Frank A., 12n
Dvořák, R., 104n

Eckstein, Alexander, 181
Economic production units, 95, 96
Economic system: basic facts of, 109
Ellis, Howard S., 164n

185

Enterprise autonomy, 70–71, 83–84, 175–178
Enterprise behavior, 84
Erlich, Alexander, 155
Exchange rates, 130–133

Fedorowicz, Z., 166n
Fekete, János, 10n, 11, 107n, 114n, 121, 171
Felker, Jere L., 158n
Finance: functional, 103–105
Financial control. *See* Control
Financial flows, 174, 177
Foreign exchange multipliers, 74
Foreign trade: Hungary, 62; policy, 76
Freedom: consumer choice of, 51
Friedman, Milton, 23n, 125
Frisch, Ragnar, 158, 162

Gadó, O., 166n
Galbraith, John K., 180n
Garvy, George, 1n, 2, 6n, 9, 10–11, 13, 18n, 20n, 23n, 28n, 105n, 166n
Gekker, Paul, 167, 173, 175, 177
Gerashchenko, V. S., 9n
Germany, East, 33, 166, 176
Ginzburg, A. M., 172n
Gluck, L., 25n
Gold and convertible currencies, 136, 137, 144, 148, 150
Gold parities, 132, 138
Goldberg, Leonard D., 167, 176
Granick, David, 34n
Grossman, Gregory, 1n, 9n, 20n, 23n
Growth, 31, 35
Guidelines: wage-price, 102

Hájek, M., 85n
Hansen, Bent, 29n
Hirschman, Albert O., 31n
Hlaváček, B., 84n
Hoarding, 34
Hodgman, Donald R., 24n, 161
Holešovský, Václav, 11, 106, 156, 162, 164, 165, 172, 174, 175, 176, 177, 178
Holzman, Franklyn D., 35
Hungary: effects of 1956 revolution, 62–63; foreign trade, 62, 65; inflation (1946), 58; Investment Bank, 60n; monetary and credit policy, 57–79 *passim*; National Bank of, 59n, 61, 77; National Savings Bank of, 60n; nationalization of banks, 59; reform, 11, 13, 67–79 *passim*; wages, 14; war damage, 57–58, 106–107

IBEC. *See* International Bank for Economic Cooperation
Income distribution, 115
Inflation, 10, 15, 22, 168–170; and growth, 31; hidden, 82; in Hungary (1946), 58; mechanics of, 29; open, in Poland, 42; repressed, 22, 36, 41, 42, 50, 51, 55; theory of, 39
Information, economic, 82
Innovation, 118, 121
Interest, 12, 20, 64, 78, 122, 123, 124, 170–172
Interests, conflict of, 7
International Bank for Economic Cooperation, 129–152; Council of, 135; credit, 139–142, 148; deposits with, 141; functions, 135; interest charges, 147; non-COMECON members, 142–143
Investment: finance, 9n, 91–94, 123, 181; policy, 75
Inventories, 47, 49, 65–66, 82, 124
Ivanter, B., 177

Jaroszewicz, P., 148, 150n
Jaworski, W., 18n, 19n, 25n, 41n

Kaser, Michael, 131n
Knauthe, E., 166n
Klinkmüller, Erich, 175
Knight, Frank H., 109
Komenda, B., 103
Komissarov, V. P., 135n
Konnik, I. I., 150n
Kotlicki, H., 148, 149
Kucharski, M., 28n
Kýn, O., 103n, 105n
Kysilka, H., 103n, 105n

Larionov, K., 133n
Leeman, Wayne A., 3
Lenin, Vladimir, 162n, 180
Leptin, Gert, 160, 166, 174
Lerner, Abba P., 105
Levine, Hervert S., 162
Liberman, E., 176
Liquidity, 24, 40, 56, 94
Liquidity preference, 27, 36
Lisichkin, G. S., 154n, 159n, 172n
Loans: overdue, 20, 25; supply of, 32, 33
Löbl, E., 100, 101, 128, 165n
Lopatkin, V. G., 158n
Lutz, F. A., 28n

Majewski, S., 24n, 148
Market clearing, 111
Market economy, socialist, 159
Market mechanism, 2, 8, 69, 109, 127, 157, 160, 161
Martin, William McChesney, Jr., 101
Marx, Karl, and the gold standard, 132
Musgrave, Richard A., 90
Mayer, Thomas, 17n
Messages. *See* Information
Mikoyan, A. I., 31
Mitel'man, E., 171n, 172n
Model, new economic. *See* Reform
Monetary planning, 9
Monetary policy, 9, 35, 99, 12; enhanced role under reforms, 2
Monetary reform, West German, 125
Monetization, 15
Money: active, 80; demand for, 25–28, 36, 39; elasticity of demand for, 28; elasticity of supply of, 24; Marxist theory on, 163n; quantity theory of, 27, 30, 36; rediscovery of, 164; supply of, 33, 35, 36, 39
Money balances, real private, 37
Moneyness, 4, 11, 164
Monobank, 7, 9, 13, 165
Monopoly, 114, 127
Montias, John M., 10, 19n, 40n, 169
Multilateral clearing, 138, 139, 141, 142, 151
Multilateralism, 133–135
Multilaterization, problems of, 144
Multipliers, foreign exchange, 74

Nachtigal, V., 84n
Nash, Manning, 4n, 16
Nazarkin, K. I., 136, 138n, 139n, 148n
Nevařil, F., 103n, 105n
Nosko, P., 147n
Nove, Alec, 5n

Obolenskii, N., 133n
Ownership, public, and Hungarian reform, 71

Pesek, Boris P., 11, 160, 162, 174, 178, 179, 180
Pigou, A. C., 31
Pirozyński, Z., 18n
Planning: central, 69, 73; central, and foreign trade, 146; polycentric, 80, 81, 105, 162
Plocica, A., 22n

Pohl, O., 100, 100n, 102n
Poland: budget, receipts and expenditures, 41; General Savings Bank of, 18, 28; Investment Bank of, 18; National Bank of, 18, 23
Polycentric planning. *See* Planning, polycentric
Popov, A. N., 135n
Powell, Raymond P., 38n, 40, 162, 174, 175
Price policy, 73, 103
Price reform, 74, 159, 178; in Czechoslovakia, 88–91
Price stability, 35
Prices, 158; double channel, 89; retail, 14; socialist world, 145; world, 130–31
Probst, A., 131
Production, 112
Production-assets levy. *See* interest
Profit maximization, 161–162
Profits, 172–173; distribution of, 72
Progress, types of, 118–122, 125
Pruss, W., 19n
Prybyla, Jan S., 158n

Quantity Theory of Money, 27. *See also* Money

Ratchford, B. U., 20n
Real bills doctrine, 56
Red administrators, 180
Reddaway, W. B., 32n
Reforms, economic: and management, 179; obstacles to, 157. *See also under countries' names*
Remonetization, Yugoslavia, 15
Resources: misallocation of, 118; mobilization and mobility of, 12
Roosa, Robert V., 164n
Rubles: transferable, 136, 138; convertibility of, 148–151

Savings, household, 50, 53, 54
Schmookler, Jacob, 121
Schonfield, Andrew, 101n
Seller's market, 34
Shaglov, G. L., 130n
Šik, O., 102, 126, 128, 163n
Sloan, Alfred P., 6n
Socialist market economy, 159
Solvency, 6
Spulber, Nicolas, 155
Standards fixing, 110

Stigler, George, 159n
Stupov, A. D., 131n
Subsidies, 14, 127, 178
Suliaeva, L., 139n
Sulyok, Bela, 165n, 167n
Sveshnikov, M. N., 134n

Target solution, 81
Tarnovskii, O., 146n
Thunberg, P. H., 132n
Taxes, 85–86, 94, 119–120, 178
Toms, M., 85n
Trade agreements, negotiation, 146–147
Transferable rubles. *See* Rubles, trans-
    ferables
Transition problems, 178
Trapans, Andris, 3
Trusts, 95, 127
Trusts, 95, 127

Underdeveloped countries, 182
Unemployment, 115–117

Vácha, S., 84n

Wages, 43, 178; Czechoslovakia, 14;
    Hungary, 14; policy, 116
Wan, Henry Y., Jr., 17n
Ward, Benjamin, 3
Ward, Joanne, 3
Weaver, M., 38n
Wegge, Leon, 17
Wilczyński, S., 21n
Wiles, Peter, 31n, 163n
Wilson, T., 31n
Wronski, H., 22n
Wyczalkowski, Marcin R., 151n

Yugoslavia, 15–16, 156, 170, 177, 178

Zaczek, T., 24n
Zaleski, Eugène, 158n
Zauberman, Alfred, 24n, 158n
Zienkowski, L., 33n
Zwass, A., 148n